Hazards and Opportunities

Farming livelihoods in dryland Africa: lessons from Zimbabwe

Ian Scoones

with

Chinaniso Chibudu, Sam Chikura, Peter Jeranyama, Daniel Machaka, William Machanja, Blasio Mavedzenge, Bright Mombeshora, Maxwell Mudhara, Claxon Mudziwo, Felix Murimbarimba and Bersazary Zirereza

Zed Books Ltd
LONDON AND NEW JERSEY
in association with
International Institute for Environment and Development
LONDON

Hazards and Opportunities was first published by Zed Books Ltd, 7 Cynthia Street, London N1 9JF, UK, and 165 First Avenue, Atlantic Highlands, New Jersey 07716, USA, in association with the International Institute for Environment and Development (IIED), 3 Endsleigh Street, London WC1H 0DD, in 1996.

Cover designed by Andrew Corbett
Set in Monotype Garamond by Ewan Smith
Printed and bound in the United Kingdom
by Biddles Ltd, Guildford and King's Lynn

A catalogue record for this book is available from the British Library

US CIP data is available from the Library of Congress

ISBN 1 85649 353 9 cased
ISBN 1 85649 354 7 limp

Contents

Tables

Figures

Boxes

Acknowledgements

This book is the result of a collaborative research project involving the Farming Systems Research Unit of the Department of Research and Specialist Services (DRSS), Ministry of Agriculture, Harare, and the Drylands Programme at the International Institute for Environment and Development (IIED), London. We are grateful to our respective institutions for supporting the research throughout. We would particularly like to acknowledge the support of the Director of the DRSS, and Camilla Toulmin, Drylands Programme Director at the IIED. We would also like to thank Kim Collins of the Environment Group at the Institute of Development Studies (IDS), University of Sussex, for secretarial and administrative support.

This research has been largely funded by the Science and Technology for Development programme of the European Commission (contract number: TS2-0304-M). We would particularly like to thank Mario Catizzone of the EC, who has provided constant encouragement. Additional funding for the project came from the Government of Zimbabwe through the DRSS and from the IIED. The final writing and editing was carried out at the IDS, Sussex, UK.

A number of people kindly reviewed earlier versions of the text. In particular we would like to thank Andrea Cornwall, Ben Cousins, Mike Drinkwater, Tim Lynam and two other reviewers for their comments. In addition, the participants at the Lake Kyle workshop held in November 1993 were especially helpful in reviewing the policy conclusions being reached by the research. However, all errors and omissions are, of course, our own responsibility.

Above all, our special thanks are due to the many people in Chivi who, through their commitment to the research, allowed it to happen. In particular, thanks are due to the people of Zivhu, Tandare, Havurovi, Madzivadondo, Mazhambe, Shanduka and Mapuvire who hosted the research and continue to keep the process of learning going through the farmer research groups and on-farm trials. In addition, we would like to acknowledge the assistance of district officials – in the District Administrator's office, in Agritex and in the Veterinary Department – who were most supportive of our work. Various NGO workers have also influenced our ideas, most notably Kudakwashe Murwirwa and colleagues of ITDG-Zimbabwe and Zephaniah Phiri of Zvishavane Water Projects, who, in different ways, are putting many of the lessons of this book into practice.

Preface

This book is about the challenges faced by people living in dryland areas. Lessons for policy and practice are drawn from a detailed case study carried out during the first half of the 1990s in Chivi communal area in southern Zimbabwe. You may be asking: why Chivi? What relevance is it to me? Surely where I work is very different? As this book shows, even over relatively short distances, different histories, different ecologies and different economic and social relations mean that there are significant contrasts in responses to risk and uncertainty: different hazards, different opportunities and so different livelihoods. However, some central themes of this book are of wide relevance to dryland development in Africa and elsewhere. These themes focus on processes rather than site particularities, and so suggest common policy issues with general relevance. For instance, chapters in this book discuss processes of farmer innovation and experimentation and their articulation with scientific research and formal extension; the historical evolution of agricultural landscapes and how they are shaped by external policy, macro-economic factors and the agency of farmers; and the dynamics of drought impacts and response, including local-level coping strategies and the implications for food and relief policy.

All of these issues are the subject of intense debate in the search for sustainable development in Africa's drylands. All are brought into sharp relief by the case study analysis. Instead of indulging in the generalities and rhetoric of much of the sustainable development debate, the case study hopefully allows the reader to engage with the complexities and details of issues at a particular site. Through understanding the history of the area, from the pre-colonial period to the present day; through understanding the economic contexts for decision-making, from local contingencies to national economic policy; and through hearing commentaries by people from Chivi on issues ranging from crop varieties to the causes of drought, policy issues central to the wider debate on dryland development in Africa are brought alive and provided with a context.

This book is the result of a collaborative effort between a large number of people. The book is the product of work by a total of twelve co-authors from different backgrounds. We are a fairly diverse bunch: some of us have a collection of university degrees, while others of us stopped formal education at secondary school; some of us regularly farm in a dry area, while others of us draw a salary and live in a town; some of us have lived all our lives in the study area, while others of us have come to know the area only recently. This diversity has made us much more than a multi-disciplinary team; we have all contributed different skills, different insights and different perspectives. This has meant that tasks have been divided, with some more involved in the fieldwork while others have invested more in data analysis or writing. This book has been compiled by Ian Scoones, drawing on a diversity of material produced during the project. Sources range from project papers and reports to field notes and interview transcripts to analyses of government documents and archive material to computer databases of survey results.

In addition to the group of authors, there is a wider network of people who have contributed to this research. These are the people of Chivi communal area who have been the hosts to the research carried out by the Farming Systems Research Unit (FSRU) since 1982. Many of their voices are heard in the text. In writing this book we have tried to reflect the realities of living with the hazards and opportunities of a dryland area through people's commentaries, as well as our own analyses. A particular group of nearly one thousand people – men, women and children – living in 146 different households in three parts of Chivi district regularly participated in this research. This sample group has suffered our questions, pointed out our misperceptions and readily offered us their views on a huge variety of topics. During the research they have welcomed us into their homes, discussed the details of their lives, shown us their livestock and fields, and demonstrated their agricultural practices.

The approach to this research evolved over time. In 1990, when the project was initiated, it was set up in a fairly conventional research mode. Our first activity was to hold a workshop with Zimbabwean policy-makers, researchers and development practitioners in order to set the agenda for the work. But local people were not involved in defining our priorities or the initial research questions. Although we had the support of many key actors in the agriculture and development policy arena, we did not necessarily have the backing of the people we were supposed to be working with in Chivi.

As we were committed to a more participatory way of working, we had to backtrack and think again. Fortunately, a large number of our team know Chivi well. Five authors of this book live in Chivi and have done so for many years. Furthermore the FSRU, the host of the research and the employer of all but one of us, has worked in the area for over a decade, building up solid networks based on trust, friendship and collegiality. In setting up the research we drew on these networks, asking advice and getting good suggestions as to how we should go about the work. The sample groups were established with the help of village leaders and following discussions at a series of open village meetings in areas where the FSRU had successfully carried out on-farm research in the past. With good relations established from the start, the research proceeded smoothly.

An effective research process involves open learning by all parties. The research team has learned an enormous amount, but as the research progressed farmers involved in the sample survey work, the participatory rural appraisal exercises or the feedback workshops became increasingly engaged. We thus moved from conventional, extractive research to the beginnings of a co-learning, action-research process. Following the devastating drought of 1991–92, people were even more eager to make use of the research to seek out their own solutions to the problems and issues being raised. This was the point when farmer research groups began to form, first around clusters of individuals directly associated with the research activity (often members of the household sample) and later beyond. At this point the research activity began to become more responsive to local demands, supporting farmers' trials, arranging exchange visits or carrying out focused studies on key issues identified by the groups. Equipped with the understandings generated by the more formal research, the team was now able to respond more effectively to the practical issues raised by farmers.

In shifting to a more farmer-focused agenda, driven by the enthusiasm and centred on the skills of farmers themselves, we did not abandon our original primary clients for the research – the research community, policy-makers and development practitioners. In writing this book, and in the discussion papers and workshop documents that have preceded it, we have continually tried to make the links between field-level realities and wider policy issues. This brokerage role, shifting the analytical frame from the micro to the macro, from complex detail to broader policy insight, is essential if wider debates about development in dry areas are not to eclipse what is happening on the ground and so become self-referential and ultimately irrelevant. In deciding what to include in this book, we have chosen elements of our experience over the past few years that we feel highlight important insights for policy and that keep local perspectives at the top of the agenda.

The review process for the final research report (this book's precursor) was extensive, with the document, known as 'the book', travelling from home to home in Chivi getting appropriately dog-eared along the way. Towards the end of the project we held a policy workshop to discuss our findings and examine implications for policy. This was well attended by representatives from a wide variety of national agencies, including many of those who had helped frame the research several years before. The workshop was also attended by farmers from Chivi who were chosen by the farmer research groups and who were able to articulate, often very vocally, alternative, local viewpoints. Indeed, many of the policy conclusions contained in this book were sharpened and refined by participants at this workshop.

The research project formally ended at the close of 1993, but the obligations and responsibilities of action-research work necessarily persist. The FSRU continues to work in the area, providing support to the farmer research groups when requested, as well as pursuing other areas of research activity identified by farmers as of high priority. In entering an action-research mode, as new things are learned, new actions are suggested. This book represents just one point on this cycle of learning, reflection and action. In 1995, as people in Chivi face the prospect of another poor season, things have moved on still further. However, we believe that our findings are still pertinent to the struggles and dilemmas faced by people living in dry, risk-prone areas and will be of interest to all thosc committed to development in the dryland areas of Africa and beyond.

Acronyms and local terms

AFC	Agricultural Finance Corporation
Agritex	Agricultural extension service
CFU	Commercial Farmers' Union
chisi	rest day
CMB	Cotton Marketing Board
CNC	Chief Native Commissioner
CPI	consumer price index
CSC	Cold Storage Commission
CV	coefficient of variation
dambo	low-lying valley wetland; vlei
DRSS	Department of Research and Specialist Services
ESAP	Economic Structural Adjustment Programme
FPR	Farmer Participatory Research
FSR	Farming Systems Research
FSRU	Farming Systems Research Unit
GDP	gross domestic product
GMB	Grain Marketing Board
IIED	International Institute for Environment and Development
ITDG	Intermediate Technology Development Group
kraal	cattle pen or village area
lobola	bridewealth
mhunga	pearl millet
miombo	woodland type
mitoro	rain-making ceremony
n'anga	traditional healer
NC	Native Commissioner
Ndebele	Ethnic group in Zimbabwe
nyusa	rain messenger
PET	Potential Evapotranspiration
PRA	Participatory Rural Appraisal
RRA	Rapid Rural Appraisal
rukweza	Finger millet
rusengwe	contribution to territorial rain cult
sadza	porridge, made from grain
SE	standard error
Shona	Ethnic group in Zimbabwe
t	tonne
UDI	Unilateral Declaration of Independence
VIDCO	Village Development Committee
WADCO	Ward Development Committee
Zame	High God
ZANU–PF	Zimbabwe African National Union–Patriotic Front

PART ONE

Contexts

CHAPTER ONE

Exploring risk and uncertainty

Risk and uncertainty dominate people's lives in dryland areas. Whether it is variability at a field level imposed by patterns of rainfall, the impacts of crop pests or the heterogeneity of soil types, or variability at a more macro level due to changes in market conditions, shifts in wage levels or adjustments in economic policy, hazards of various sorts overshadow farming livelihoods. This book is about how people manage this variability: how farmers respond to unfolding circumstances during a cropping season; how people make use of a diversity of income sources, both on- and off-farm; and how people cope with extreme adversity and food shortage during periods of drought. Drawing on case study material from Chivi District in southern Zimbabwe, the book identifies a number of key issues for policy in dryland areas, ranging from approaches to agricultural research and extension, through food security and relief strategies to broader rural development issues.

The way livelihoods are composed, under conditions where food and income supply are always uncertain, is a central theme of this book. Both the way seasonality and inter-annual variability influence income earning strategies and the role of diversification as a way of reducing vulnerability are emphasised. These themes are addressed in the wider literature (e.g. Chambers *et al.*, 1981; Chambers 1989; Mortimore, 1989; Sahn, 1989; Walker, 1989; Gill, 1991; and Webb and von Braun, 1994), but the implications for the Southern African setting have rarely been brought out. An analysis of people's livelihood strategies focuses our attention on the wider context for rural livelihoods. Rural people are not just farmers: they are factory workers, miners, farm labourers, craftspeople, traders and so on. Making a living exclusively from the land is rare in Southern Africa.

Different people at different stages of their lives adopt different livelihood strategies. Men, women, older and younger people, rich and poor are involved in different approaches to managing risk and uncertainty in their lives. Aggregated approaches that make generalisations about rural communities or rural households are inadequate (cf. Guyer and Peters, 1987; Kabeer and Joekes, 1991); instead it is necessary to take a differentiated approach to risk analysis, looking beyond individual or household responses to wider social and economic contexts. The social and economic worlds that influence local-level decisions go well beyond the farm gate, and include networks of social relations locally and with relatives and friends in town; they include links between national economic policies, in turn affected by international economic trends, and price levels, market functioning and levels of infrastructure and service support; and they include the influence of external actors, whether government extension workers, development projects or religious leaders, on the options and possibilities of local-level action. Contexts are also historically situated. The contemporary agricultural landscape in southern Africa has been shaped by a history of intervention, both by farmers themselves and by the state. Thus by moving between analyses of macro-economic, political and historical contexts and local-level processes, the linkages between the micro and the macro are illuminated.

Responses to risk and uncertainty while farming necessarily involve continuous adaptive change in farming practice. A whole range of contingencies impinge on day-to-day farming practice. Whether it is variable rainfall or an unexpected event such as death in the village, farming must continuously adapt and change. Drawing on studies of farming practice in West Africa, Paul Richards has termed this the farming 'performance' (Richards, 1986; 1989). As Gene Wilken (1987) has shown for Central America, successful farming makes use of existing variability, in field slope and patchiness or in different soil types and fertility, as well as reshaping the environment in order to increase production and reduce risk. This book picks up these themes through a detailed study of farming practice over a number of seasons.

This analysis points to a number of important directions for farmer support services and agricultural policy. A recognition of risk and uncertainty means that simplified and standardised approaches are inadequate. A more flexible approach, recognising variability and diversity, is required, suggesting new approaches to research and extension that go beyond a technology transfer approach to agricultural development to a more participatory mode, allowing farmers to have a much more active role in the technology development process (Chambers *et al.*, 1989; Reijntes *et al.*, 1992; Okali *et al.*, 1994; Scoones and Thompson, 1994). This book addresses the current concerns with farmer participation through an examination of the Zimbabwe experience, both past and present, and points towards new directions for policy and practice that offer the opportunity for risk and uncertainty to be taken seriously.

Alongside the day-to-day hazards that form the backdrop of all farming activity, there are occasional shocks with more dramatic impacts. Drought is a recurring phenomenon in the dry zones of sub-Saharan Africa, and the Southern African region has been particularly badly hit in the last decade (Thompson, 1993; SADC, 1994). Drought impacts are often ignored in the process of development planning. When drought strikes, as it inevitably does, the result is a hurried and often inadequate relief response.

Taking an entitlements approach (Sen, 1981; Swift, 1989; Drèze and Sen, 1989; 1990) this book focuses on the experiences generated by the 1991–92 drought, looking at both official responses and local coping strategies.

This opening chapter introduces a number of ways of understanding risk by first asking: what is risk? The following sections then examine economic, psychological and sociological ways of looking at risk and uncertainty, each with different methodological and practical implications. Following this brief review of the risk literature, the chapter looks at how farming systems research deals with risk analysis and concludes that previous approaches have many shortcomings. Finally, the case study area and the structure of the book are introduced.

What is risk?

Exploring risk in agriculture presents a range of methodological problems. First, what is risk? The Royal Society special study offered the following definition: 'Risk is the chance, in quantitative terms, of a defined hazard occurring. It therefore combines a probabilistic measure of the occurrence of the primary event(s) with a measure of the consequences of that/those events' (Royal Society, 1992: 4). Measuring risk is, however, not easy. Within the literature there is no agreement on what is an acceptable measure of risk.

Most approaches to risk analysis are rooted in probability theory. Probability emerged as a core concept in scientific analysis in the mid-nineteenth century, following a long history of social survey and census work (Hacking, 1975). Through understanding probability, the unruly, chance-dominated world could somehow be 'tamed' (Hacking, 1990). In terms of the moral discourse of the time, risk, like gambling, and deviation, like criminal behaviour, was bad, whereas probabilistic description provided the potential for order and control. From this time onwards, the frequency approach to probability theory has remained the dominant route to analysing variability. Risk analysis has thus tended to focus on the analysis of simple probabilities, ignoring the more complex solutions suggested by considering sequential learning. Risk assessment has been developed particularly in the engineering sciences where probabilities of technical failure are calculated for design purposes (Royal Society, 1992). In addition, the insurance industry has developed sophisticated actuarial approaches to assessing risks to life and property. In economics, normative decision theories assume individuals (or households) are rational economic actors. Choice between options is based on the maximisation of utility, according to the assessment of expected utility outcomes from different options (Anderson *et al.*, 1977; Roumasset *et al.*, 1979). Simplified decision rules (such as safety-first, safety-fixed etc.) may approximate utility maximisation through the ordering of options, but the overriding assumption is that outcome probabilities are known to some degree. As Frank Cancian (1972) points out, 'the distinction between risk and uncertainty seems to be overwhelmed by the demand of the micro-economic model to characterize decision-making into calculable terms'.

Where data are readily available and the type of risk is well defined, modelling approaches have proved useful. However, in more complex situations, where problems are more loosely defined and where the perception of hazards greatly influences action, probability-based approaches to risk analysis have been found wanting (Krimsky and Golding, 1992). This is particularly the case when dealing with broader environment and development issues. In such situations, uncertainty and, perhaps more importantly, fundamental indeterminacy or simple ignorance dominate (Wynne, 1992). In these cases, it is not possible to get quantitative measures of the probabilities of different outcomes and so therefore a measure of risk is very often elusive. Without knowledge of the probabilities of different outcomes, the future remains uncertain. Uncertainty is thus formally different to risk, as the term relates to conditions where probabilities of future events are unknown.

The difference between risk and uncertainty is, in practice, blurred. Some would argue that it is not a useful distinction, because all events are fundamentally uncertain in some way, particularly where human agency is involved. As Mary Douglas notes, 'every choice we make is beset with uncertainty. That is the basic condition of human knowledge. A great deal of risk analysis is about trying to turn uncertainties into probabilities' (1985: 42). The engineering approach to risk, where factors are reduced to probabilistic formulations, is therefore inseparable from questions of risk perception. In other words, all risk assessment is in some ways subjective, whether this involves the subjective specification of a risk model or the measurement of risk behaviours. Within risk studies, there are always several sources of uncertainty. These may be parametric uncertainties ('what you know you don't know') or systemic knowledge uncertainties ('what you don't know you don't know'). Recognising these uncertainties, as well as situations where fundamental indeterminancies ('what you know cannot be known') exist, is vital for effective decision-making.

When something is known about likely outcomes, risks can be taken. For instance, farmers know that certain crops respond to poor rainfall conditions in particular ways and that the likelihood of such conditions, at least on the basis of past experience, is of a certain order of magnitude. Farmers can thus knowingly take or avoid such risks through their crop planting decisions. A variety of factors, such as resource constraints, may affect the choice (Chapter 5), but options can be weighed up and trade-offs assessed. However, in many other instances uncertainty prevails. In such cases, outcomes are unknown and decisions cannot be prejudged. For instance, chance events, such as an unexpected illness or a death in the family, may affect the course of agricultural activities, requiring adaptive responses and adjustments. Equally, with the introduction of a new technology, farmers do not know how it will respond under local circumstances; 'they neither know the odds against which they are gambling, nor the outcomes' (Huijsman, 1986: 34).

A large body of work has explored individual perceptions of risk. Surveys have examined risk perceptions in relation to a wide variety of risks, from rare technological risks (nuclear power stations, chemical plants) to daily risks (household injury, transport dangers) to health risks (smoking, diet) to natural disasters (earthquakes, floods). Comparative studies have highlighted the ways in which people's perceptions influence their judgements about the acceptability of a particular risk (Lichtenstein *et al.*, 1978; Slovic *et al.*, 1980; Fischoff *et al.*, 1981; Kahneman *et al.*, 1982; Johnson and Tversky, 1983). Such studies have shown that people find probability approaches difficult to conceptualise, that people perceive risks differently if the decision option is framed in terms of benefits or costs or willingness to pay or accept, and that people have difficulty in accounting for a wide range of variables in decisions and instead use simple decision rules. Studies have also found that certain risks are ranked as less acceptable if they have particular characteristics (Box 1.1).

The way people respond to risks is therefore not reducible to a product of probabilities: values, preferences and normative judgements inevitably intervene and perceptions guide people's response. As Mary Douglas and Aaron Wildavsky point out, 'the perception of risk is a social process' (1982: 6). Risk perceptions thus emerge from the complex interactions of history, politics, socio-economic conditions and institutional dynamics. As Brian Wynne observes, 'Science is … often partial, temporally contingent, conflicting and uncertain' (Wynne, 1991: 119). With all forms of knowledge, whether derived from agricultural scientists or farmers, being seen as conditional, policy processes for dealing with risk must be negotiated between different actors, each with different perceptions of the nature of a hazard and the likely risks associated.

With complex risk problems, such as are faced in dryland development, there are no neat and tidy answers, as might be expected for an engineering problem. This means that new methodologies for risk analysis are required that take local insights seriously. Silvio Funtowicz and Jerome Ravetz argue for the creation of a 'post-normal science':

> When problems do not have neat solutions, when phenomena themselves are ambiguous, when all mathematical techniques are open to methodological criticism, then the debates on quality are not enhanced by the exclusion of all but the academic or official experts. Knowledge of local conditions may not merely shape the policy problems; it can also determine which data are strong and relevant. (1992: 271)

Box 1.1 Unacceptable risks

- Risks with catastrophic consequences (at low probability)
- Risks with the potential for high-level fatality
- Risks that are associated with dread
- Risks which are seen to be outside personal control
- Risks that are unfamiliar
- Risks that are unequally shared
- Risks where blame can be ascribed to someone else
- Risks that are perceived as preventable
- Risks where causes are assumed to be technological or human, rather than natural

Enriching science through incorporating practice is therefore a necessary way of tackling the complexities of variability, risk and uncertainty that dominate complex development and environmental management problems (Schön, 1983). As Wynne argues, including local perspectives in risk analysis allows the opportunity to 'place scientific knowledge on a more legitimate, properly conditional and ultimately more effective footing' (1992: 279). Ensuring this implies a number of major institutional challenges for the management of risk information (Otway and Wynne, 1989). For, as Douglas points out, 'the institutional filter through which risks are perceived imposes a consistent distortion upon probabilities' (1985: 92). Institutions for managing risk must therefore draw on an extended network of different peer communities, be open and transparent about doubts and uncertainties, encourage trust through participation, and share control with a variety of interest groups (Funtowicz and Ravetz, 1992). These are, of course, major challenges for the design and reform of public institutions dealing with the management of risk and uncertainty.

Exploring risk in farming systems research and development

Most farming systems research has adopted a static view, and considerations of risk have been limited (Anderson and Dillon, 1992). Early formulations of farming systems research adopted a linear approach to the investigation of the farming system which started with descriptive or diagnostic studies, moved into the design and testing of technology, involving the adaptation of existing off-the-shelf technologies developed on-station, through on-farm research, and finally led to dissemination through demonstration and extension (cf. Byerlee *et al.*, 1980; Gilbert *et al.*, 1980; Norman, 1980; Shaner *et al.*, 1982).

Although farming systems textbooks and manuals offer a nod in the direction of risk analysis (e.g. CIMMYT, 1988; Upton, 1987), the uptake in practice is limited. Those analysts who take risk seriously tend to take an economic expected utility approach and attempt to model farming decisions. But most of these models are too data-hungry for regular application, and despite their complexity they often fail to capture farming system dynamics. Attempts to make such approaches accessible to a broader audience fail to achieve their aim, because the mathematical and statistical requirements of even highly simplified models are too daunting for many practitioners.

There has been very limited work in farming systems research on risk perceptions. Studies of risk preference have been limited to gaming simulations as an input to larger modelling exercises (cf. Binswanger, 1980). Decision analysis using decision trees has received some attention (e.g. Gladwin, 1983), but has not been widely adopted. However, qualitative agricultural anthropology studies have a long tradition of taking variation and diversity seriously (cf. Richards, 1939; de Schlippe, 1956; Richards, 1985). More recently, rapid and participatory rural appraisal techniques have been used to look at risk and decision-making through matrix ranking exercises, personal construct analyses, simulated board games and to focus group discussions (cf. Chambers, 1992).

But why is risk of concern in farming systems research and development? Two reasons stand out. First, underinvestment in technology or management may be the result of people not being willing or able to take risks. Second, risks, shocks and stresses may undermine rural livelihoods in a way that increases vulnerability, resulting in impoverishment and powerlessness. These two themes are addressed in different parts of this book. In Part II (chapters 4–8), the impact of risk and uncertainty on agricultural decisions is explored. The case material suggests that although farmers are constrained from taking risks or dealing with uncertainty by a variety of resource constraints, they have a wide range of strategies for managing variability in both space and time. However, this range of risk management strategies is rarely taken account of in the design and implementation of research and extension programmes in dry areas. In Part III (chapters 9–11), the impacts of drought are examined. During drought, longer-term stresses on asset entitlements and investment strategies are combined with more sudden shocks affecting production and consumption patterns, resulting in shifts in levels of vulnerability. Too often, policy responses deal with immediate consequences, such as food deficits, without considering underlying causes, such as changes in entitlement patterns. Instead, a more sophisticated policy agenda is suggested whereby the

Figure 1.1a Map of Zimbabwe showing Chivi and major towns

ways people are exposed to risks, shocks and stresses and the dynamics of vulnerability are taken seriously.

The analysis contained in this book thus suggests a wider scope for farming systems research and extension, one that is not limited to technology testing, but also involves policy analysis and the assessment of impacts beyond the farm. Taking risk seriously means using a variety of analytical approaches that increase the understanding of change and variability at various scales. Models of change that over-simplify, standardise and aggregate in order to ease computation can be highly misleading; instead a methodological pluralism that includes qualitative and quantitative methods is seen to be most appropriate for increasing our understanding of complex, diverse and risk-prone agricultural systems (Chambers *et al.*, 1989).

The case study

This book draws on a detailed case study carried out at three sites – Chivi central, Takavarasha and Ngundu – in Chivi District in Masvingo Province, a largely Shona-speaking part of Zimbabwe between 1990 and 1994 (see Appendix 1 for details on site choice, sampling, data sources and methods used). This period coincided with perhaps the most severe drought this century (chapters 9–11). The scenes of people queuing for relief food or moving *en masse* to the major rivers to pan for gold stood in sharp contrast to the confident image of agricultural success that Zimbabwe had come to be known by. During the 1980s, Zimbabwe had become renowned for the dramatic expansion of smallholder crop output levels since Independence in 1980, which had resulted in the enviable position of the

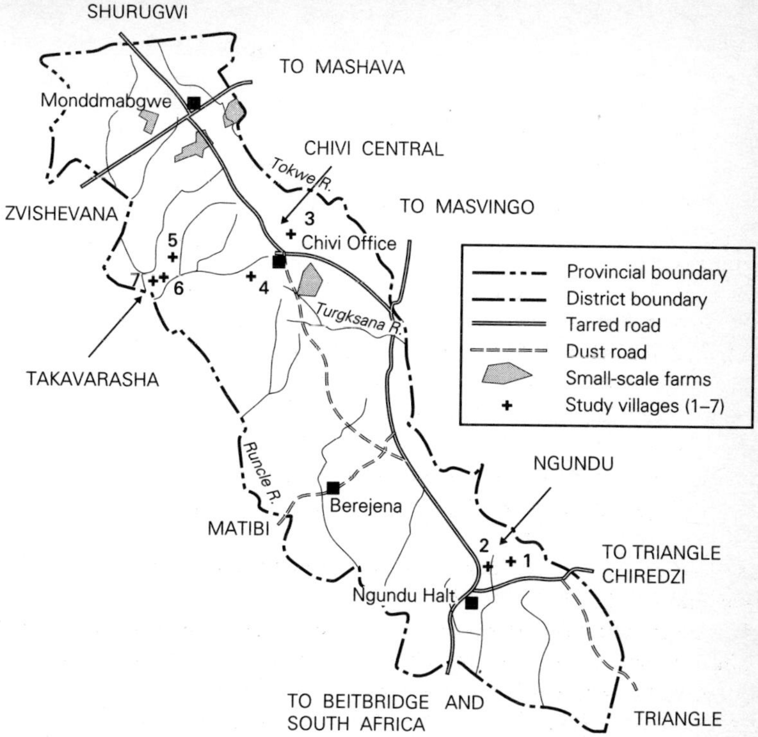

Figure 1.1b Map of Chivi showing the study sites

country having large reserve stores of grain and the ability to export grain in most years (Rukuni and Eicher, 1994). Yet despite this apparent success, there remains a hidden, untold story of poverty and vulnerability in the rural areas. At a household level, there is now known to be widespread food insecurity resulting in deleterious impacts on health (Christensen and Stack, 1992; Chisvo and Jayne, 1992). This is particularly acute in the drier areas of the country, where poor land quality combines with regular drought to make agriculture marginal and off-farm sources of income, whether through wage labour or self-employed activity, vital. Chivi District is one such area, typical of the communal areas of the dry south of the country.

The following sections introduce various aspects of variability faced by people living in the three study sites in Chivi. First, environmental variation is examined with a look at spatial patterning, ecological dynamics and temporal variation in rainfall patterns. Second, socio-economic differences at a household level are introduced, with some basic data presented from the household sample. Further information on the social and institutional context is introduced in later chapters, where questions of intra-household resource access, networks and social relations between households, and institutional forms at a community level are discussed.

Environmental variation

The productivity of resources in savanna environments such as Chivi is highly dependent on the trade-off between available soil moisture and fertility (Frost *et al.*, 1986; Scholes and Walker, 1993) determined by a combination of rainfall patterns, soil properties and landscape form. Soil types range from heavy clay soils to sodic soils to mixed soils to granitic sands (Chapter 7). Heavy soils are usually associated with *Colophospermum mopane*, *Combretum* spp. and on lower slopes, particularly in old field sites, *Acacia tortilis*. By contrast, the sandy soil areas are typified by a *miombo* woodland, with *Brachystegia spiciformis* and *Julbernadia globiflora* being key tree species. The response of crops to rainfall on these different soils suggests fundamentally different ecosystem dynamics in these different environments. Low infiltration rates in the heavy soil areas means that high rainfall levels must be received before effective crop production occurs. However, the relatively higher natural fertility in such soils means that potential production under good rainfall conditions or appropriate water management and response farming techniques is higher than on the sandy soils. The sandy soils show the opposite pattern, with relatively lower rainfall levels allowing earlier planting and the opportunity for some yield in low-rainfall years. However, low natural fertility means that without significant inputs high yields are unlikely even with good rainfall conditions. This pattern of variation and crop management responses in different savanna types is captured diagrammatically in Figure 1.2.

Within these broad environments a range of microenvironments and landscape patches can be found. Variations in topography in the undulating landscape are particularly important in forming this micro-level spatial variation. Catenal sequences typically involve a gradation from upland areas through transition zones to sink areas at the bottom of the slope. Differential transport and deposition of soil and water across slopes creates different components of the landscape with differing agricultural potentials. Whether at the landscape level, with differences between topland, sandy soil fields in the *miombo* areas or at the field level, with differences between erosion source and sink sites within a small area, farmers must respond to this microvariation and differences in agro-ecosystem dynamics (Chapter 6).

The three study sites in Chivi have differing agroecosystem properties. The Takavarasha site is dominated by heavier, clay soils associated with *C. mopane* woodland (Figure 1.2: quadrant 1). By contrast, the Ngundu and Chivi central sites have a mix of clay and sandy soils (quadrants 1 and 4), with interspersed low-lying wetland (*dambo*) areas within the sandy soil

← *Plant-available moisture* →

↑ *Plant-available nutrients* ↓

1: Heavy clay soils with low infiltration rate and high fertility (e.g. *Acacia, C. mopane* areas) = Water management; response farming	2: Low-lying key resource areas: *dambos*; riverbanks; other deposition zones and micro-environments = Dry-season and drought cropping; limited inputs
3: Degraded sites: poor soil structure; leached nutrients = Rehabilitation investment	4: Sandy soils with high infiltration rate and low fertility (e.g. *miombo* areas) = Intense fertility management

Figure 1.2 Interaction of plant-available moisture and nutrients on crop management priorities.

areas (quadrant 2). Within each area there are degraded areas or areas that are naturally unusable for arable production (e.g. rocky areas; sodic patches etc.) (quadrant 3). Rainfall patterns vary between sites, but in general Ngundu receives more rainfall due to local micro-climatic conditions.

Seasonal rainfall differences are superimposed upon spatial variability, making agricultural production highly risky. At Chivi Office the average annual rainfall between 1914 and 1992 was 548 mm. This varied between a maximum of 1,160 mm in 1917–18 and a minimum of 143 mm in 1991–92, with an overall coefficient of variation (CV) of 37% for the period. The pattern of deviation from the long-term mean is shown in Figure 1.3, illustrating the high level of variability in precipitation levels.

There is no evidence for any decline in annual rainfall for Chivi, nor any significant shifts in season starting dates, frequency of mid-season droughts or rainfall intensities. Rainfall patterns are characterised by unpredictable variability. However, rainfall levels appear to follow a cyclical pattern in Southern Africa with a periodicity of between 13 and 19 years (Zimbabwe Department of Meteorological Services, 1981; Tyson, 1986; Mazvimavi, 1989), possibly related to the El Niño-Southern Oscillation (ENSO) effect (Downing, 1992). In Chivi, wetter periods occurred during the mid-1920s, early 1940s, early 1950s and the 1970s. These periods of good rainfall have been important for building up livestock populations and for the recovery of grain stores. The likelihood of shifts in climate patterns in Southern Africa due to the impacts of global warming remains the subject of hot debate. Estimates based on models of maize yields under different climatic conditions suggest that an increase in temperature of 2°C would substantially increase the level of food insecurity of people in the semi-extensive farming zone of Zimbabwe (Downing, 1992).

Rainfall variation also occurs within years, with mid-season droughts being frequent occurrences. The variability of January rainfall in Chivi is

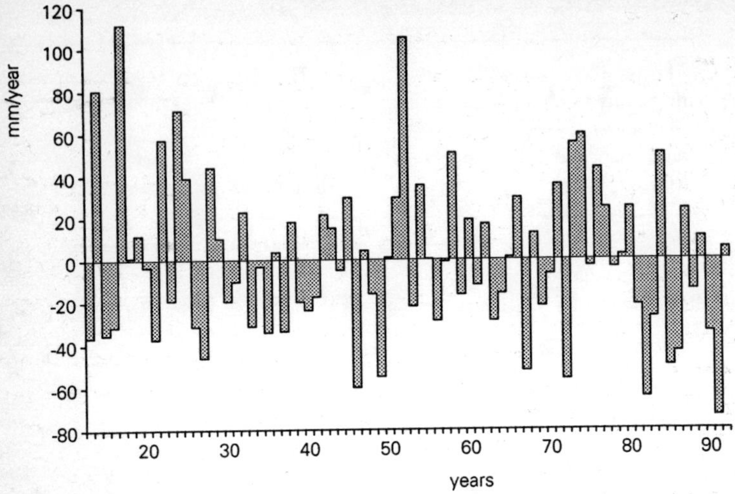

Figure 1.3 Deviations from mean rainfall, 1914–92, for Chivi Office

very high (CV = 78%), and 45.5% of years have January rainfall 25% or more below the long-term average. Mid-season droughts are particularly disastrous for drought-vulnerable crops such as maize. A simple water balance model for three consecutive seasons is shown in Figure 1.4. Rainfall data come from Chivi Office, and Potential Evapotranspiration (PET) data are based on a modified Penman equation calibrated with data from Chivi (Hussein, 1987). Using rainfall and PET data from the period 1954–55 to 1983–84, analysis shows that the median season start date (when rainfall is greater than 0.5PET) is 16 December and the median ending date is 76 days later on 26 March. However, season length is immensely variable, with a CV of 40%. The three seasons studied in depth and discussed in subsequent chapters illustrate the range of this variation.

- The 1990–91 season was poor (total rainfall at Chivi Office = 359.7 mm), with a start date in late November. There was no point in the season when rainfall exceeded PET, so little opportunity for effective crop growth. A mid-season drought struck between mid-December and mid-January when rainfall levels fell below 0.5PET. Late rains in February and March offered some chance of late planting, but much of the maize crop had been lost.
- The 1991–92 season was a disaster (total rainfall = 143mm), and rainfall did not reach 0.5PET at any point. Late March rains were wasted as crop production had been abandoned. The drought caused major mortality in livestock, resulting in a collapse in draught power availability.

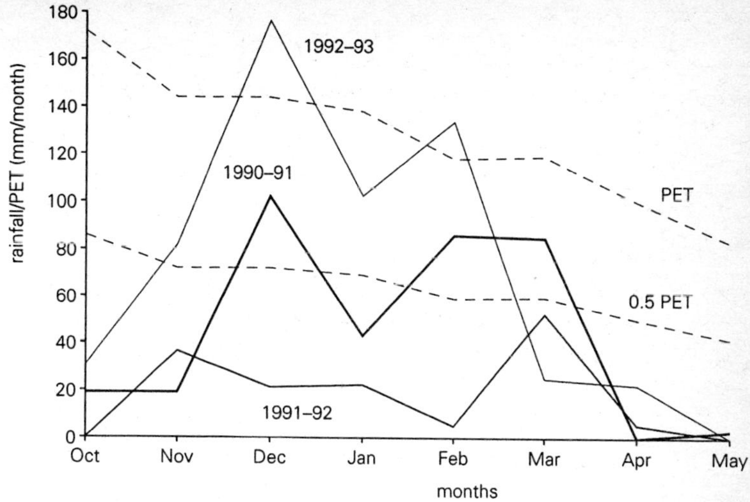

Figure 1.4 Rainy season characteristics (1990–91 to 1992–93)

- The 1992–93 season was much better (total rainfall = 577.1 mm) with reasonably evenly spread rainfall through the season. The season started in early November and continued through until late February. There was a dip in rainfall levels in late December to January, but this did not drop to critical levels.

Chapters 4 and 5 focus on the 1990–91 and 1992–93 seasons when rainfall was sufficient to allow crop production. The impacts on agricultural practice of different patterns of rainfall, combined with other environmental, economic and social factors, are discussed. Since agriculture was effectively abandoned in 1991–92, this year is treated separately and is discussed in detail in chapters 9 to 11.

Socio-economic differences

Not all farmers have the same access to the necessary elements for effective farming – land, labour and capital assets. Effective farming thus depends on the judicious and responsive employment of a variety of inputs and production factors. For those who do not own draught animals or do not have enough labour, the negotiation of access to such inputs is key. Table 1.1 provides a summary of differences between two groups within the household sample: those with and those without draught access.[1] As the table shows, this measure of 'wealth' is highly correlated with other forms of asset ownership (e.g. land, equipment, off-farm income access) (Scoones, 1995a). There are no significant differences between the three study sites

Table 1.1 Socio-economic differences between those with draught access and those without (fewer than two adult cattle and/or donkeys). (Data are for 1991, unless otherwise specified.)

Dimension	Full sample N = 146	Draught access N = 80	Without draught N = 66
Field area (ha: average and range)	5.5 (0.4–16.4)	6.2	4.5
Cattle (N: average and range)	3.5 (0–28)	6.1	0.4
Donkeys (N: average and range)	1.1 (0–10)	1.9	0.05
Goats (N: average and range)	5.9 (0–95)	8.9	2.36
Ploughs	69%	100%	38%
Grain output (bags: average and SE): 1990, 1989, 1988 harvests	12.5 (1.1) 12.4 (1.1) 24.2 (2.1)	19.2 (2.1) 19.2 (2.1) 26.1 (3.9)	7.3 (0.9) 7.4 (0.6) 14.9 (1.4)
Maize sales (bags: average and SE) 1990, 1989, 1988	1.7 (6.3) 1.4 (4.6) 4.1 (9.9)	2.9 (7.2) 2.5 (6.4) 7.6 (13.0)	0.8 (5.5) 0.6 (2.6) 1.6 (5.9)
Household size (N: average and range)	7.2 (1–36)	8.3	5.88
Age of household 'head' (years: average and range)	45.3 (23–83)	46.1	44.4
Remittance access	59%	72%	44%

in terms of the majority of factors. The exceptions are field areas and livestock holdings. Field areas are on average higher in Chivi (6.9ha) and Takavarasha (5.5ha) than Ngundu (4.0ha), reflecting the fact that there are a few very large land holders in both areas. The Takavarasha sample group on average had more livestock than the other two sites, especially Ngundu, reflecting the greater importance of the livestock economy in Takavarasha (Chapter 2).

The structure of the book

This book is divided into four parts. The remainder of Part I provides the context for the detailed case study contained in the following chapters. Chapter 2 introduces the case study area and provides an historical overview examining the various forms of risk imposed by environmental change, government intervention and shifts in the wider economy.

Economic factors are further discussed in Chapter 3 with a look at the process of economic change and the impacts of market liberalisation on people's income-earning strategies. The way different livelihood options are chosen under changing economic conditions is also discussed.

A detailed examination of farmers' practices at a field level is contained in Part II. In chapters 4 and 5, cropping decisions over several seasons are examined in relation to a variety of factors affecting decision-making, including individual preference, economic situation and social context. The next chapters explore farmers' agronomic practice further with an examination of the spatial use of agricultural landscapes (Chapter 6) and the management of soil fertility (Chapter 7). Chapter 8 picks up the themes highlighted in previous chapters and explores the prospects for participatory research and extension approaches that take local conditions seriously.

Responses to drought are the subject of Part III. Here the emphasis shifts from individual field- or farm-level agronomic decisions to questions of livelihood and survival under conditions of extreme stress. The focus thus changes to a wider consideration of entitlements including the mobilisation of assets, claims and exchange opportunities. The analysis thus moves to a wider assessment of on- and off-farm income sources and the importance of social networks and claims on assistance in providing support in times of stress. Understanding people's perceptions of drought is essential to understanding responses. Chapter 9 documents perceptions of the 1991–92 drought, illustrating how differing views on drought and its causes influence the diversity of responses at different levels. Following an historical review of drought response, Chapter 10 looks at people's coping strategies during the 1991–92 period and the patterns of recovery since then. Chapter 11 continues the analysis with a look at the impacts of drought and recovery dynamics of livestock populations.

Part IV of the book contains a single chapter (Chapter 12) which examines the policy implications of the case study findings for Zimbabwe and beyond. This final chapter focuses on four policy areas, namely economic policy and rural livelihoods, land and natural resources policy, agricultural research and extension policy and policies for livelihood security.

Note

1. The initial survey was carried out during early 1991. Households were defined by local people in terms of discrete residence units; field areas were measured by pacing; livestock numbers relate to direct access: all animals held at the home *kraal* (including borrowed animals and not including loaned-out animals); crop outputs relate to field plots only; household size relates to total resident people, including children, excluding migrant workers away for more than six months of the previous year; household head relates to the identified head, sometimes including an absent male; remittance access includes all those receiving some money or gifts in kind in the past year.

CHAPTER TWO

Farming livelihoods in southern Zimbabwe: environmental and economic change

Chivi is commonly perceived as being poor, backward, drought-prone and environmentally degraded. On the rare occasions when Chivi gets a mention in the national press it is usually in connection with drought. Yet Chivi is home to over 150,000 people who, in a variety of ways, make a living in the area. The immediate impression of Chivi differs dramatically depending on the time of year and the quality of the rainy season. In the dry season the area is dry and dusty, with squalls of wind blowing across the sparse, brown landscape. But with adequate rainfall the environment is transformed, with lush grass in the valleys, vigorously growing crops in the fields and green trees covering the hillsides.

Most people drive through Chivi without noticing what happens in the hinterland. The district is dissected by the main roads between Masvingo, Beitbridge and Zvishavane. The administrative centre for Chivi district is Chivi Office, an old settlement established in the early part of the twentieth century. Today it is a collection of government offices and houses, together with the usual range of bottle stores, small hotels and general shops. The rest of the district is largely rural, except for a few small business centres scattered among the villages and Ngundu Halt in the south, where business activity is attracted by the intersection of two main roads. Chivi communal area covers some 3,534 km^2. The farming and grazing lands can be found in a diversity of environments, ranging from the hills of central Chivi to the open plains in the southwest. Settlements are generally scattered in the hills area, with farm plots located in the available cultivable land in the valleys. In the plains, more regular settlement has been imposed and farms are found in the upland areas, with grazing along the rivers and in the valleys.

This chapter introduces Chivi and analyses historical changes in farming landscapes and livelihoods since the turn of the century. This analysis provides the historical context for examining the nature of risk in today's farming and livelihood systems in the chapters that follow.

The transformation of farming landscapes and livelihoods[1]

Travellers who passed through Chivi in the nineteenth century recorded an intensive system of cultivation of valley wetlands (*dambos*), combined with some limited cultivation of upland areas and red soils when conditions were right. Mauch, travelling in 1871, noted: 'Between the kopjes [rocky outcrops] or on other sides of a small perennial river are the furrows of cultivated ground that is intended for growing rice' (in Burke, 1969: 144). Similar impressions were documented by Thomas Leask in 1867: 'The hill was surrounded by rice gardens. These rice fields are in low swamp places and, the better to hold water, they are under ridges' (in Wallis, 1954, quoted by Wilson, 1990). W.H. Brown, travelling with the pioneer column, talked of: 'A thickly populated region and the valleys filled with fields of rice, mealies [maize] and kaffir corn [sorghum]. The people ... built their houses in rocky fastnesses' (Brown, 1899: 93, quoted by Wilson, 1990).

At this time, most settlements were on secure, hilltop sites where people and livestock could be protected from Ndebele raids (Beach, 1980). Livestock populations held by local Shona farmers were limited and the plains were grazed by the wide-ranging herds of the Ndebele (Cobbing, 1976; Mudenge, 1988). Hoe cultivation of rice and root crops (e.g. *Coleus esculentus*, locally known as *tzensa*) in valley wetlands was the most important farming method and labour was mobilised through lineage clusters (Wilson, 1990). The colonial conquest following 1890 saw the end of Ndebele raiding into Chivi and surrounding areas and the beginning of major changes in the agricultural system. During this time, enterprising lineage groups were able to break away from a tight control of labour imposed by the tribute system and embark on new agricultural enterprises in areas now safe from raids. This new-found security, combined with rapid technological changes, encouraged agricultural expansion into dryland farming (Wilson, 1990).

During the first decades of the twentieth century there was an expansion of cultivation into the plains area around the new administrative centre at Chivi Office, with Chief Chivi and his followers establishing claims to large areas of land in the central portion of the district. Here, dryland cropping in large fields became the dominant mode of farming, although many retained small riverbank gardens (*majeke*). Movement from the hills occurred slightly later in the Takavarasha area, with key lineages establishing villages in the clay soil plains and along the banks of the Runde river. This was good grazing country, and large herds built up in the area, while the extensive farm plots were ploughed for millet and sorghum. Major settlement of the Ngundu area in southern Chivi only occurred during the 1950s, with the arrival of people expelled from farms designated for European occupation further north. Prior to this time the area was sparsely populated with wetland farming and opportunistic dryland cropping persisting.

Population pressure has had a major impact on farming landscapes in Chivi. At the turn of the century the estimated population was only around 15,000; by 1930 the population had grown to an estimated 28,500, in part due to population movements into the reserves. Censuses in 1962, 1969 and 1982 showed district populations of 57,220, 80,580 and 103,656 (CSO, 1985). The 1992 census shows a total population for Chivi District (now including Mashava communal land) of 157,428, with a growth rate of 1.98% and a population density of 44.5 people per km^2. Human population growth is likely to continue as the age distribution of the population shows that 48.7% of the population is under 15 (CSO, 1992; 1993).

In the early part of the twentieth century, significant shifts in land use occurred. The colonial government began allocating large tracts of land to European settlers and commercial companies. Following a series of commissions and the passing of the Land Apportionment Act in 1930, 'reserves' for African farmers were established. The reserves made up only 25% of the total land area of the country, while around 50% of the land was allocated for European occupation. Land areas became increasingly constrained in Chivi as more and more people were forced to settle within the boundaries of the communal areas. Land pressure has resulted in an increasing proportion of land being used for farming. The percentage of total arable land increased from under 10% in the mid-1940s to over 20% by the early 1960s. By the late 1980s around 45% of the total area in the district was arable land, the rest being settlements, woodland, rough grazing or granite rock (ICRA, 1987).

The expansion of arable areas has meant that available woodland and grazing has decreased. Livestock must increasingly rely on small patches of grazing within the landscape, found along riverbanks, in uncultivated valley sites, on remote hillsides, along roads and around settlements. With the decreased availability of grass, browse has become ever more critical in livestock diets. Arable areas are now also an important source of fodder, with field-edge grazing and crop residues key to dry season livestock nutrition (Scoones, 1995b). All parts of Chivi have experienced similar patterns of change, although over different time periods. In the past, herds were often allowed to roam over long distances with limited herding. The dangers were more of potential predation by wild animals than of causing crop damage to neighbours' fields. Today, much more intensive herding management must be employed to avoid animals straying into fields and to ensure adequate fodder intake.

The woodlands of Chivi used to provide an abundance of wild products. Oral histories and archival accounts record the importance of hunting for bush meat, particularly in times of drought. In addition, wild vegetables and fruits could be collected in order to supplement cultivated products. Similarly, desired woodfuel species could be harvested easily and large stores were built up during the winter months. Woodland products are still extensively used in Chivi for a variety of uses, including food, fuel or other manufactured products (Cavendish, 1993), but today they often come from sources outside the woodland areas. Changes in the agricultural landscape have thus resulted in the use of new products derived from new landscape niches. For instance, firewood is now collected extensively from farmed areas, with sites around homesteads, on contour bunds and around field boundaries being especially important (McGregor, 1991). Similarly, the once-plentiful wild harvest gathered or hunted in the woodlands is now increasingly derived from arable areas, with fruit trees being retained in fields, wild vegetables collected during cultivation, and field pests, such as rats or mice, being hunted (Wilson, 1990). Some areas in Chivi, however, still benefit from abundant wild resources. For instance, areas close to the sparsely settled hills have easy access to the resource-rich *miombo* woodlands, while others neighbour privately owned commercial ranches where illegal hunting forays are sometimes carried out.

From the 1940s, a series of land-use planning initiatives and enforced natural resources legislation increasingly constrained farming opportunities. The centralisation policy was initiated in nearby Shurugwi by the Chief Agriculturalist of the Native Department, Emory Alvord, in 1929. The policy aimed to modernise local farming systems, which were perceived to be backward, unproductive and unsustainable. Farmers were allocated land holdings of designated sizes, made to shift farm plots and settlements to new areas, and encouraged to adopt a package of technical advice based on improved varieties of grain and cash crops, rotational cropping and the manuring of arable lands (Alvord, 1930). Legislation during the 1940s and early 1950s increased the level of intervention in farming practice in the reserves, further transforming the landscape. The Natural Resources Act of 1942 reinforced the ban on riverbank and *dambo* cultivation and ushered in the era of destocking, in which livestock populations were culled to fit in with official 'carrying capacity' targets. The Native Land Husbandry Act of 1951 consolidated the policies initiated by the centralisation programmes of the 1930s, with a concerted effort to reorganise and modernise small-scale agriculture (Garbett, 1963).

During the liberation war of the 1970s the restrictions imposed by state intervention in land-use management were no longer obeyed, particularly by younger people without access to large land holdings. 'Freedom farming' (*madiro*) became a popular protest around Chivi as people claimed land areas previously reserved for grazing. The good rainfall of these years ensured a growth in crop output, although livestock populations declined due to disease incidence.

Following Independence in 1980, a number of the policies pursued in the colonial era were revived (Drinkwater, 1989; 1991). Bans on riverbank gardening and *dambo* cultivation were again enforced and people were shifted into consolidated gardens some distance from the water sources.

In addition, grazing schemes were reintroduced and land reorganisation and villagisation were pursued vigorously for a period (Cousins, 1992). The new government also announced an ambitious plan to resettle communal area populations on commercial farmland. In 1982 a resettlement target of 162,000 families on 10m ha of land was set. However, by 1989 only 52,000 people were settled on 3.1m ha (Roth, 1990; 1994). Within Masvingo Province, 402,262ha of land has been resettled since 1980, mostly in 'Model A' schemes which, in the drier regions, allow for 6ha of arable land, 0.25ha of residential area and 20ha per livestock unit for grazing (Agritex Masvingo, 1993). Despite the new opportunities opened up by the 1992 Land Acquisition Act, the pace of resettlement remains slow, as the high costs of land acquisition and resettlement infrastructure prevent any major expansion of the programme. Today, around 42% of the total land area of the country is communal area, three quarters of which is found in the drier regions (Natural Regions IV and V) of the country. Only 8.4% of the total land area is made up of resettlement land, while the remainder includes large-scale commercial farms (29%), small-scale commercial farms (3%), state farms (1.3%), parks and wildlife areas (13%) and other areas, including urban settlement (3.8%) (World Bank, 1991).

Box 2.1 lists chronologically the range of state-imposed interventions; each has dramatically affected the lives of Chivi farmers, transforming landscapes and changing the nature of both hazards and opportunities encountered by farmers in Chivi.

Environmental impacts of landscape change

The natural resource base which supports farming livelihoods has changed dramatically over the past century. At the beginning of the colonial period sparse populations were able to make use of a wide range of resources for wetland and dryland agriculture, for grazing and browsing of livestock and for the hunting and gathering of wild products. As landscapes have changed, through agricultural expansion and policy interventions, options have shifted.

Agricultural policy debates in Zimbabwe have been dominated by concerns about environmental change since the early colonial period (Beinart, 1984). Fears of a repeat of the American dust bowl in Southern Africa dominated discussions from the 1920s. The publication of the South African Drought Commission report in 1922 marked a significant turning point in Southern Rhodesia (as Zimbabwe was then known). From this time, more and more attention was paid to issues of soil erosion, overgrazing and deforestation. A major commission of enquiry into the natural resources of the colony (Southern Rhodesia, 1939) set the stage for the passing of the Natural Resources Act in 1942 and the establishment of the Natural Resources Board.

Box 2.1 Some government interventions affecting land-use

1914 Native Reserves Commission outlines a policy for the subdivision of land along racial lines.
1925 The Carter Commission recommends the category of Native Purchase Areas, in addition to African reserves.
1928 The Water Act is passed restricting the cultivation of land close to public waterways and streams.
1929 The centralisation policy designed by Alvord is launched.
1930 The Land Apportionment Act sets in law the designation of all land in the country, with one quarter being allocated for African inhabitation, largely in the low-potential zones of the country.
1939 The McIllwaine report on the condition of the natural resources of the colony recommends the establishment of Natural Resources Board and a range of legislation to protect the environment.
1942 The Natural Resources Act is passed, its provisions include compulsory destocking, prevention of stream bank cultivation and the enforced implementation of soil conservation measures.
1944 The Godlonton Commission reports on 'Native Production and Trade' and recommends the enforcement of good land husbandry.
1950 The Land Apportionment Act is revised to accommodate growing land pressure. New areas, such as Special Native Areas and some Crown Land, are added to the reserves, including Chivi.
1951 The Native Land Husbandry Act is passed and the centralisation policy is enshrined in law. Major financial support from the World Bank allows the government to implement the policy on a wide scale.
1961 The Native Land Husbandry Act is abandoned due to nationalist opposition.
1967 The Tribal Trust Lands Act is passed giving chiefs and headmen the authority to allocate land.
1969 The Land Tenure Act is passed, replacing the Land Apportionment Act. New names are given to various land categories; reserves become Tribal Trust Lands.
1980 Independence; the new ZANU-PF government announces an ambitious plan for resettlement under the terms of the Lancaster House agreement.
1982 The Communal Areas and District Councils Acts set up local administrative structures for the renamed communal areas. District Councils are given the authority to allocate land, with chiefs and headmen given ceremonial duties.
1984 Village and ward development structures are announced by the Prime Minister, and Village Development Committees (VIDCOs) and Ward Development Committees (WADCOs) are formed.
1988 The Rural District Councils Act is passed, with all land whether previously European or African coming under one district-level authority
1992 The Land Acquisition Act gives government opportunities for compulsory purchase of under-used farm land for resettlement.
1993 The Land Tenure Commission is convened to investigate future tenure options for the communal lands.

Concern about soil erosion in Zimbabwe was expressed during the first decades of the century; a series of articles warned of the dangers of inappropriate cultivation measures (e.g. Watt, 1913). These concerns with erosion translated into policies and interventions. From the 1920s major campaigns to conserve arable lands were launched. Between 1929 and 1939 some 46,212ha of arable land in the reserves had been conserved with contour ridging (Southern Rhodesia, 1939). This increased significantly with the expansion of the centralisation policy (Aylen, 1942) and the implementation of the Native Land Husbandry Act (Floyd, 1959). By 1957 over 200,000ha had been contour-ridged and the technique had been applied to nearly all arable areas in the country by the early 1970s (Whitlow, 1988).

Alarmist reports about overgrazing in the communal areas have appeared regularly since the 1930s (Scoones, 1995c). The destocking programme from the mid-1940s was aimed at conserving pasture areas by reducing animal numbers to specified 'carrying capacities', and was carried out in most communal areas, including Chivi. However, the impact of draconian attempts to reduce livestock populations was limited as animal numbers soon recovered. By the mid-1960s, Cleghorn (1966: 60) observed that 'nearly half of the rangeland areas in the communal lands were either bare or very overgrazed'. During the 1960s and 1970s, rangeland conservation measures switched away from destocking to the encouragement of grazing schemes and rotational grazing. By 1973 there were over 300 such schemes in Masvingo Province alone, including a number in Chivi (Dankwerts, 1974).

The impacts of and responses to these policies were mixed. Many people strongly objected to the compulsory imposition of mechanical soil conservation measures and the destocking of cattle. This became a focus for nationalist opposition to the government (Ranger, 1985). For instance, people argued that traditional methods of natural resource management were effective and that contour ridging, combined with land reorganisation, potentially increased the risks of erosion (Wilson, 1988). Where ridges were constructed inadequately, due to the use of unmotivated, forced labour or due to hurried surveying by Land Development Officers eager to meet targets, this was certainly the case. Equally, destocking was based on an inappropriate understanding of range ecology and livestock management in the communal areas. The reduction of livestock populations to levels appropriate to commercial beef ranching undermined the livestock economy in the communal areas (Scoones, 1989). Due to the high levels of climatic variability and the spatial heterogeneity of the grazing resources, static notions of carrying capacity are misleading (Behnke *et al.*, 1993). The non-equilibrium dynamics of the grazing resource meant that paddocked, rotational grazing schemes were also inappropriate interventions. The need for flexible grazing management, requiring movement to grazing resources in different parts of the landscape, could not be accommodated in restrictive, fenced schemes. Dissatisfaction with the schemes, combined with growing insecurity in the rural areas, led to most being abandoned during the 1970s.

Following Independence, concerns about the environment resurfaced. Henry Elwell argued that in many communal areas the effective soil life was only 35–50 years and in some areas, such as the Save Valley, as little as 10 years (Elwell, 1983). An estimate that soil loss from arable land was 50t/ha per year and 75t/ha per year from rangeland was made on the basis of a nationwide survey (Elwell, 1985). Erosion hazard modelling suggested that 39% of the land in communal areas was at high or very high risk from sheet erosion (Stocking and Elwell, 1973). Examination of aerial photographs implied that 83.3% of all communal areas were eroded; 27% of this erosion was regarded as severe or very severe (Whitlow, 1988). Erosion levels were found to be correlated with population density, land tenure, crop land area and presence of rock outcrops (Whitlow and Campbell, 1988), as well as agricultural history and patterns of settlement (Stocking, 1978). Levels of dam siltation appeared to support the claim of serious soil loss: over 50% of the 132 dams surveyed in Masvingo province were severely silted (Elwell, 1985). Most analysts conclude that soil erosion will have a major negative impact on crop yields over time, incurring major economic costs. For instance, Stocking (1986) estimated that soil nutrient losses of nitrogen and phosphorous were equivalent to Z$94/ha per year at 1985 prices.

These studies produced a flurry of environmental concern reminiscent of the 1930s. For instance, Elwell proclaimed in doomsday terms that: 'There is absolutely no doubt whatsoever that malnutrition and death through starvation of the communal land population is inevitable if present rates of soil erosion are allowed to continue' (Elwell, 1983: 145). This was translated into policy advice. For instance, environmentalists argued for more investment in soil conservation measures (Elwell, 1985); they suggested that resettlement would inevitably result in environmental damage and by implication should be slowed down (Whitlow and Campbell, 1988: 26); and they supported the implementation of national plans to halt environmental degradation (Zimbabwe, 1987).

But what is the evidence for environmental degradation? How appropriate are the policy initiatives being proposed? Despite the evidence that soil is lost from fields and measurement plots, the impact of soil erosion processes on production is less clear. Estimates of loss rates are often many times higher than actual losses, especially from well-conserved arable plots (Roberts and Lambert, 1990); sediment yield measures in major rivers do not match up with soil losses (Walling, 1984), showing that soil is often being redistributed rather than lost; and studies of gulley changes over long periods do not support claims of major increases in soil erosion (Elliot, 1989).

A more tempered view of environmental impact is suggested by an examination of agricultural output levels over time. If erosion and land degradation in the communal areas were as severe as has been claimed over such a long period of time, then it could be expected that they would have had an impact on crop yields or on the ability of the land to sustain livestock populations. In fact, there is no such evidence, as crop yields have increased significantly since the 1950s (Tattersfield, 1982). Although this is partly due to improved technology, notably hybrid seeds and fertiliser inputs, there is little evidence that widespread reductions in yield potential have occurred due to land degradation. Instead, crop yields in the communal areas are largely influenced by annual rainfall variations rather than long-term declines in soil productivity. A similar story applies to livestock. Data over a 60-year period show that cattle productivity has been maintained or increased and that population fluctuations are due to rainfall rather than any secular decline of land productivity (Scoones, 1992a).

This does not mean that there has been no environmental degradation. It is clear that some areas have suffered irreversible declines in potential productivity due to soil erosion, livestock disturbance or other human-induced impacts. However, these tend to be focused on particular sites, with a variety of causal factors impinging all at one time. Within Chivi, degraded sites can be seen close to settlements or water points where human and livestock paths converge, near roads with poor drainage, or where cultivation has been attempted on inappropriate soils. At such sites production potential is clearly reduced as soil nutrients are washed away or compaction reduces water infiltration.

Environments in communal areas such as Chivi have been transformed, but not necessarily degraded. The fact that land has been cleared for new land uses or grasses grazed in order to feed livestock does not constitute degradation unless the production potential, and particularly the economic return from the land, has been impaired (Abel and Blaikie, 1989). At the aggregate level, the transformation of the Chivi landscape over the past century has increased the value of production considerably. During the 1920s, the area cultivated was only 10% of the total land area, with crops yields on average only 300kg/ha. Today, the cropped area represents nearly half of the total area with average crop yields around 1,000kg/ha. During this time real prices of crops have also increased, meaning that the total value of crop production in Chivi has more than doubled. The same applies to cattle value: the total real value of cattle increased by over 100% between 1925 and 1990. Whilst there is no room for complacency, there is equally little evidence to suggest that such increases in output value cannot be sustained.

Agricultural and technological change

The arrival of the plough was probably the single technological change with the most dramatic impact on agricultural production in the twentieth century. Across the communal areas only one in 333 people owned a plough in 1910, by 1920 one in 45 people did and by 1940 nearly every family owned one (CNC Annual Reports). This pattern was repeated in Chivi, where the Native Commissioner reports the presence of only 18 ploughs in the district in 1902, 1,300 a decade later and over 5,000 by 1939. This shift in cultivation system from one concentrated on labour-intensive cultivation of wetland patches, combined with some shifting cultivation, to land-extensive cultivation of dryland areas brought with it many changes in risk exposure.

Dryland cultivation offered the potentials for high overall output if large areas were cultivated with millets and sorghum. Individuals and families could now plant large areas with relatively little labour; the constraining factor increasingly became livestock for draught, instead of human labour for intensive hoe cultivation. However, opting for dryland cultivation had its pitfalls, as the variability in season quality meant that crop output levels fluctuated dramatically. Food security thus had to be ensured by an increased emphasis on storage of crops, as well as continuing the practice of wetland gardening for drought insurance (Wilson, 1990).

Opportunistic dryland cropping involved concentrating on small grains. Colonial officers in Chivi regularly recorded their importance for food security. For instance, the Native Commissioner for Chivi noted in 1928: that '*Mhunga* [pearl millet] did extremely well despite the drought and it was this crop that saved the district from famine. Mealies [maize] were an absolute failure throughout the district' (NC Chibi, 1928). Pearl millet was the principle crop in Chivi at this time. Flint varieties of maize were also grown in more favourable sites, but usually for green consumption, rather than for grain. There was an enormous genetic diversity of sorghum and millet to draw upon, with varieties suitable for most conditions and uses (Wilson, 1987).

New patterns of differentiation between households emerged in this period, as the lineage cluster as the basis for production organisation decreased in importance. Farming entrepreneurs, with access to large areas of land and with sufficient draught power, were able to accumulate large stores for sale or exchange in times of need. Risks of crop failure were thus offset by ownership of livestock assets and opportunities for local exchange through barter and sale. By bartering or selling grain stores during drought such individuals, known locally as *hurudza*, gained large herds of cattle, as well as other assets such as carts or even motor vehicles.

Crop management

In the early years of the twentieth century, the technical advice offered by colonial officers and agricultural demonstrators was largely rejected by farmers in Chivi. People preferred low-input, land-extensive opportunistic dryland farming of small grains to the labour-intensive crop rotation and manure fertilisation recommended by the authorities. The Native Commissioner for Chivi regularly complained about the lack of adoption of manuring practices in his reports, explaining that farmers rejected the idea because manure encouraged weed growth and entailed a lot of extra work in transport in small baskets from the cattle *kraal*. However, a combination of increased population pressure and changes in technology began to transform the farming system from the 1940s. Land scarcity necessitated an intensification of dryland farming, and the greater availability of animal-powered transport meant that manuring was increasingly practised. Certainly the availability of transport was rising in the district as people invested in carts of various types. In 1926 only three scotch carts, twelve ox wagons and one donkey wagon were recorded for the district as a whole, but by 1939 there were 54 two-wheel scotch (ox-drawn) carts, nine four-wheel wagons, as well as four motor cars and two lorries (NC Chibi, 1926; 1939).

The 1950s saw the beginnings of the adoption of other new technologies for boosting production, including hybrid maize, a variety of cash crops, such as cotton, and inorganic fertiliser. At first only the relatively resource-rich shifted their production strategy at the encouragement of the agricultural demonstrators. But the arrival of hybrid maize, in particular, transformed the agricultural landscape in Chivi. The major yield breakthroughs achieved with the release of SR52 and its successors (Chapter 8) meant that maize, although prone to drought conditions, was a viable competitor with small grains on dryland fields. By 1970 nearly everyone was planting at least some hybrid maize in Chivi (Rohrbach, 1988). Since Independence the use of hybrid maize seed has steadily increased, although, with the removal of subsidies in the 1990s, this pattern may reverse.

The spread of the use of inorganic fertiliser has been less dramatic, since the returns are variable and often negative (Chapter 7). By the 1970s only around 15% of farmers in Chivi were using fertiliser regularly and usually only in small amounts (Rohrbach, 1988). Use increased with the post-Independence credit packages, but since 1990 use has decreased to a minimal level due to high costs. Until recently, diversification into cash crops was also limited to a few farmers. Attempts to encourage cotton-growing date back to the 1930s in Chivi, but they were largely unsuccessful as people had alternative cash sources.

Following Independence, the new government committed itself to support the growth of the agricultural sector in the communal areas. Support included a major expansion of the agricultural extension service, the expansion of the formal Grain Marketing Board (GMB) and Cold Storage Commission (CSC) crop and cattle marketing network into the remotest of communal areas, as well as a variety of subsidies on both agricultural inputs and outputs. The support of the post-Independence

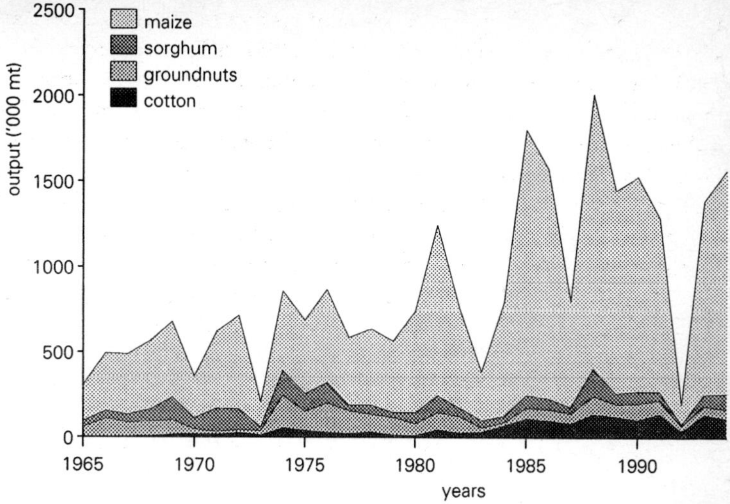

Figure 2.1 Crop production in the communal areas of Zimbabwe, 1965–93 (selected crops)

government offered many communal farmers a real opportunity for increasing the value of their output and a new set of incentives for investing in agriculture. This resulted in a massive increase in overall agricultural output from the communal area sector following Independence, with major increases in maize areas planted, as well as diversification into sunflower, cotton and other cash crops (Weiner *et al.*, 1985; Rukuni and Eicher, 1994; Figure 2.1).

However, the benefits have been unevenly distributed (Stack, 1994). Those living in regions of the country with better rainfall were able to make better use of cheaper inputs. Equally, those who sold crops regularly were able to profit from better market access and increased producer prices in the communal areas (Jayne and Rukuni, 1993). Most farmers in Chivi, however, have been unable to reap the benefits of the post-Independence boom in agricultural production (Chapter 3).

Livestock

At the turn of the twentieth century cattle populations were very low. They had recently been decimated by the 1896 rinderpest epidemic (Mack, 1970) and had suffered repeated raids from the Ndebele (Cobbing, 1976). However, from the 1910s cattle numbers in Chivi started to recover (Figure 2.2). Favourable rainfall conditions, access to large grazing areas and a reduction in disease incidence meant that animals thrived. The importance of livestock in people's livelihood increased significantly in the early colonial

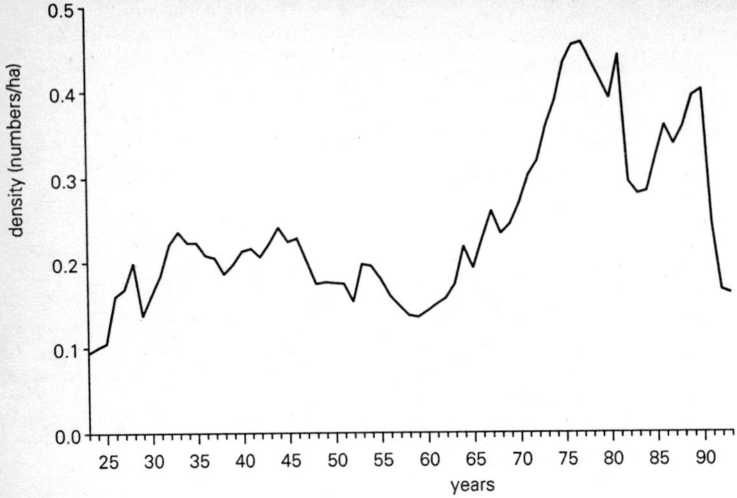

Figure 2.2 Cattle population density in Chivi, 1923–93

period as cattle became an increasingly important production input, through the expansion of draught power, and an important source of exchange entitlement in times of food shortage (Chapter 10).

Most livestock interventions in the colonial era were focused on cattle production. Early initiatives concentrated on developing a disease control programme in the reserves, and by the early 1920s there was the beginnings of a network of dip tanks in Chivi. This expanded significantly over the following decades, and soon all cattle were being regularly dipped. Foot-and-mouth disease was a perennial problem in the Chivi area, especially during the 1930s, and there were regular movement restrictions imposed to stop the spread of the disease to neighbouring commercial ranches. From the late 1920s attempts were made to improve the indigenous cattle breeds through the supply of grade bulls across Chivi. In 1929, 50 Hereford bulls were purchased and distributed to trusted headmen across the district. Each year more bulls were introduced in the hope of breed improvement. However, by 1940 the policy was abandoned; no bulls were left and it was realised that the indigenous breeds were much hardier and more suited to the harsh environments found in Chivi.

Smallstock populations expanded dramatically too in the early decades of the century. Goats, in particular, thrive in the *Acacia* savannas in some of the drier areas. For both men and women, goats have always been a good investment, providing both guaranteed growth and security for drought periods. Donkeys were first imported from South Africa around 1905 and they have become an increasingly important source of draught power over time. In 1907 only 18 donkeys were reported in the whole of

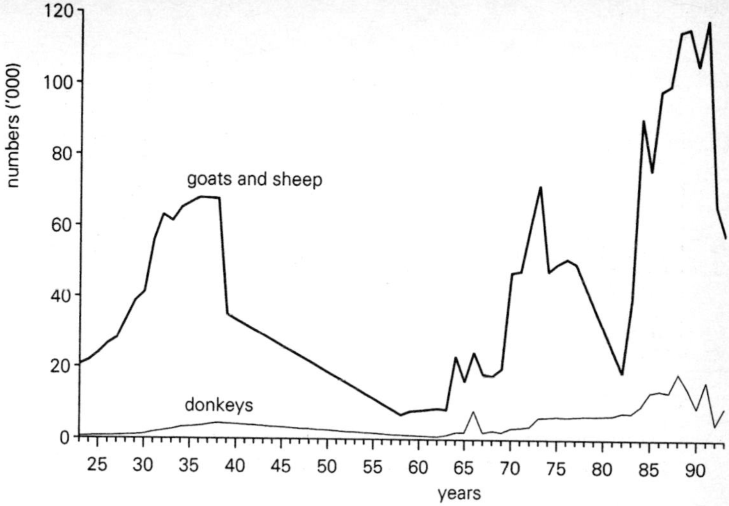

Figure 2.3 Smallstock and donkey populations in Chivi, 1923–93

Chivi, but by the early 1920s there were several hundred. Since then the donkey population has expanded enormously, particularly with the increasing vulnerability of cattle to drought (Chapter 11).

By the early 1980s livestock populations had recovered from the losses suffered during the liberation war. Numbers had almost returned to the high levels of the good rainfall years of the early and middle 1970s when drought struck. The 1982–84 drought saw a massive loss of cattle; mortality rates in some areas of Chivi were as high as 60% (Chapter 11). This was a severe blow to the fragile agricultural economy. The bumper harvest of 1985 provided some compensation, but further disasters were to follow. Major droughts in 1987 and 1991–92 meant that cattle populations have been unable to recover to former levels; the result has been severe draught power shortages for many farmers. Through this period, smallstock and donkey populations fared much better. Although kidding rates were depressed, goat mortality hardly increased during the droughts of this period. Donkeys were only hit by the severest of drought conditions, being able to survive off very limited grazing.

Agricultural prices and marketing

The market orientation of agricultural production has seen major changes over time. While local bartering and sale has always been an important route for exchange, other options opened up with the growth of the wider economy in the first decades of the twentieth century. Traders took advantage of new market opportunities arising with the establishment of

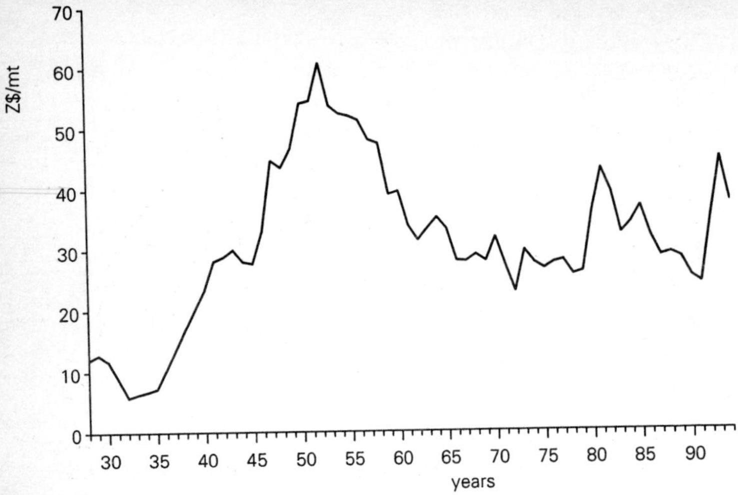

Figure 2.4 Maize price, 1928–94 (deflated price with CPI base = 100 in 1960)

mining centres and agricultural schemes nearby Chivi during the 1920s; sorghum, millet and maize were increasingly sold for cash. However, during the 1930s, fearing competition with the emergent white commercial farming sector already suffering from the effects of economic depression, the colonial government imposed a series of restrictions. The Maize Control Acts attempted to channel all maize sales through a marketing board which offered low prices to African producers. This resulted in the collapse of maize prices during this period, reducing the incentives for marketing through formal channels. There were ways round the restrictions, however, and traders continued to operate illegally in Chivi. As real prices of grain crops rose during the 1940s, and incentives to grow maize increased, maize again became an important source of cash income (Figure 2.4).

Price incentives for crop-growing have varied over time. For instance, there was a long period of decline in real producer prices of maize during the 1950s and 1960s. Maize prices increased at Independence, but the 1980s saw another real decrease in prices, until prices were raised again in the early 1990s. Until very recently, centralised price-setting by the government, following negotiations with representatives of the major farming unions, has characterised the pricing system, with political considerations often highly influential in the final outcome.

Prior to Independence, the crop marketing infrastructure in Chivi was very limited. There was only one government-approved buyer in the district, who started in the early 1960s; all other crops had to be transported to the Masvingo Grain Marketing Board (GMB) depot if they were to be sold through formal channels. At Independence only 5% of all

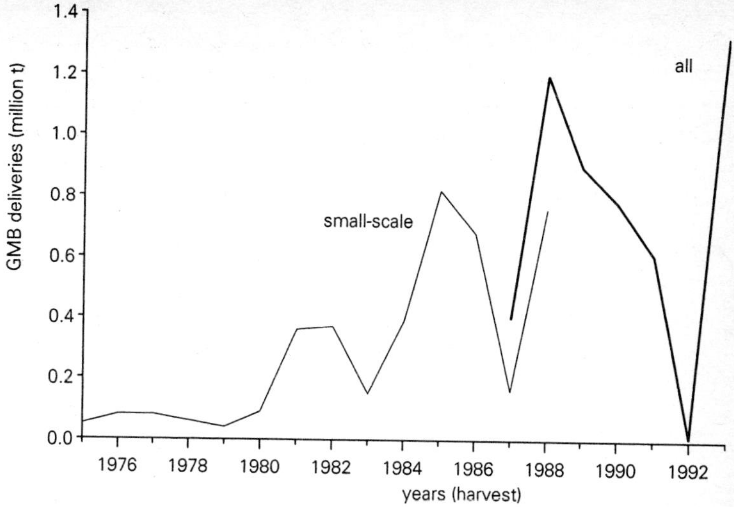

Figure 2.5 Maize deliveries to GMB depots in Zimbabwe, 1975–93 (1975–88 small-scale sector; 1987–93 all areas)

crops were sold to the GMB (Rohrbach, 1988), but this changed with the establishment of three GMB collection points in the district in 1985–86 and the initiation of a network of approved buyers. In 1985, around 30% of all crops were sold through the GMB when producers found that prices were higher than on the local market due to the subsidisation of transport costs by the board (Rohrbach, 1988). This changed pattern of deliveries to the formal marketing system is reflected in data for the country as a whole (Figure 2.5). However, crop marketing is an irregular affair in Chivi and so the new GMB depots were used only rarely, with significant sales only occurring in 1981, 1985 and 1988 (Chapter 3).

After Independence, livestock sales were encouraged by an expansion of Cold Storage Commission (CSC) sales pens in Chivi. Weight grade sales at fixed prices were offered and real prices were high, except during droughts, when poor condition combined with oversupply to depress price levels. The competitive prices offered by the CSC meant that marketing through the formal channels became increasingly favoured. This contrasted starkly with the situation in the late 1940s when the Native Cattle Marketing Act (1947) and the Native Development Fund Act (1948) were passed resulting in high levies on cattle sales. Combined with restrictions on itinerant traders imposed by the colonial authorities, this limited the sale of cattle except under conditions of duress when drought struck or tax demands were made.

Until the 1990s, agricultural policies in Zimbabwe have been characterised by intense government intervention (Rukuni, 1994). In the colonial era, legislation restricted marketing opportunities for Africans (e.g. Maize Control Acts), while post-Independence this was reversed with subsidised parastatal marketing boards (GMB, CSC) offering communal area farmers controlled prices for certain commodities. In Chivi this subsidy benefited those farmers who sold crops or cattle regularly, but not the vast majority of farmers who rarely, if ever, marketed their products. Restrictive sales channels also meant that commercial millers operated an effective monopoly over maize meal distribution, with a negative effect on consumers – the majority of Chivi households in most years. With the removal of subsidies and the liberalisation of the marketing system from 1991 to 1992, a wider range of marketing opportunities have been opened up (Chapter 3).

Households, lineages and social networks

The risks to agricultural production in a dryland environment such as Chivi are mediated by a range of networks, institutions and organisations. Individuals are not alone in the pursuit of livelihoods, they are part of the social fabric making up rural society. This is highly complex and always changing.

During the nineteenth century a lineage-based production system based on tribute labour formed the basis of agricultural organisation. Labour relations, settlement patterns and land use were all constituted around a tight network of relationships centred on the elder, male lineage head. Through a tribute system (*zunde*), he was able to control labour and so production. This tight control was weakened during the expansion of settlement and agricultural activity during the early colonial era (Wilson, 1990). Male lineage heads established new villages and their immediate families farmed on individual plots, often with men and women having separate fields. The lineage mode of production, however, did not cease completely, since access to cattle became important. Younger members of the village would normally be reliant on lineage elders for supplying draught animals for ploughing their fields. Sometimes loaning arrangements (*ronzera*) would allow stockless families to hold cattle of a resource-rich relative in return for herding labour.

Relationships between households also included the sharing of labour for herding or agricultural activities, such as weeding or harvesting. Pooled herding systems were common, as were work parties (*humwe*). These co-operative activities within lineage clusters continue today. They persist particularly in villages where large families live in close proximity and ties remain strong. In other instances, sharing occurs as a form of charity when someone who is old or infirm is helped out (Chapter 4). But most people observe that co-operation is on the decline. This is attributed to a variety of factors, ranging from increased individualisation due to the cash orientation of farming, the emergence of markets for draught and labour, and the break-up of tight lineage-based groups through population growth, lineage fission and the in-migration of 'outsiders'. Others put it down to a change in attitude and the loss of a sense of community and belonging brought about by disputes, jealousies and witchcraft. It is difficult to assess these claims, as reflections on a past characterised by co-operation and community spirit may be somewhat overblown. However, it is clear that agriculture today is often individualistic, with farming households increasingly going it alone. But in times of trouble, such as following drought when draught power is scarce and labour is critical to ensure a good harvest, networks are re-established and co-operative behaviour is very evident (Chapter 10). Social networks based on lineage relations and friendship thus may not be critical to agricultural production in all years as they were in the past, but they are certainly of vital importance as a means of offsetting extreme hardship.

Relationships within households have also changed over time, affecting the deployment of labour and the nature of agricultural production. Following marriage, a woman is expected to provide both children and agricultural labour. Since most assets, including land, are controlled by men, women have limited formal entitlement to productive resources. However, in practice the nature of conjugal relationships is immensely varied (Jackson, 1994), with many women, particularly in cases where the husband is absent working in town, taking control of joint finances, managing the land, providing food for the household and overseeing children's upbringing and education. Women may also have independent sources of income derived from smallstock raising, gardening or craftwork which may be invested in building up assets at the parental home away from the acquisitive eye of any husband.

Children's roles in agriculture have also changed. In the past, children were ready sources of labour for all activities. Young boys were sent herding animals from a young age and girls always helped their mothers both in the fields and at home. Whilst children's labour is still vitally important today, it is no longer so available as previously, due to the commitments of schooling. Nearly all children in Chivi go to primary school (e.g. 96% of eleven-year-olds attend school in Masvingo Province; CSO, 1992) and a large proportion attend secondary school. This expansion of schooling since Independence has meant that fewer and fewer children are now full-time agricultural labourers.

Land tenure and institutions

Following the colonial conquest and the establishment of the 'reserves', land previously held by chiefs was expropriated and allocated for alternative uses, much of it for European settlement. In the early part of the twentieth century, arable land was allocated by the village head under the direction of the overall chief in the area and, because of relative land surplus, large tracts were claimed by individuals. Livestock were allowed to graze uncultivated areas during the rainy season, but were permitted to roam freely once the end of the cropping season was declared by the headman.

This situation changed with the implementation of the Native Land Husbandry Act from 1951 when land was reallocated and standard portions were given to male heads of household. Village headmen (*sabhuku*, literally 'keepers of the book') were allocated larger portions in recognition of their services and on account of their obligation to feed visitors to their village. Through this process, women lost independent rights of access to individual holdings, although husbands often allocated portions of land as women's plots. All land was registered and those who were absent during this time became effectively landless. The aim was to develop a title-based system of land holding where rights to arable and grazing land could be exchanged. During the 1950s a certain amount of land was bought and sold (Weinrich, 1975), but basically the imposed system did not wholly override the customary pattern of allocation and control by lineage heads.

With the passing of the Tribal Trust Lands Act in 1969, chiefs and headmen were again allowed to allocate land. This was an attempt by the government to co-opt traditional leaders and dissipate nationalist opposition to the series of land husbandry interventions carried out in previous decades. This period saw an attempt to strengthen a tradition of ward (*matunhu*) management of natural resources by chiefs and headmen, building on earlier analyses of land administration and management (Holleman, 1969). However, the pattern of collateral inheritance, where the eldest male inherits all rights, meant that there was a proliferation of disputes over chieftaincy titles as sub-sections of lineages competed for authority. In many cases, following painstaking negotiations over kinship relations, the state had to intervene and appoint chiefs.

Chiefly authority broke down in most of Chivi during the 1970s at the height of the liberation war, and there was limited control over land allocation, with 'freedom farming' and an effectively open-access situation the result. Following Independence, authority was reasserted by the ZANU-PF government and new administrative structures were imposed. The authority over land allocation was once again captured by the state, with district councils becoming the legitimate authority over all land issues following the passing of the Communal Areas Act in 1982. Local administrative structures were planned and a hierarchical village and ward committee structure was announced in 1984. The establishment of the elected village and ward development committees (VIDCOs and WADCOs) presented a direct challenge to the previous authority structures in the rural areas. The chiefs and headmen were now relegated to nominal posts in charge of a limited legal function, together with ceremonial and ritual roles. The 1980s thus saw a major battle between the newly imposed village and ward committees and the so-called traditional authorities.

The form this contest took varied from place to place. In central Chivi the younger, more politically active inhabitants became elected to the committees with the previous authorities largely by-passed. A similar situation arose in the Ngundu area where, with the help of a strong party organisation in the area, in-migrants usurped the authority of the longer-term inhabitants through the offices of the councillors and committees. A much less confrontational situation arose in the Takavarasha area. The pattern of settlement in this area meant that there was no single lineage leader and much internal competition between different factions. The lineage politics of the area were played out within the committees with lineage leaders becoming elected to key posts alongside younger political activists, businessmen and teachers. In many areas the political in-fighting between lineage leaders, party politicians, in-migrants and longer-term residents incapacitated the new structures for many years. Their inability to deliver the promised fruits of post-Independence development frustrated many and there has been a general return to faith in the chiefs, headmen and lineage elders. This has been increasingly recognised by government, first tacitly and then more explicitly, with the government recognising the right of chiefs to allocate land once again in 1992.

The consequence of this complex history is that tenure patterns are complex, overlapping and often ill-defined (Scoones and Wilson, 1989). The fission of lineages into competing sub-groups and disputes between and among families have combined with the effects of government intervention that has continuously redefined boundaries through land reorganisation initiatives, as well as imposed parallel administrative structures. The overall picture is thus confused and varied.

Off-farm work and employment

The migrant labour economy of Zimbabwe has, since the early colonial era, relied on a supply of labour to work in the mines, in the towns and on the commercial farms. In the early part of the twentieth century the low wages, poor conditions and insecurity of this formal employment was only occasionally attractive to people (largely men) from Chivi. Many preferred to remain farming their land and only to seek employment on a seasonal basis or in periods of drought. Colonial administrators often despaired at the uncertainty of the labour supply, and so they encouraged a permanent labour force drawn from Malawi or Zambia in preference (Palmer, 1977; Phimister, 1988). The Native Commissioner for nearby Belingwe (now Mberengwa) commented in 1934:

> Sufficient labour was offered in the first part of the year ... but there have been shortages latterly. This is usually the case ... as there is a general exodus of indigenous natives at the commencement of the rains to return to their villages to plough ... there can be little inducement for an able bodied native, with a

wife and family to support, to work from sunrise to sunset for 15 shillings. (NC Belingwe, 1934)

The emergence of the dual, migrant labour economy presented many familiar dilemmas for the government. The Native Commissioner of Selukwe (Shurugwi) reflected upon the question in his 1947 annual report: 'The government say all natives cannot be farmers and some must go and stay out of the native areas for work. Can present industries absorb the surplus? ... What are we to do with the natives in employment who become too old to work?' (NC Selukwe, 1947)

The relative returns to formal employment versus agricultural incomes have been an important factor determining migrant labour in Zimbabwe since mines, commercial farms and other urban-based industries were established from the 1920s. With increased real wage rates and improved conditions, periods of full-time employment became increasingly attractive for men, particularly in drought-prone areas like Chivi. By 1945 participation in the formal labour economy had increased significantly and 40% of the 'indigenous' African population over the age of fourteen was employed. By the mid-1960s, this rate had increased to 55% (Arrighi, 1970). This reliance on periods of formal employment has become characteristic of the livelihood strategies of Zimbabwe's rural areas. Agricultural or livestock production is insufficient to sustain households, especially under conditions of high environmental uncertainty and a diminishing resource base. A study carried out in Chiweshe during 1960 showed that on average 33% of total household income was derived from remittances (Johnson, 1968). By the mid-1980s this high reliance on remittance income was still the case. A national survey in the good agricultural season of 1984–85 found around 19% of total income was from remittances (Jackson and Collier, 1988). In the poorer season of 1986–87, around 37% of total income was from this source in the dry, Mazvihwa communal area (Scoones, 1990).

Since the mid–1980s, the contraction of the economy has led to increasing levels of unemployment and declining real wages (ILO, 1993). The devaluation of the Zimbabwe dollar, following the implementation of the Economic Structural Adjustment Policy (ESAP) policy, has had an inflationary impact on the economy. In the short term at least, this has exacerbated the trend of decreased real wages and increased unemployment, especially as the loan conditions require major retrenchment in the public sector.

Services: agriculture, education and health provision

Agricultural extension services have a long history in Chivi. The first agricultural demonstrators arrived in Chivi in 1927 when two were appointed by Alvord to work alongside ten demonstrator farmers. A third demonstrator was posted to the district in 1939. Around this time, the Master Farmer training scheme was initiated in the district. This training scheme, and much of the extension support, focused on relatively resource-rich farmers who were able to make use of the information offered and adopt the technologies recommended. Following Independence, a new extension service (Agritex) was formed with an expansion of field-level extension workers, and improved transport provision. In 1993 there were 33 extension workers in the district, supported by district and provincial-level specialists. However, the extension service has largely retained its pre-Independence focus on high-input, technological solutions to farming problems, tending to underestimate the problems of the risk-prone, resource-poor farmer.

During the colonial era, research support was virtually exclusively focused on the problems of the large-scale commercial sector (Tawonezvi, 1994). There were, however, some beneficial spin-offs for farmers in Chivi, including the spread of hybrid maize from the 1950s (Chapter 8). Since Independence, research has been redirected towards the needs of the small-scale sector, and increased attention has been paid to drought-resistant crops such as millet and sorghum, water harvesting technologies and draught power issues. The Farming Systems Research Unit has been working in Chivi since 1982 attempting to examine problems identified by farmers. However, despite this shift in research emphasis, the last fifteen years have not seen any major technological breakthroughs appropriate to resource-poor farmers in dry areas, nor has research had much impact on the type of recommendations offered by the extension service.

Since Independence, government has been joined by an increasing number of non-government organisations (NGOs) working in agriculture and resource management. In Chivi, NGOs have been working on a variety of themes, including tree planting and woodland management (ENDA–Zimbabwe), water development and small-scale gardening (Lutheran World Federation, Oxfam), and soil and water conservation (ITDG-Zimbabwe). These efforts have complemented government activities including food-for-work projects, although the mixture of approaches, the diversity of messages, and the differences in incentive packages have sometimes confused local communities.

Formal financial services have been very limited in Chivi. Prior to Independence, credit options for communal area farmers were practically nonexistent. After 1980, the Agricultural Finance Corporation (AFC) offered credit and this was eagerly taken up. However, a sequence of poor harvests meant that massive default rates arose and the credit package was soon abandoned. Since then, formal credit options have been very limited, although a variety of informal savings mechanisms are important (Chapter 3).

The level of schooling has increased dramatically since Independence, incurring large increases in government expenditure (Chung, 1988). Today the literacy rate (measured as attendance at school to Grade 3 or above) is 77% (CSO, 1992), with much higher rates among younger people, who have benefited from post-Independence schooling opportunities. This contrasts with a national literacy rate of only 55% prior to Independence. In 1979 only 42% of primary-school-age children attended school, and only 20% of primary-school leavers attended secondary school (Chung, 1988). In Chivi there was a rudimentary network of primary schools, supported by the government. Those who were lucky enough to reach secondary education usually attended one of the few mission schools in the district. Since Independence, primary schooling is near-universal and secondary schooling to O-levels is the norm. Schooling is regarded as a critically important investment and both girls and boys are encouraged to attend. Many parents go to great lengths to pay the school fees, often sacrificing their hard-won assets such as goats or cattle in order to raise the needed money. The costs of school fees have risen dramatically. Whilst primary schooling remains relatively cheap at Z$20–30/year in 1994, the costs of sending a child to secondary school have escalated to around Z$160/year, some 300% higher in nominal terms than a decade ago.

A similar expansion in service provision following Independence is seen in the health sector. Whereas the Chivi population used to have to rely on mission hospitals or limited government hospitals in the main towns, today the network of rural clinics and village health workers provides an important service of basic health care (Loewenson and Sanders, 1988). Between 1979 and 1992, infant mortality, child mortality and maternal mortality all fell, and life expectancy increased in Masvingo Province (CSO, 1993), although the impacts of HIV/AIDS mortality have yet to be fully felt. Department of Social Welfare food relief schemes have also been important, particularly during drought. The extent of free provision has decreased in the last few years and some commentators suggest that this is beginning to reverse previous gains (Chisvo, 1993). What is clear is that the post-Independence expansion of health care has significantly decreased mortality and morbidity and has especially benefited women. Improved health status has positive impacts on agriculture as work is not disrupted by illness and anxieties about health do not add to the risks faced in everyday life.

Conclusion

Agricultural landscapes today are products of history, shaped by wider economic forces, government policies and the management interventions of generations of land users. Understanding this historical context is key to the understanding of people's livelihoods. Knowing what hazards exist and what opportunities are on offer for farming families today requires insights into this process of change.

This chapter has shown how resource entitlements, and so the exposure to risk and uncertainty, of people living in Chivi have changed dramatically over the last century. While the productivity of the resource base upon which people depend may have not declined so much as some commentators claim, access to and potential claims over resources have altered significantly. Overall, field areas have declined, as have livestock herd and flock sizes. Equally, access to common property resources, such as grazing and woodland, has also diminished. These changes have hit some harder than others. In particular, in-migrants, younger men and women of all ages have less access to such resources than they did in the past. For many, these changes have increased vulnerability, as farm production is inadequate to tide people over during drought.

Increased vulnerability has been compounded by state intervention, with land-use planning and legal restrictions often reducing opportunities for flexible land management. Uncertainties over resource access have also been introduced by interventions which have regularly shifted tenure rights and administrative arrangements. The failure to address effectively national land distribution inequalities since Independence has also meant that people are more reliant than ever on off-farm income sources. Farm production is simply inadequate to satisfy regular needs, even with the support of extended networks of kin and friends.

With a decrease in local resource entitlements through the erosion of the asset base, there has been a shift to a greater reliance on public support. The post-Independence record of public service provision has certainly been impressive, acting to reduce some of the risks associated with food shortage or poor health, as well as offering improved educational opportunities. However, expenditure restrictions mean that such provision is increasingly under threat, shifting the risk burden back onto the rural population.

Despite this rather grim picture, some brighter lessons can be drawn from this historical review. Today's agricultural landscapes and livelihoods have been shaped by continual adaptation and innovation over time. With new constraints, new opportunities have been found. Much of this innovation has come through local experimentation, sometimes with technologies supplied from outside, but often not. While there remain many constraints at both local and wider levels, effective support to such locally determined processes of change will be vital if rural livelihoods, in places like Chivi, are to be sustained into the future. The ways in which this might happen are pursued in later chapters; first, however, economic factors influencing people's livelihoods are discussed.

Note

1. The agricultural history of Chivi is based on a combination of key informant interviews and archival research. This work would not have been possible without the important work carried out by Ken Wilson, Billy Mukamuri and others. Data sources for the figures contained in this chapter are included in Appendix 1. Archival sources can be found at the end of that appendix.

CHAPTER THREE

Money and markets: the rural economy and farming livelihoods

Money is a rare commodity in Chivi communal area. It comes irregularly and unpredictably. Securing the household money supply and fulfilling investment plans are both dominated by uncertainty. There are various sources of money, each of which is affected by different patterns of risk. Over the last 50 years, perhaps the major source of money for rural investment has been income from remittances. Cash from crop or livestock sales are next in importance. Small amounts of money are also generated by local piecework, craft, manufacturing or trading activities. The likelihood of receiving cash income from any of these sources is dependent on a variety of factors at the household level and within the wider economy.

People of different ages, at different stages in the household demographic cycle, have access to different opportunities; people with different levels of formal education equally have different chances, particularly in the formal labour market; men and women may pursue different livelihood careers, raising money from different sources and so on. Money also comes in different amounts, pulsed seasonally and interannually by variations driven either by the environment or factors in the economy. Crop incomes in Chivi are sporadic, being dependent on the occasional good harvest. Equally, cattle sales are rare, only being possible for those whose herds have grown large during extended periods of good rainfall when forage was plentiful. Crop and cattle sales tend to realise large amounts of cash at one time, offering the opportunities for lumpy investments which happen only once in a while. The same applies to one-off payments of bridewealth, pensions or redundancy pay. By contrast, other forms of income, such as from goat or chicken sales, vegetable production, crafts and trading and most remittance flows, provide relatively small amounts of money, but on a regular basis. These sources service the regular expenditures on groceries, clothing and other daily necessities.

This chapter starts by looking at changes in livelihoods over time with a series of case studies from men and women of different ages. Following a discussion of the macro-economic backdrop to current livelihood strategies, the diverse ways of raising money – through crop farming, livestock sales, remittance income and off-farm work – are discussed. These are related to the need to provision recurrent expenditures, purchase capital assets and make long-term investments. The ways the flow of money are managed within the rural economy are also examined with a consideration of savings, credit and investment strategies. Throughout this discussion a differentiated view of the rural economy is taken, highlighting both inter and intra-household, as well as seasonal and interannual, differences in income and expenditure patterns.

Case studies: economics and livelihoods

Patterns of circular migration, with periods of work away, preceded and succeeded by farming activities, characterise the lifecycle of men in the migrant labour economies of Southern Africa (Murray, 1987; Potts and Mutambirwa, 1990). The flow of remittances from off-farm work helps to sustain the rural economy and to structure social relations. In Chivi many buildings, most agricultural equipment and nearly all first cattle were purchased from the pay packets of migrant workers. Similarly, marriage payments are also paid from this source, with initial bridewealth (*lobola*) payments now often being paid by the prospective husband rather than his father as in the past (Jackson, 1994).

The importance of remittance incomes must be set within an understanding of the household demographic cycle (Ellis, 1988). A classic pattern would be when a young man is reliant on his parents until marriage. After marriage he would be expected to establish a new home, but it is likely that he would still be reliant on parents or older relatives for the supply of draught power, equipment and maybe labour for farming. He would usually seek formal employment around this age. As men are increasingly expected to contribute to the payment of their own bridewealth, seeking employment may be a prerequisite of marriage. Formal employment is a route to investment in the rural home through marriage, acquisition of cattle, purchase of farm equipment and the building of a home (increasingly a square, brick-built structure with an asbestos or tin roof), as well as the regular provisioning of the family through payment in cash or kind for groceries, medical expenses, school fees and other expenses. Responsibilities include immediate family (wife, children), as well as older parents and younger brothers or sisters. During older age men usually return home to farm, taking on the responsibilities of an elder within the family. Women, by and large, are expected to remain at the rural home and manage the farm, as well as bring up children. Their money-earning opportunities are thus limited to local income-generating activities. This idealised pattern of the demographic cycle, of accumulation and disposal of assets over a lifetime, is of course highly variable. The case studies below show the great variety of life courses followed by a group of men and women of different ages, from different parts of Chivi.

Men's life histories

Matye (age 72)

I am now 72 years of age and I was born in Mapuvire near this place. I never went to school and learned my skills from others in the area. I started to stay behind the spot where the school now is and used to have my fields there. The village was small and we had good lands. I decided to move to a new site and establish our new home around 1945. I came with close relatives only and all the people had access to good fertile lands. At that time contour ridges were being dug in the area and I joined as an assistant to the Land Development Officer. I was, however, soon dismissed and I travelled to Kadoma in search of work. There I worked under a ginnery and married my first wife who was from the area. My first child was born in 1951. While working I was able to buy some cattle and I came back to Chivi to farm. I later divorced my first wife, but married again in 1954. My second wife has given birth to nine children and my third wife to seven. I did not think about going back to work and committed myself to farming. With the help of my family I was able to cultivate a large area and we sometimes reaped good harvests. Through farming I have managed to purchase cattle, goats, scotch carts and farm implements.

Phillimon Midzi (age 63)

I was born in 1931 in the Zwamapere area. My father died while I was still an infant so I grew up under the guidance of my brother Nyengerai. I attended school from 1944 and studied up to Standard 5. Then I ran away from school and got a job as a conductor on Amos Makombe's bus service. I was getting £3 every month and an allowance of 12c each day. During the time I was working on the buses I got married. This was in 1957. The next year I established my home in the very place it is today. The Native Commissioner allocated me a field area and I began to plough. In the same year I left my job on the bus services, I moved to Bulawayo where I acquired a hawker's licence. I worked with my brother, Mangudze, buying and selling clothes until 1962. In 1963 I married again and I returned home to join my two wives. I now have eight children. My first-born, Elfas, was born in 1959, but sadly he died during the liberation war. My other son, Kudakwashe, was born in 1966 and got married in 1988. Seven other children are living at home, with one at secondary school at the moment. While I was a bus conductor I bought four heifers at £5 each. Later, while hawking, I bought another three. Through these jobs I was also able to pay *lobola* which cost £35, equivalent to seven beasts. In addition to livestock I have two scotch carts; one was acquired from my brother who migrated to Gokwe, the other was exchanged with a bicycle which was bought following some success at gambling. My other money was gained through farming which allowed me to build my home, purchase more livestock, buy agricultural implements and educate my children.

Newton Zivhu (age 46)

I was born in 1948 in Gomana village. I married Rose Sunday in 1970 and we now have eight children – five daughters and three boys. My home was established in 1978 when we were granted a field and garden. My eldest daughter was married in 1993 and the eldest son completed his O-levels in 1989, but is still not working. The other children are all still at school. I worked in Triangle as a general worker in the mid-1960s and then later in South Africa from 1977 to 1981. When I was working in South Africa I managed to buy a bicycle, build a new house, purchase a sewing machine and radio and also livestock. Since 1981 I have been at home and have been farming. In years of good harvests there are no problems and I sometimes sell my crops and buy things. For instance, last year we had a good yield and I bought some more farm implements to replace those bought long ago. However, with the costs of things today – school fees, clothes, groceries and so on – things are getting increasingly tough.

Bowas Kuzipa (age 41)

Our family originated in Zimuto area near Masvingo. Our parents migrated from Zimuto riding on donkeys and first settled in the Mandamabwe area. Here they found fertile sandy soils and very few people. They farmed successfully, exchanging food for cattle and goats. As the sandy soils became tired, they got less and less produce. They decided instead to move to Takavarasha where the in-laws were staying. They were welcomed in the area and given fields with rich red soils. I was born soon after their arrival in this area in 1953. I grew up herding cattle and started school at Chiware in 1962. In 1970 I went to Harare and got a job at Isella bakery as a general labourer. This job lasted until 1974 when I went to Mashava mine where I was employed until 1979. As soon as I returned home I got married and my daughter was born the following year. My father paid all the *lobola* costs, as at that time he had plenty of cattle. I had very little and struggled to make ends meet through farming. In 1985 I managed to exchange grains for donkeys. I also worked for the District Development Fund as a labourer and managed to buy more donkeys sufficient to make a span. In 1992 I built my own home – there are two houses of brick and thatch. I am now a farmer and I will not return to work.

Livison Dube (age 26)

Our family originated in Nyajena and my father lives near Chiredzi in Mhuka village near the Save river. I was born in Chiredzi in 1968 and grew up in that area. During this time I herded cattle and attended school. I was forced to leave school after Grade 7 in 1987 due to lack of school fees. In 1990 I went to Checheche area and worked as a general labourer moulding bricks. After this I went to Chiredzi and worked cutting sugar cane on the estates. I left the job after only six months and accompanied my father's young brother to his new home in Chasiyatende in Chivi. I helped him at his new home and later married in the area while I was working as a herdboy for Mangweza of Runai village. I arranged for payment of some of the *lobola* money myself, as my father was living far away. My first child was born in 1991 and we stay together at my father's young brother's home. I was granted a field in 1993, but I have yet to build a home of my own. My field is inadequate for survival, so I continue to work for others. This time I work for Mr Maranbire who is a headmaster at the local primary school.

Women's life histories

Jester Sihambe (age 54)

Our family comes from Chivi central and my parents are both living in Sihambe village. I was born at this village in 1940. In 1958 I married Kefas Chanda. We established our home the following year and have farmed the land ever since. I now have seven children in the family, including four daughters and three sons. My eldest is working as a policeman in Harare, my fourth born is a bank teller also in Harare and my daughter, Sibongile, is working in a supermarket. The other children are not working and some live nearby. All our assets, including the money spent on our children's education, have come from farming. For instance, we built our house in 1959 following a good harvest. Equally, livestock were purchased in 1960 once crops were sold, and farm implements were bought following a good harvest in 1972. These days the harvests are not so good due to drought, but we get enough to feed ourselves.

Enita Zivhu (age 42)

My family originated in Gutu, but my parents currently live in Hurungwe. I was born in 1952 and went to school between 1960 and 1968, but had to come home because the mission school did not have sufficient accommodation. I married a soldier, Kangai, in 1969. I have three children – two sons and one daughter. The home was established in 1970 and we got a field and a garden in the same year. While he was working my husband purchased some livestock. Sadly, my husband died in 1974 and I had to start non-farm activities in order to survive. I do sewing and crocheting, as well as keeping poultry. Most of my assets are from my farm work, as well as poultry sales, in addition to my husband's pension. I bought a sewing machine from the 1981 harvest and a cultivator from the 1985 harvest. I also did some house building following the harvest in 1986. The most recent harvest allowed me to purchase a wheelbarrow. Poultry sales have also allowed me to buy a scotch cart and a radio.

Mai Makadara (age 35)

I was born at Maregere village. I did primary education in Mazorodze school, but I failed to get as far as secondary school due to money problems. I went to Gweru to stay with relatives where I hoped to retake Grade 7. But my uncle wanted me to be a maid and also help with his market stall. I failed Grade 7 and so came home and stayed here during the liberation war. At the end of the war, when the comrades returned from Mozambique, I married an ex-combatant who came from around here. We were married in 1979. I am now the mother of five. My first-born is doing Grade 6, my second-born is in Grade 3 and my third-born has started Grade 1. My husband is working away and works as a builder in Norton. He married a second wife there, but she does not come home. After this happened my husband failed to send me money, so I reported the issue to the Community Court. I was offered Z$250 per month and I get it automatically one day after his pay through the Post Office. When my husband found out, he came straight to Chivi. Now he comes regularly and I give him some of the money. When I was receiving no support I turned to farming. I farmed seriously, making use of the cattle that my husband had bought in order to plough the land. At that time my husband's parents also helped me out. Now I have money, it makes life a bit easier as I can hire people to help. The cattle have all died due to drought, so again I must hire spans for ploughing. I am also a vegetable vendor, buying and selling vegetables in the area. Since we have tapped water close to our home it is easy to carry out gardening throughout the year.

Lucia Z. Madzivadondo (age 25)

My family originally came from Mashava-Bere area, but when my grandparents died my parents moved to the Masunda area where my aunt was married. They were very young at that time and they had gone to seek help from relatives. The fields they were allocated were, however, very small and of poor quality. For this reason they moved again to the Musvuugwa area. Here they were given better fields and although they started very poor, they were able, through hard work, to improve their situation. They bought cattle, donkeys and goats. They also acquired a scotch cart, a wheelbarrow, two ploughs and a cultivator. My father became a very successful farmer. He is still alive and now he specialises in cash crops like cotton and sunflowers. I was born in 1969 and grew up in the Kokera area, attending school up to Form 4 between 1977 and 1987. After leaving school I got married to Zanda Madzivadondo who was by that time still a schoolboy. Our first child was born in 1987 and our second in 1990. We established our own home in 1990 and were given a field of only one contour by the *kraal* head. This field is too small to live from, so I have joined food-for-work and I also do sewing and crocheting. From 1989 Zanda went to work in Chiredzi as a general labourer, but this only lasted a few months. In 1991 he went to Kadoma to get a job and was lucky to get temporary work. In 1993 he got another job as a storekeeper in Chivi. All the money had to be used for paying off *lobola* and providing food for the family. We have made attempts to improve our lives through getting loans for cattle, seeds and fertilisers, but all the money was eaten and we had to sell the seed and fertiliser to others. I have also tried to get a passport in order to take up trading, but the lack of money has meant that this is impossible. These days, life is difficult without a job and with only a small field.

The increasingly constrained opportunities for income earning are highlighted by these stories. For younger men, the chances of finding off-farm work are increasingly slim, allocations of land in the communal areas are getting smaller, and the costs of getting married and raising a family are escalating. A different set of problems are highlighted for women. A number of women commented on the dangers of relying on men for income, particularly in the context of polygamous marriage arrangements. However, the opportunities for independent income-earning activities are limited, especially when other obligations, such as child rearing, cultivation of the main field and management and herding of livestock, compete for time and attention. With data from the Chivi study sample, the following sections pursue the themes highlighted by the case studies, asking how different people's income portfolios are composed and what trade-offs must be made between different earning opportunities and expenditure demands. Before examining the data in detail, the macro-economic context for money earning and market transactions in Chivi is discussed.

Macro-economic change and the impact on rural incomes

Zimbabwe has a relatively well-developed economy, with a high degree of linkage between sectors. Farmers living in Chivi are part and parcel of this wider system. The economy is composed of a dual agricultural system, with quite distinct commercial and communal area sectors, a substantial manufacturing and industrial base and a growing service sector, including quite sophisticated private and state-controlled financial services. Zimbabwe's macro-economic performance since Independence has been disappointing. Slow rates of growth in the economy have meant that budget deficits rose as the burdens of subsidies and an expanding civil service increased. The post-Independence government maintained a strategy of restricting imports, limiting foreign exchange availability, artificially maintaining the value of the currency, combined with high levels of regulation, including price regulation, labour practice restrictions and the control of investment flows (World Bank, 1991).

In an attempt to reverse the pattern of low investment and economic stagnation, in 1991 the government embarked on an ambitious programme of economic reform (Zimbabwe, 1991), with support from the World Bank. The aim was to reduce the budget deficit through a rationalisation of the civil service and the parastatals, to shift the exchange rate policy to achieve a realistic currency value, to encourage agricultural trade, notably the boosting of exports, and to increase employment opportunities (World Bank, 1991). The economic structural adjustment policy (ESAP) has provoked much controversy. In the years since its implementation it certainly has not proved the economic miracle that some of its more ardent advocates claimed. Indeed much hardship has been caused, with reverberations throughout the economy (ILO, 1993).

The policies of 'stability through control' of the UDI period and the first decade after Independence resulted in an inflation rate of around 15% during the 1980s. Since 1990, inflation rates have increased dramatically, reducing purchasing power and depressing the real value of incomes. Inflation peaked at 49% during the drought of 1992 before declining to 18% in early 1994. High interest rates mean that borrowing has been expensive and investment depressed. Escalating costs have meant that there have been large numbers of retrenchments and a contraction in the job market. The failure of government to deal with civil service and parastatal restructuring has meant that expenditure cuts have been made in other public services with declining standards of provision and an increasing move towards cost recovery in the health and education sectors.

The droughts of 1982–84, 1987 and 1991–92 have taken their toll on the economy. With a shift in food production from the commercial farms to the communal areas following Independence, there has been increased volatility in the supply of basic foodstuffs. The inflationary consequences of drought have hit the low-income consumer hardest. In addition, the manufacturing sector contracted significantly during these droughts because water and electricity shortages disrupted critical industries. The high costs to government of importing and distributing food have meant increased levels of internal borrowing. In the 1990s, all these factors have exacerbated the recessionary effects of structural reform (Benson and Clay, 1994).

These wider economic changes have had a major impact on the income-earning opportunities of farmers in Chivi. Because of the close linkages between the different components of the agricultural sector and between agriculture and industry, impacts in one area will be felt in another. People living in Chivi are not immune. Farmers in Chivi are both food producers and food consumers; they are both workers and farmers; and they are both rural and urban residents. Differences within households, between generations and genders and over time, with changes in the demographic cycle, mean that people in Chivi are affected by every change in the wider economy.

Sources of income

The structure of rural incomes is, as we have seen, immensely varied. Moreover, the composition of rural incomes is not static. With the high variability in returns from agriculture, crop incomes may be high one year, but nonexistent the next.

Rural incomes in the dry communal areas of Zimbabwe are generally low and highly skewed. Estimates put total household income (including the value of subsistence agricultural production) during the mid- to late-1980s at on average under Z$1,500 per household per year (Jackson and Collier, 1988; MLARR, 1989; 1990; Mudimu *et al.*, 1990; Stack and Chopak, 1990; Scoones, 1990). During the 1990s real incomes have declined, especially during and following the 1991-92 drought and the implementation of the structural adjustment programme. The relative contribution of agriculture to total income varies significantly from place to place and from year to year. A national survey for 1989–90 showed that crop incomes made up 58% of gross incomes for all sites, while livestock income was 8.3%, off-farm income 15.6% and remittance income 17.6% of a total gross income of Z$1,451 per household (MLARR, 1990). However, in some areas remittance incomes are much more significant; this is especially the case in drought years when agricultural incomes collapse (Scoones, 1990; Corbett, 1994).

Differentiation within rural communities is highly significant, with all income streams being very skewed. This is particularly so for cash incomes from agriculture, as very few people are able to regularly sell crops or livestock. A national survey carried out in 1984-85 showed that 42% of measured income was controlled by the top 10% of households, and only 4% of all income was controlled by the bottom 25% of households (Jackson and Collier, 1988). This skewed distribution was found across all communal areas, but was particularly pronounced in the drier regions. Income studies in Chivi show a similar pattern, with over 50% of households having annual household incomes below Z$400, and under 10% having incomes above Z$1,200, during 1990 (Corbett, 1994).

Exploring how rural incomes are structured is an important step if we are to understand how people buffer their livelihoods against the hazards of living in a dryland environment (Maxwell and Smith, 1992). Patterns of income diversification allow the mixing of different income streams by individuals and households in relation to seasonal and interannual variations in income-earning opportunity. The way people trade off the various options in relation to the risks faced is the subject of the following sections.

Crop incomes

Crop sales are rare events in Chivi. Since Independence there have only been four occasions where significant proportions of households have sold crop surpluses. These good harvests were in 1981, 1985, 1988 and 1993. Sales in other years were practically zero. Even in the good years, not everyone sells. Some farmers' land areas are too small and their food provisioning commitments and debt burdens too high to expect any surpluses for sale. On the other hand, others are able to sell regularly and orient their production towards cash sales of maize, sunflower and cotton. The skewed pattern of crop income in Chivi is reflected in national statistics, where it is found that around 40% of farmers sell no crops, 40% receive half the crop income, and the top 10% of farmers receive the other half (MLARR, 1989; Christensen and Stack, 1992). Patterns of differentiation in Chivi are thus most acute in the good harvest years. In droughts, by contrast, these days nearly everyone suffers (Chapter 10). Table 3.1 shows the sales pattern for the Chivi sample farmers in the harvest years between 1988 and 1993. No sales were recorded during 1991 and 1992. Between 1988 and 1990 average sales of maize ranged from 1.7 to 4 bags, realising under Z$100.

The patterns of sales are comparable between the three Chivi study sites. Ngundu farmers tend to sell a greater percentage of their crops compared to farmers from Chivi and Takavarasha, reflecting their greater concentration on maize production for sale. Takavarasha farmers sell the smallest proportion of their crops on average, reflecting their different cropping strategy, which incorporates a greater range of small grain crops and the low yield potential for maize in this area. Farmers in all areas market most of their sorghum and practically all of their sunflower and cotton.

Table 3.1 Average number of (91kg) bags (and SE) sold in harvest years 1988–93 by Chivi farmers (N = 146)

CROP	1988	1989	1990	1993
Maize	4.14 (0.83)	1.7 (0.39)	1.69 (0.52)	3.90 (0.70)
Pearl millet	1.16 (0.38)	0.2 (0.06)	0.30 (0.13)	0.13 (0.08)
Sorghum	2.32 (0.52)	0.74 (0.20)	0.42 (0.19)	0.74 (0.17)
Groundnuts	0.54 (0.15)	0.32 (0.12)	0.53 (0.15)	0.62 (0.36)
Sunflower	2.03 (0.42)	1.40 (0.28)	2.56 (0.40)	2.01 (0.30)
Finger millet	0.58 (0.11)	0.25 (0.07)	0.21 (0.06)	0.24 (0.08)
Cotton (bales)	0.45 (0.14)	0.39 (0.12)	0.24 (0.06)	0.17 (0.07)

Livestock incomes

Livestock sales provide a useful source of cash income, but their role in the rural economy varies between livestock species and producer. Sales of cattle are rare, usually provoked by a particular cash crisis. Most farmers in Chivi do not have sufficiently large herds to allow for regular commercial sales of cattle. Prior to the 1991–92 drought, 55% of the sample population in Chivi owned no cattle at all. By the end of the drought this proportion had increased to nearly 70% (Chapter 11). Most estimates assume that a viable breeding herd that allows regular offtake is around ten, given the existing sex and age structure of cattle populations (GFA, 1987). Prior to the 1991–92 drought, fewer than 10% of the sample households had cattle herds of greater than ten, while after the drought this percentage had dropped to around 1.5%. In other words, commercial production of cattle for sale is a non-starter. Sales and slaughter rates over the last decade for a neighbouring communal area are shown in Table 3.2.

These data show cattle sales and slaughters peaking in times of drought (1983–84, 1986–87, 1990–91) and decreasing in the later periods of drought due to poor condition, as well as in the post-drought recovery period in order to rebuild herds. This pattern of sales following rainfall cycles is shown for longer time series for the same area (Scoones, 1990). Sales may be to the Cold Storage Commission (CSC) or to other local farmers. The CSC runs a network of cattle sales pens in the communal area where regular purchases are made on a simple grading basis. Other sales may be to local farmers who want to buy breeding stock or draught animals. In some parts of Chivi, commercial ranchers operate an exchange system where older animals are exchanged for young heifers (Chapter 10). Because of the small herd sizes, most cattle sales are distress sales, either in drought when owners know there is no other option, or in response to particularly pressing cash needs, such as school fees. For most people, cattle are therefore a last-resort cash-generating option. The value of cattle derives

Table 3.2 Cattle sales and slaughters as percentage of total herd size (Mazvihwa communal area dips), 1983–94 (all years October–September, except 1993–94, October–May).

Year	% Sales	% Slaughters
1983–84	13.1	8.2
1984–85	0.7	2.6
1985–86	1.1	2.1
1986–87	3.2	2.4
1987–88	0.9	1.3
1988–89	2.3	2.6
1989–90	1.7	2.3
1990–91	5.4	3.6
1991–92	2.0	0.7
1992–93	1.4	0.9
1993–94	1.3	1.3

Source: Veterinary Department files, Zvishavane.

much more from their other functions, such as draught power, milk, manure etc. (Scoones, 1992b).

Goat sales are more common, particularly in the drier areas of Chivi where goats thrive. Goat population dynamics show different patterns to those of cattle. Droughts do not hit as hard; indeed, if water is still available for drinking, goats often do well in dry periods due to the decreased disease risk and a lower parasite burden. However, supply usually exceeds demand, because there are few marketing opportunities. There are no organised marketing outlets for goats, so sales tend to be opportunistic and dependent on contacts with people who have disposable incomes, such as civil servants and people living in town. But with reduced real wage levels, the amount of money circulating in the rural economy has been depressed, resulting in fewer sales.

Chickens provide a regular source of cash income for many households. Individuals in five households in the sample established commercial broiler chicken operations during 1993 which yielded significantly more income than the raising of free-range indigenous chickens, so long as the initial investment capital and markets were found. By 1994, another six individuals had started broiler operations as a way to raise money and recover from the impacts of drought (Chapter 10).

Remittance incomes

As the case studies presented earlier have shown, the employment situation today has changed significantly from that encountered in the past. Real wages have declined since the mid-1980s, unemployment has also risen steeply, and employment security is now much lower than it was in the past. In the mid-1990s the chances of getting a job, particularly for inexperienced, unskilled school leavers, are small, and if you are lucky enough to find one it probably will not pay well or offer good job security (Bennell and Ncube, 1994). This situation is having a number of major impacts on the rural economy, particularly in areas like Chivi where a sole reliance on agriculture is impossible under current land pressures and where remittances have become the lynch-pin of rural investment and household provisioning strategies.

In all three study areas over 50% of households regularly received remittance income, either in cash or in kind. The three Chivi study areas, however, differ in the level of remittance income. The Takavarasha area shows the highest proportion of people receiving remittances, along with the highest cash amounts. This contrasts with Chivi area, where fewer people receive remittances; when they do, smaller amounts are received. Ngundu shows an intermediate situation. This pattern can be explained in relation to the out-migrancy history of each area and the pattern of job seeking found in each community. Takavarasha area has a long history of out-migration to the mining towns of Zvishavane, Shurugwi and Mashava (Chapter 2). The limited agricultural potential of the area has made out-migration a necessity over the years. Families in the Takavarasha area have an established network of contacts working in the formal sector, and this

Table 3.3 Remittance patterns in the Chivi study areas

	Chivi (N = 48)	Ngundu (N = 47)	Takavarasha (N = 35)
% Receiving remittance in cash in 1991, 1993 and 1994	1991: 54 1993: 48 1994: 68	21 15 55	83 85 75
% Receiving remittance only in kind, during 1991	10	63	87
Average amount/year in 1991 ($Z)	28	267	589
Types of job	Recently employed short-term jobs	←→	Longer term stable jobs
Source head	Relatives	←→	Household
Redundancies 1992–93	1	10	1

encourages others to join them, as it is easier to secure a job and find accommodation in town. People living in the Chivi area have less of a tradition of out-migration to particular areas. Most of those who are currently employed from this area are young sons, with low incomes offering few remittance opportunities, rather than older male household heads. Others are short-term employees, again with low wage levels. The Ngundu area has a mix of both situations, with some longer-term employees in established, salaried jobs and others with shorter-term employment, particularly those with seasonal jobs on the large sugar estates at Triangle and Hippo Valley.

The value of remittances has decreased over time, as wages have not kept pace with inflation. From 1982 to 1989 the low-income consumer price index (CPI) increased by around 300%, while wages increased only 190% for private domestic workers and 125% for agricultural workers (Christensen and Stack, 1992). Inflation rates during the 1980s were around 15% annually, but they worsened during the early 1990s, reaching nearly 50% in 1992 before dropping back again (CSO, 1994). Figures 3.1a and 3.1b show the trend in real wages, alongside employment trends, over the last 30 years, highlighting the notable decline in purchasing power of employed people in low-income jobs in the last decade. Unemployment and underemployment also remain a problem as the economy has failed to grow as fast as hoped for. Currently, there are only about 60,000–70,000 jobs for the 200,000 school leavers who enter the job market each year (World Bank, 1991: 5).

Off-farm income

There are a whole range of off-farm activities that provide significant income-earning opportunities for both men and women (Adams, 1991). These are discussed in detail in Chapter 10 for the drought situation. In other years, such activities are still important (Table 3.4). The 1993 and 1994 dry seasons followed a reasonable harvest, so plenty of beer brewing was carried out in all the study sites, although religious prohibitions meant that there was less in Ngundu than elsewhere. Once crops were sold, there was some surplus income for investment in building or repairing homes. Activities are differentiated between genders, with some, such as vegetable gardening being virtually the sole domain of women; others, such as hunting, are dominated by men. Some off-farm activities require specialised skills and apprenticeship training. For instance, there are usually only a few specialised builders or traditional healers in each area. Activities are also differentiated between wealth groups, with the poor hiring out their labour and the rich hiring out their capital assets, such as ploughs and animal-drawn carts. Some activities, such as broiler production, require a certain amount of up-front capital, whereas other activities require limited

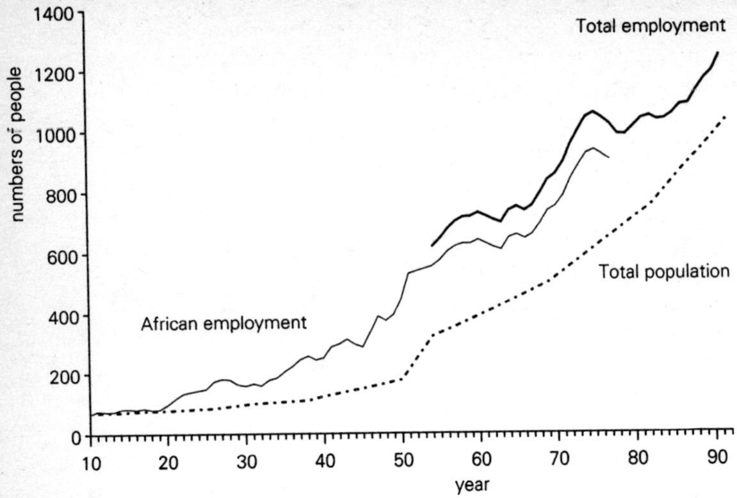

Figure 3.1a Total population ('0000s) and employment levels ('000s), 1910–93

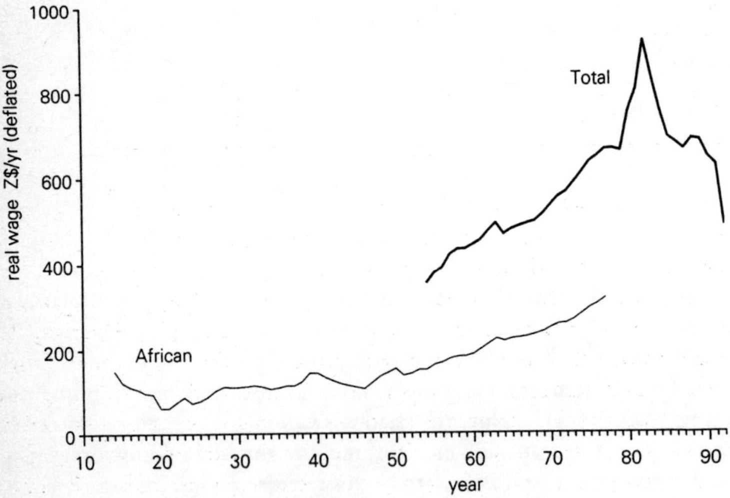

Figure 3.1b Real wage labour rates, 1910–93
(deflated with CPI base = 100 in 1960)

start-up costs. Trading activities by women often start with very small exchanges. For instance, salt or sugar may be exchanged with small amounts of grain. The grain is accumulated and later sold for a profit. This profit may then be transferred to another activity with higher returns but greater capital requirements. The availability of markets is an important

Table 3.4 Off-farm income-earning activities found in Chivi during the 1993 and 1994 dry seasons (M = mostly men; F = mostly women; M/F = both)

Off-farm activity	M/F	% households 1993	% households 1994
Vegetable gardening	F	39.8	28.6
Beer brewing	M/F	36.8	50.4
Building/thatching	M	8.3	11.3
Trading	F	6.8	15.0
Equipment hire	M	6.0	–
Prostitution	F	5.3	4.5
Labour/piecework	M/F	3.0	27.8
Sewing/crochet	F	3.0	12.8
Carpentry	M	2.2	0.75
Carving	M	2.2	–
Peanut butter sale	F	2.2	0.75
Gold panning	M	2.2	6.0
Hunting	M	1.5	–
Gambling	M	1.5	0.75
Pottery	F	1.5	3.7
Healing	M/F	1.5	1.5
Church official	M/F	1.5	1.5
Brick making	M	0.75	–
Hides and skin sale	M	0.75	–
Tailor	M	0.75	–
Blacksmith	M	0.75	0.75

factor in the choice of off-farm income-earning activities. There is a much greater variety of activities among the Ngundu households, who have access to the roadside market for the sale of craft products to tourists travelling to or from South Africa along the Beitbridge road. Equally, the relatively low transport costs mean that women are able to get involved in trading along this road without seeing their profits disappear in exorbitant bus fares. Local markets also vary depending on the proximity to rural business and service centres where civil servants with guaranteed pay packets create some demand. Otherwise the flow of rural money is very limited, resulting in few opportunities for cash earning and in the limited development of small-scale rural enterprise (Moyo, 1991; Helmsing, 1987).

During the wet season there are some piecework opportunities on other people's farms. Labour markets exist during reasonably good seasons and young people and women are hired for such tasks as weeding or harvesting. Jane Corbett (1994) found that 63% of households in an area in southern Chivi had their labour hired on occasions during the cropping season, but wage levels were very low, with average total income from this source being only Z$58. Dry season piecework was very limited in 1993, but increased in 1994 as people were employed to help with the harvest, and later to clear the land and repair fences.

Markets: sites of exchange

The inheritance of colonial restrictions on marketing by Africans (Chapter 2) persisted following Independence. A combination of strict licensing of trading activities and the concentration of agricultural produce marketing in formal channels characterised the marketing system during the 1980s. Sites of exchange have thus been limited. Crop marketing and livestock marketing have been dominated by parastatal marketing boards, the Grain Marketing Board (GMB) and the Cold Storage Commission (CSC) being the most important. Local marketing does occur and is increasing, but exchanges tend to be through informal networks and relationships, rather than at a particular marketing site.

Local markets occur at various business centres in Chivi, most activity being at Ngundu and Chivi Office. Here traders sell vegetables or second-hand clothes to local residents or travellers passing through on buses. Beyond this, the retail trade is dominated by a few businessmen who have licences to run general stores. These stores supply a range of basic grocery items, agricultural inputs, and grain and meat. Many people also travel to the regional towns, particularly Masvingo, for shopping. Here the major commercial stores can be found and products can be purchased at a lower price than in the rural areas. The well-developed commercial retail sector, combined with the costs of trading imposed by licences and other restrictions, undermines attempts to establish local informal trading activities, except in a few key commodities such as vegetables.

Crop marketing

Opportunities for the sale of crops in Chivi differ dramatically according to crop type. Following Independence, the GMB purchased maize at a guaranteed price agreed prior to the harvest. This reinforced the incentive to plant maize, as farmers were sure of a sale in the event of a good harvest. During droughts, local markets emerged and local prices rose above the GMB floor price, but under most conditions bulk sales were directed to the marketing board. The GMB experimented with a period of offering guaranteed prices for millets, but this was abandoned when a storage glut occurred. Sorghum, by contrast, does have a commercial market in the brewing industry and the GMB has been an important channel for sale. The same applies to sunflowers and groundnuts, although the latter are mostly absorbed by the local market and for home consumption. Cotton is marketed separately through the Cotton Marketing Board (CMB), often with specific agreements with producers.

The situation up until the early 1990s was typified by a centrally controlled marketing system for certain crops, with prices set independently of area or season. For instance, sales of maize were channelled to the formal marketing system via the GMB, onto the industrial millers and back to rural consumers in the form of commercially processed grain flour. This arrangement benefited rural producers in places distant from urban centres, as transport costs were effectively subsidised through pan-seasonal and pan-territorial pricing (Masters and Nuppenau, 1993). However, the costly process of exporting grain out of areas only to reimport it as processed meal was borne by rural consumers in places like Chivi (Jayne and Lawrence, 1993).

Since the inception of market reforms, the situation has changed (Jayne and Nuppenau, 1993; Takavarasha, 1993). Restrictions on sale have been removed and it is now legal to move grain around the country, and to sell direct to small-scale millers and so to take advantage of spatial and temporal price variations. The result has been a dramatic growth in entrepreneurial activity in crop marketing following good harvests. The maintenance of a floor price for maize allows for a sales channel of last resort if demand in local markets is minimal. More important for the Chivi population, who are net consumers of grain, the maintenance of at least a limited network of marketing points means that grain is available for purchase within the area when local markets fail.

Between 1988 and 1990 the main outlet for crop sales in Chivi was the GMB (Table 3.5). However, over this period an increasing proportion of crops was sold locally. By 1993, following major market reform, the proportion of local sales had risen even further, especially in Ngundu where there is good access to private transport. The advantages and disadvantages of the different market outlets were illustrated by Chivi farmers in a simple ranking exercise (Table 3.6).

With the changes in the marketing regulations governing crop sales, the opportunities for a wider diversity of sale options opened up following the harvests in 1993 and 1994. In 1993, the good harvest across Chivi,

Table 3.5 Maize sales to GMB and local sources in Chivi as a percentage of total production, 1988–93 (nd = no data)

Sales	Area	1988	1989	1990	1993
GMB sales	Chivi	16.1	13.2	1.2	nd
	Ngundu	30.5	2.2	0.0	13.8
	Takavarasha	20.4	3.7	1.1	9.0
Local sales	Chivi	12.2	12.2	11.4	nd
	Ngundu	8.9	7.8	2.9	25.5
	Takavarasha	3.2	1.8	4.0	1.0

Table 3.6 Pros and cons of different marketing outlets according to Chivi farmers

Market	Advantage	Disadvantage
GMB	Buys in bulk, so the money is also received in bulk.	Force people to buy bags which are expensive; offer low prices considering expenses; high transport costs; late payment; remove money from old credit; no payment for over-filled bags; rejects underweight bags; unfair grading system.
Approved grain buyers	Immediate payment; farmers able to solve immediate cash problem.	Sometimes give payment in kind not cash; prices very low; no grading criteria; over-filling of bags.
Local markets	No transport costs; usually offer higher prices.	Only buy in small quantities; over-filling of bags.

Source: FSRU/IIED, 1991

together with a high demand for cash following the devastating drought of the previous year, meant that crop sales were a priority for most households. Sales, particularly in the early part of the season, were dominated by private traders; only later did people send grain to the GMB. Private traders entered the market at a time when Chivi farmers were seriously in need of cash. After the failed harvests of the two previous years, most people had accumulated debts or were in need of clothes, blankets, shoes and other commodities. The early harvest was quickly sold to traders who arrived in the area and exchanged grain for clothes, blankets, sugar, salt, dried fish, tea and other items in high demand in the area. The rate of exchange was not favourable (e.g. 2kg of sugar worth Z$7.50 was exchanged for 1.5 buckets of maize worth Z$15–18), but rural farmers were happy to part with some of their harvest in order to acquire much-needed goods.

Various groups of people started trading in the period immediately following the harvest. These included outsiders who arrived in the area with transport, and local store owners who made it known that grain could be exchanged for goods in their shops. Another group of traders included government workers (teachers, council staff, extension workers) resident in the rural areas who had some salary income to provide a capital base for trading but needed to supplement their declining wage levels with additional economic activity. As the season progressed, more people started becoming engaged in trading. This was particularly pronounced in the Ngundu area due to the good transport access to Beitbridge. Women increasingly took up a grain exchange business whereby maize was acquired in the villages in exchange for salt, sugar or second-hand clothes. These women then transported the grain in sacks on local buses some 200km to Beitbridge, taking advantage of the substantial price differential. In Beitbridge they would replenish their supplies of second-hand clothes imported from South Africa and return to Chivi for another round of trading. This pattern persisted for several months. Other buyers in Chivi included some relief NGOs who were operating in the Beitbridge area. Their need for maize grain for free distribution as relief was satisfied by buying in Chivi, in both Ngundu and Chivi Office. The immediate cash payments offered and the reasonable price meant that farmers preferentially sold their maize to this source. The marketing board only became the major outlet for crop sales later in the season. In Chivi area the GMB depot saw purchases of maize grain increase through the season and GMB still remained the preferred selling point for sunflowers. In Ngundu, the lack of a local GMB selling point encouraged farmers to persist with informal selling strategies. However, some farmers did join together and

Box 3.1 Crop marketing in Ngundu area, Chivi, 1993 and 1994

During July 1993 a trader from Harare came with a truck. He was buying sunflowers at Z$1/kg. Even though the price was very low, we were happy to sell because we needed money. We had so many debts after the drought. The second time he came he wanted sorghum. Now he is back and wanting to buy maize. People are happy because it is so difficult to sell to GMB these days. We have hired a truck to take grain as far as Masvingo and this should happen next week. We will sell it there for around Z$75/90kg bag. Another option is the 'donor' in Ngundu who is buying maize for Z$41/50kg bag. Early on in the season another businessman from Ngundu was exchanging grain with blankets: four tins of maize for one blanket. Others are taking bags of maize on buses, two at a time, to Beitbridge where the prices are high (up to Z$15–20/bucket) compared to here (now Z$10/bucket). The traders are still fearing the GMB, but we are relying on them. Farmers are selling like mad this year. We are desperate for cash. Many have forgotten the drought.

Transport to the GMB in Masvingo was too expensive during 1994, so most people tried to sell locally. Some were lucky and made deals with truckers who were travelling between Johannesburg and Harare. For a relatively small payment they would load bags of grain onto their lorries and take them to the GMB depot in Masvingo or to Beitbridge where aid agencies were buying up grain for relief. Others moved small amounts of grain on buses or in scotch carts. The price differences made it worthwhile. The price of a bucket of maize after the harvest was Z$12–15 in Ngundu, but Z$20 at Chivi Office and Z$25 in Beitbridge or Triangle. By the end of the dry season, prices had risen in Ngundu to Z$20/bucket due to scarcity, but those who were able to sell outside the district could realise Z$35/bucket.

Source: Discussions in Ngundu, September 1993 and November 1994

hire transport to ferry their grain to Masvingo. This increased the costs of marketing dramatically, however, and only with large organised sales were the transport costs offset by the higher prices offered.

The pattern of sales seen during 1993 and 1994 was dramatically different to previous years. A much greater regional and seasonal variation in price provided incentives for a larger variety of traders to enter the market. Initially the market involved only those with some starting capital, including a group of government employees new to crop trading who were finding it increasingly necessary to supplement their salaries. But later a wider variety of traders became involved, including local women involved in complex barter and exchange transfers.

Following deregulation of maize meal prices in mid–1992, the prices of purchased meal increased dramatically. By mid–1994 the price in Chivi was Z$82 per 50kg bag. This meant that locally produced maize meal became increasingly competitive. Most town dwellers now purchase locally milled maize meal or bring it directly from the rural areas. Maize meal, processed at rural hammer mills, was being transported to Harare, Bulawayo, Triangle, Beitbridge and all places where relatives of rural residents live and work. As someone pointed out, 'it is only rich bachelor school teachers who buy Palenta (commercially processed maize meal) these days'.

The growth of an informal grain market has brought a number of advantages. The greater flexibility afforded by informal trade has meant that localised responses to food deficits are possible, without recourse to centralised decisions about food allocations. Price differentials between areas and over time increase the incentives to transport grain, as well as to store it for later resale. Although major traders with access to private transport are all men, the opportunities for women to extend their trading enterprises into barter and exchange of small amounts of grain was important for drought recovery. The increasing role of barter in the grain economy has meant that goods are provided direct to the home, rather than via a marketing board cheque or cash, usually paid to a male household member. This means that women's control over and access to agricultural incomes has increased.

The limitations of an informal grain market are also highlighted by recent experience (Chisvo *et al.*, 1991). The lack of transport infrastructure in certain parts of Chivi, such as Takavarasha, has meant limited opportunities for people to benefit from competitive transport or grain milling services. Poor roads, few trucks, scattered grain mills and monopolistic practices have all combined to undermine marketing opportunities and raise costs for both producers and consumers in such areas. The experience of such areas, combined with the experience of drought periods, when food was unavailable and GMB depots were important as selling and distribution points, should remind policy-makers that a free-market solution only works well when the conditions are right. Ensuring such conditions, through rural infrastructure investment, as well as market liberalisation, remains a major policy priority (Chapter 12).

Investments, savings and credit

Household investment may occur through short-term expenditure (e.g. agricultural inputs), purchase of durable assets (e.g. livestock, agricultural implements, buildings and furniture) and long-term investments (e.g. education and marriage of children). Different income sources tend to be channelled to different expenditures, in line with their size and frequency. Sporadic crop incomes tend to be invested in durable assets that require a one-off purchase. Livestock tend to be sold only when a particular need arises; this may be for marriage obligations or for school fees. Smaller, more frequent expenditures (e.g. agricultural inputs, groceries, some school fees) may be serviced by regular off-farm income or remittances.

Savings in the rural economy tend to be in the form of assets, such as livestock. Also, some individuals have bank or building society accounts, especially those who have been working in towns. However, most people do not have sufficient savings as a hedge against risks. Mobilising cash for major expenditures is a perennial problem. Regular incomes tend to be in small amounts which are easily spent on groceries, beer or other items. Most people find it difficult to save sufficient cash for major investments. They therefore rely on windfall cash payments, such as *lobola* or GMB cheques, or the disposal of major assets, such as cattle.

However, local savings mechanisms do exist through such institutions as savings clubs (*kukandirana*), beer brewing groups (*baroni*) or burial societies. Regular payments are made and each member receives a large amount on a rotation basis. Such money can be directly invested rather than frittered away. During mid-1994, 16% of the Chivi sample households were involved in *kukandirana* savings clubs, 26% in *baroni* beer brewing groups and 22% were members of burial societies. Most arrangements had started up in early 1994, following the harvest of the previous year, and continued through the dry season of 1994. *Kukandirana* clubs are dominated by women, who invest small amounts derived from vegetable gardening or portions of remittance incomes sent from husbands or sons. Beer brewing club membership is mixed, often with husbands and wives joining separately. During 1994, such clubs were concentrated in the Takavarasha area, where plentiful millet had been harvested. In other areas, notably in some villages in Chivi central, religious restrictions prohibited people from participating. These savings clubs usually follow reasonable harvests and are based on networks of 10–25 savers, often associated with shallow lineage groups living in close proximity. This was the first time since 1988 that such clubs had featured in the local economy, as the long period of drought had prevented people from saving. Burial societies are a more recent innovation in Chivi, having been introduced to the area by Malawian or Zambian in-migrants. These savings systems involve regular saving for funeral expenses, with savers usually guaranteed a coffin and a certain amount towards the burial ceremony. In addition to these informal savings mechanisms, around 60% of households had one or more members who held a post office savings account or a building society account. Nearly all of these are held by men, as such accounts are used for receiving wages, pensions or GMB cheques.

Formal credit systems have had a poor history in the communal areas of Zimbabwe, especially drought-prone areas like Chivi (Bratton, 1986; World Bank, 1991). The Agricultural Finance Corporation (AFC) extended loans widely in the early 1980s, but the level of default was so high that the loan package was withdrawn. Few credit options are now open for small-scale farmers without complex requirements for collateral security. The risky nature of agricultural enterprises in dry areas means that agricultural credit liability or insurance premiums are necessarily very high, and large-scale commercial credit arrangements are therefore usually not viable. However, alternative options for credit provision have not been fully explored. Certain investments are less risky (e.g. irrigation pumps, garden fencing etc.) than dryland agriculture, but credit is not available for such ventures, as schemes are currently tied to particular activities (e.g. dryland farming with a specified seed/fertiliser package). In Chivi these are not financially viable, so default on repayments is almost inevitable. Small-scale revolving loan funds have had some success in dryland areas, if based on existing saving scheme mechanisms, where social responsibility and accountability are strictly regulated by the group (Nhuvira, 1992).

Income portfolios and livelihood trade-offs

The trade-offs between different income sources are conditioned by a range of factors. Some are more climate-dependent than others, some require certain types of labour or skills, some become more or less favourable with changes in the macro-economy. These factors are continually in flux, introducing a high degree of uncertainty into people's lives. In order to reduce income insecurity a portfolio of income sources is needed that provides high and stable returns.

Returns to agriculture are both low and uncertain. Returns to labour for all field crops are estimated at between Z$0.00 and Z$0.57/person day (1988–89 season) and between Z$0.00 and Z$1.26/person day (1989–90 season) (MLARR, 1989; 1990). Returns to land are also low and often negative. There is also major within- and between-year variation in returns to land and labour. Over the period between 1982 and 1988 the coefficient of variation in maize yields for communal areas was 64% (World Bank, 1991: 93), which is compounded by variability in producer prices between years and between areas. These calculations of returns to agricultural production are based on producer prices of the crops concerned. However, a more realistic assessment of returns to agricultural production would be based both on the opportunity costs of not growing food crops and on the consumer prices of food purchased (Jayne and Chisvo, 1991). As consumer prices in rural areas such as Chivi are high, this would increase returns to cropping.

Livestock appear to offer a better investment in dry areas, with relatively high returns. Various estimates suggest that the value of cattle production (including inputs into agriculture and capital growth) may be as high as Z$750 per animal/year. This translates to a return of over Z$100/ha per year from cattle production at current stocking rates (Barrett, 1992; Scoones, 1992b). Returns from smallstock production are also high, with estimates of around Z$5 per animal/year. The labour inputs into livestock production are relatively low, with limited herding requirements during the rainy season, implying very high returns to labour from livestock. However, these returns are uncertain as they are affected by climate. The use of cattle as inputs to agriculture depends on there being a reasonable agricultural season. Similarly, other outputs are also climate-dependent, with the production of manure and milk being reliant on reasonable fodder supplies. The risks of high levels of mortality, particularly among cattle, make livestock production risky. If 30–60% mortality rates occur every five years, as they have done during the 1980s and early 1990s (Chapter 11), this reduces the advantages of livestock production significantly, especially as livestock mortality means the loss of significant assets.

Local off-farm income sources generally provide very low returns to labour. The high labour inputs required for craftwork such as carving, pottery, sewing or crocheting, and the low prices gained means that these are poorly paid occupations. However, since the labour is often non-competitive with other productive activities this means that such income sources are often supplementary. They may provide relatively stable, although small, income sources during the dry season or for women with other tasks such as child care. Some off-farm income sources may be much more lucrative, however. Examples include beer brewing, which adds significant value to small grain production. A bucket of finger millet, for instance, might realise Z$25 as grain, but Z$50 if brewed and sold as beer. The additional labour costs of collection of firewood and brewing means that this is a good return on labour input. Gold panning is another example of a non-farm income source with high returns. Panning proved highly popular during the drought of 1991–92 (Chapter 10), with returns ranging between Z$5 and Z$20 per person day.

Formal employment, however, provides the greatest pull. Most people regard a full-time job as the occupation with the highest return and with the most security. Wage rates during 1994 ranged from Z$180/month for a day labourer to Z$400/month for an unskilled mine worker, to over Z$1500/month for a government employee such as a teacher or agricultural extension worker. This is clearly significantly higher than any other option in the rural sector. It is not surprising therefore that most young people see secondary school education as the route to employment and a source of income other than farming. Spells of employment have historically been important in the processes of capital accumulation and investment in the rural economy, and remain so today. Models of household economics for Southern Africa (Low, 1986) also emphasise the importance of the migrant labour option as an alternative to household farm production. However, not everyone is able to gain full-time employment. This is an option that is mostly open to younger men, although younger women are increasingly engaged in the informal sector. Changes in the macroeconomy, as noted above, are currently having some major impacts on the prospects for such employment. High inflationary pressures, combined with a contracting labour market, mean that the returns to formal employment, particularly in the unskilled wage groups, are declining and job security is decreasing. High levels of unemployment also mean that the chances of finding a secure job is lower now than it has been before. However, despite these negative trends, the importance of periods of formal employment should not be underestimated. Formal-sector jobs generally are independent of climate and so are uncorrelated with returns from agricultural and livestock production. Exceptions are jobs in the large agricultural estates, which are important particularly for the Ngundu population. During the recent drought large numbers of workers were laid off because the lack of water supply to the sugar estates meant that production collapsed. Generally, however, in times of drought, when agricultural returns drop to zero, a job can be a vital part of a household's coping strategy (Chapter 10).

Conclusion

Coping with income insecurity means having a comprehensive portfolio of income sources, derived from both agricultural and non-farm activities. Building a portfolio, however, requires assets, both material and human. Larger households with a greater diversity of income-earning activities tend to be more income-secure than others, even though they have more people to support. Such households tend to be older, possibly with a husband or older son at work and older children and wives working at the home farm. Households are, of course, not homogeneous income-earning units: men, women and children within a household may have independent income sources which may or may not be pooled, depending on the situation and the need. In times of severe drought and food scarcity, there is a greater combined effort in generating income and providing food than in times when conditions are not so adverse (Chapter 10). In more plentiful times, different individuals may pursue more private strategies of income generation and accumulation without jeopardising the survival of others. Portfolios of income-earning potentials are not only reliant on individuals within a household, but may also depend on others. In Chivi, households tend to be clustered in lineage or family groups and many income-earning activities may be done jointly. For instance, labour may be shared for agricultural activities, beer brewing circles set up to allow for savings generation, or groups may come together to produce and market craft products. This cluster-based activity is an important aspect of the lineage mode of production found in rural Zimbabwe and a significant element of patterns of livelihood security. Farming is thus one of a number of income-earning opportunities, making up a variable proportion of people's livelihood portfolio. The relative contribution of agriculture to livelihoods varies from year to year, season to season and between different people, depending on their gender, their asset base or their age. It is not surprising that farming is an opportunistic affair in Chivi, where the benefits of a good harvest are reaped eagerly, but when the harvest fails, as it often does, other livelihood options are available.

PART TWO

Opportunistic farming

CHAPTER FOUR

Opportunistic farming: agriculture in a variable environment

Farming is a practised response to a huge range of risks. What actually happens in a field in any particular season is the cumulative outcome of a range of responses and decisions. The vast variations in asset ownership and entitlement, in access to support from others, in off-farm employment or remittance earnings are compounded by the variability of the natural environment. Rainfall, soils, weed infestations and pest incidence all vary in both space and time. The result is a highly variegated mosaic of opportunity for farming activities that belies any simple explanation of cause and effect. These multiple sources of risk and uncertainty require opportunistic responses in all farming activies.

This chapter examines the various dimensions of opportunistic farming during the 1990–91 and 1992–93 seasons in order to provide a clearer picture of the complex nature of dryland agriculture, illustrating why simple classifications of agroecological zone, farming system or recommendation domain are inadequate routes to simplifying complexity. Instead, the chapter argues for a more detailed understanding of farming under risk, that focuses on actual activities in the field rather than idealised classifications. By exploring the day-to-day activities of farmers in their fields, it is possible to identify the range of factors that impinge on decision-making in a more realistic way. The focus is less on the global optimum for decisions under a set of alternative states, but more on the conditions that give rise to variability. Using the concept of 'agricultural performance' (Richards, 1989; 1993), the diversity of agricultural practice is explored. Rather than viewing variability as noise interfering with an underlying equilibrium, the focus is on the forms of variation, contingency, risk and uncertainty that guide farming practice.

Variation in farming opportunity

Before trying to examine the diversity of agricultural activities as a whole, it is important to understand the sources of variability and diversity that impinge on individual farmers. Box 4.1 provides a profile of three Chivi farmers, each with different asset holdings, income-earning potentials and social networks. None are of course 'typical', but the cases give an idea

Box 4.1 Constraints and opportunities in farming practice – profiles of three farmers

Case 1. M. has recently migrated into the area from further south. She was previously a prostitute and established a home while unmarried. She was granted a plot of land by the headman and she built her house where she lived with her young children and her elderly mother. A few years ago she married and became the fifth wife of a man from Murewa. This marriage did not last and she returned to her home in Chivi. She now has six young children, four of school-going age. She is in her mid-thirties and has decided to settle in Chivi and farm. She has no cattle, no plough and only three goats. When she arrived in Chivi she was granted a field of 3ha, most of which is of poor-quality soil. She has no relatives in the area and must rely on friends to help her out when she wants to plough. She ekes out a living on her land, or migrates seasonally to Chiredzi where she works as a casual labourer on the sugar estates.

Case 2. D. is a 45-year-old soldier and is away from home for most of the year, returning only for Christmas, Easter, Independence Day and annual leave. Mrs D. therefore looks after the farm, as well as their four children who are all under thirteen. Regular remittances are sent home and this allows the family to live a reasonable life, able to buy tea and sugar, as well as bread. This is supplemented by farm produce. Mrs D. has a small vegetable garden which she manages during the dry season. This supplements food from the main fields. Sometimes they employ extra labour to help cultivate the area, but mostly land is left fallow. Prior to the drought, they owned four cattle. The first cow was purchased from D.'s early pay packets. The herd has grown since then. These formed a span and were able to plough the fields. Unfortunately the drought of 1991–92 badly affected the herd, leaving only two animals. The family home was constructed soon after the couple's marriage fifteen years ago and consists of a corrugated-roofed house and two round, thatched huts. The family also own a plough, a cultivator and a scotch cart, all purchased with D.'s pay. The scotch cart can be a useful source of additional income when it is hired out. Their income is also supplemented by the sale of poultry which are kept by Mrs D.

Case 3. Mr M. is 60 years old and is an important figure in the community and acting headman when his brother is away in Bulawayo. His relatives, including two brothers, live in homes around him. They often work together, sharing labour for farm work or child care as well as borrowing assets from each other. Prior to the recent drought Mr M. owned 28 cattle, nearly 100 goats and 25 sheep. He had built these up over the years through the sale of crops from his large field of 13ha. This field is always fully ploughed using the several oxen spans he owns, as well as the abundant family labour. Since he lives in a particularly dry area with heavy soils, he likes to plant pearl millet. This yields reasonably well and he always has a store of some bags. He even had stored millet right through the 1991–92 drought, although he kept this very quiet lest neighbours should want to get hold of it. Mr M. usually sells grain in exchange for goats or money. Through this route he was able to build

Box 4.1 *(cont.)*

up a large holding of livestock, which in turn are sold for the payment of school fees or other expenses. Such expenses grow and grow, particularly with the increasing cost of school education. Mr M. has ten children, seven of whom still go to school and live at home. Mrs M. manages the large home and is involved in gardening, goat rearing and beer brewing. Beer brewing is a particularly important activity and usually raises significant amounts of money, especially when it is done in rotation with friends and relatives in the neighbourhood. Due to the large amounts of millet in the stores, Mr M.'s home usually continues to brew well into the dry season and even during droughts. The home is therefore a well-known location for gatherings of all sorts, with drinking and gambling sessions being regular occurrences. Following the drought Mr M.'s lifestyle had to change. The grain stores were exhausted and a large proportion of the livestock either died or were sold for food. Mr M. and his family had to rebuild their wealth again through agriculture, and much effort was invested in the family fields during the 1992–93 season. They also had to rely increasingly on the small amount of money sent by their son and daughter as remittances.

of the range of constraints and opportunties that are imposed on farming activity.

All three people profiled in Box 4.1 farm within the same farming system and in the same agroecological zone, yet their farming activities are vastly different due to a range of socio-economic factors. This chapter is about how farmers in Chivi responded to variability during the 1990–91 and 1992–93 seasons,[1] sketching out the pattern of response during the farming year, from land preparation, through weeding to harvest.

The farming year: choices under uncertainty

As the heat rises during October, conversations in Chivi usually begin to revolve around the coming of the rains. The waiting game is loaded with expectation, speculation and concern. Everyone has a theory about the likelihood of a good or bad year, but no one knows quite what will happen. Some farmers carefully observe the changing patterns of the winds and the movement of the clouds, developing specialisations in local meteorological patterns. Others observe the signs, waiting for the cuckoo bird (*hwaya*) to start calling, or particular hills to catch fire in the intense heat. Others speculate on the past cold season and the relationship between cold winters and good rainfall or the patterns of good and bad seasons over the years.

During the long dry season, brushwood fences are rebuilt, ploughs and hoes are repaired or replaced and, if they can be afforded, inputs are purchased. As the rainy season approaches, some farmers begin to prepare their fields, clearing the woody regrowth, winter ploughing or dry planting. Sometimes the rain known as *bukurahundi* falls in August or September, which helps to moisten the ground for winter ploughing (Wilson, 1985). It can also catch people out, as some may still have grain laid out on the winnowing grounds.

The end of the dry season is also a time when appropriate rituals are performed to ensure sustained rains and a successful harvest. In the many churches scattered across the district, prayers for a good rainy season are said. Some of the newer African churches make pilgramages to particular sites and hold services. At the same time, preparations for rain-making ceremonies (*mitoro*) are made. Intense discussions begin about the site, timing and appropriate form of the *mitoro*; later, finger millet beer is brewed and goats for slaughter are collected. Payments to the territorial cult of Zame are also made and the messenger carries the collection (*rusengwe*) to the Matopos hills in order to ask for rain (Chapter 9). Once the fields and agricultural equipment and inputs are prepared, and the necessary ritual is completed, there is nothing more to do but sit in the deepest shade and wait for the rain. The waiting game can be long, tense and hot.

When the rain does come, furious activity commences. Once people are satisfied that the rain has arrived for a period and that the soil is sufficiently moist, ploughing starts in earnest. The rain that signals the start of the rainy season comes from the north; this is known as *nhuruka* – the rain that brings food. Draught animals are at a premium in Chivi, so any will do. It is not uncommon to see a mixed span of a single oxen, a donkey or two and maybe a cow or heifer pulling a plough. By the end of a long dry season, these animals are usually in poor condition. The grass has long since dried out and animals must seek green grass along the river banks, in the hills and in the valley bottoms. It is the rich browse fodder that keeps animals alive, especially once the *miombo* trees provide a late dry season flush of green leaves. Those farmers who do not own a full span of draught animals must rely on sharing networks or the hiring of draught services; others simply hoe the land.

Land preparation and ploughing

Many farmers like to carry out winter ploughing during the dry season if they possibly can. This eases land preparation during the main rainy season and encourages water infiltration, making limited rainfall more effective. However, winter ploughing depends on access to a draught team fit enough to pull a plough when fodder supplies are limited. Sometimes light rains fall sufficient to moisten the ground and allow winter ploughing on the heavier soils. If such rains fail to arrive, then only the lighter, sandier soils are prepared. During 1990–91, 38% of the land was winter-ploughed, 45%

of which was in plots that were subsequently planted to maize. Draught owners winter-ploughed around 40% of their land, while non-owners ploughed 35%. For land subsequently planted to maize, there was no significant difference between those owning draught animals and those not, as sharing networks allowed access to non-owners for their high-priority land. Winter ploughing was most prevalent in the Ngundu area, where farmers follow a predominantly maize cultivation strategy. Winter ploughing was, by contrast, practically non-existent during the following two years due to the poor condition of the animals and widespread livestock mortality during the drought. For instance, only 3.5% of the land was winter-ploughed in 1992–93. With the recovery of herd numbers and the condition of animals, winter ploughing resumed during the 1993–94 and 1994–95 seasons, with new networks of draught sharing being established (Chapter 10).

Dry planting of small grains, particularly pearl millet, is a common phenomenon in the drier areas of Chivi, especially at sites like Takavarasha. The amount of ploughing and planting activity during the period before November is always significantly higher here than in other areas, as people plant millet in the hope that it will germinate with the first rains (Figure 4.1). This cropping strategy is risky and reliant on reasonable seed stores, as very often the early crop fails when the rains arrive in fits and starts. Farmers often have to in-fill patchily germinated fields by transplanting

Box 4.2 Prudent planting

Dry planting. In order to capture the very first rains, many farmers dry-plant crops. This is particularly the case for pearl millet and finger millet. Mrs Mahonye is no exception as all her millet plots were dry-planted during 1992–93. This allows for replanting if there is a failure, or if only partial failure, transplanting from other areas can result in complete crop coverage. Dry-planting into winter-ploughed or hand-hoed soil depresses yield compared to ploughing and planting with the first effective rains, explains Mrs Mahonye, but it is impossible to do this on all plots because of labour and draft shortage. It is best to reserve this practice for the more expensive seed maize, which requires good rains for survival.

Transplanting. The practice of transplanting small grains, particularly finger millet, was very noticeable during 1992–93. This was in part due to a lack of seed provoked by the previous year's serious drought, replanting being impossible because of seed shortages. But also transplanting is a regular response to the patchy germination and initial growth response of plants in such a variable environment. Rather than replant failed crops, it is less risky to transplant from areas where the crops have germinated. For instance, Mr Isaac Demba had suffered very variable germination of finger millet in his large field adjacent to his house. So during good rainfall in February he and his wife engaged in an extensive transplanting operation.

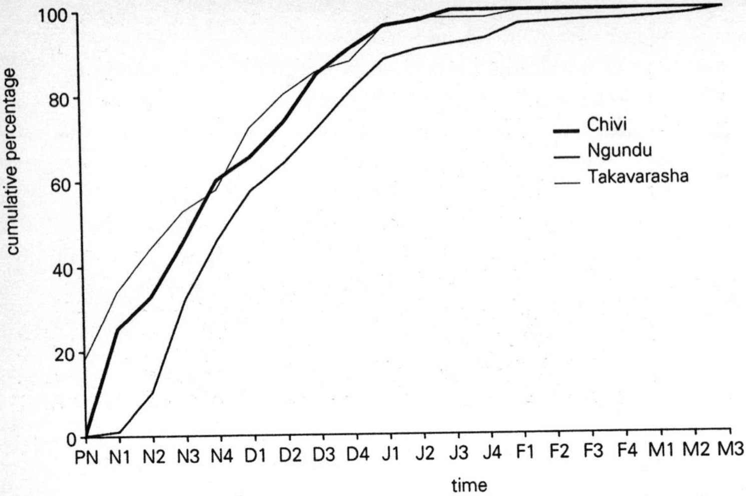

Figure 4.1 Land preparation patterns between sites, 1990-91 (pre-November, PN, to third week of March, M3)

(Box 4.2). During 1990, around 5% of the field area was dry-planted, most to pearl millet. During the period before November in 1992, even more dry planting took place, with around 12.5% of the total land area being dry-planted and much of the land preparation being carried out by hand using hoes. Following the drought, farmers were desperate to ensure at least some harvest and so invested huge efforts in preparing the land to catch the first rains.

During the 1990–91 season, responsiveness to rainfall events was key to farming success (Figure 4.1). Ploughing and planting occurred with each major rainfall event. The rains started earliest in the Ngundu area and people planted large areas of maize with the first rains. The sporadic nature of rainfall in dry areas means that timing is critical. With drought-vulnerable crops such as maize this is particularly so because mid-season droughts can wipe out a crop. Small grain crops, such as millets, are more suited to the sporadic rainfall pattern as they can physiologically shut down during a dry period. In all areas people planted maize first; there was no significant difference in the pattern of planting of maize between draught owners and non-owners. Since maize is the most valuable crop, requiring investment in hybrid seed and potentially yielding significant cash returns, non-owners of draught power make sure that their limited opportunities for sharing draught spans are focused on the maize areas. Other grain crops, such as pearl millet, get lower priority and non-owners planted later than others with immediate access to draught power. Alongside the main grain crops, a variety of other crops are grown.

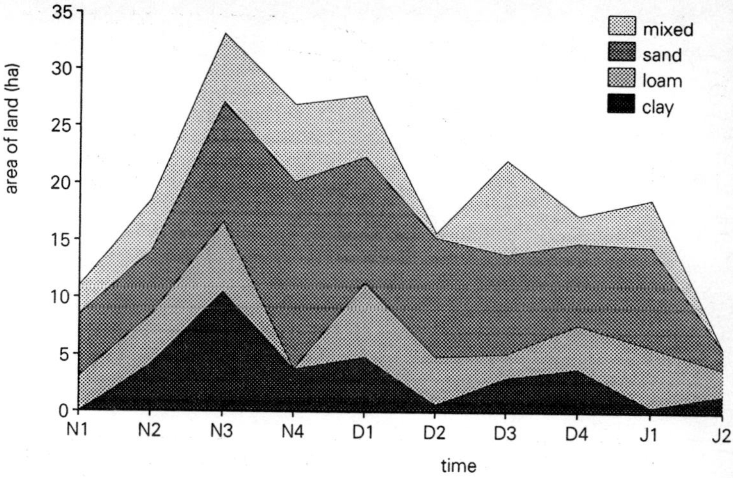

Figure 4.2 Maize land preparation patterns according to soil type, 1990–91 (first week of November, N1, to second week of January, J2)

Groundnuts are planted early and tended intensively, largely by women. Early-planted groundnuts, especially those planted on low-lying, wetter land can be reaped early and so achieve a good price on local markets. Sunflowers are sometimes given priority in a planting sequence, especially if a farmer intends to produce large quantities for sale. More normally though, sunflowers are planted late, often as second plantings in maize areas when the early-planted maize crop has failed and it is too late to plant more.

Ploughing patterns also differ between soil types (Figure 4.2). Heavier clay soils respond only to significant rainfall events and must be ploughed and planted with rain. Sandier soils have higher infiltration rates, so smaller rainfall amounts can be used for land preparation and planting. On the heavy clays, an on–off activity is seen, with rapid responses to heavy rainfall being key. On the sands more continuous activity is feasible, with ploughing continuing, even when rainfall is limited.

The pattern of ploughing and planting during 1992–93 was significantly different. Due to the lack of draught power and labour to carry out hoeing, a pattern of rapid response to rainfall events was not feasible. Instead, land preparation was much more spread out, starting with the first rains in early November and continuing into December (Figure 4.3). The first bout of land preparation was almost entirely by hand. Those animals that were alive were just too weak to be able to pull a plough. However, by December they had begun to recover condition and more people were able to use draught teams to prepare their lands. A similar prioritisation and sequencing of crop planting was seen, with maize re-

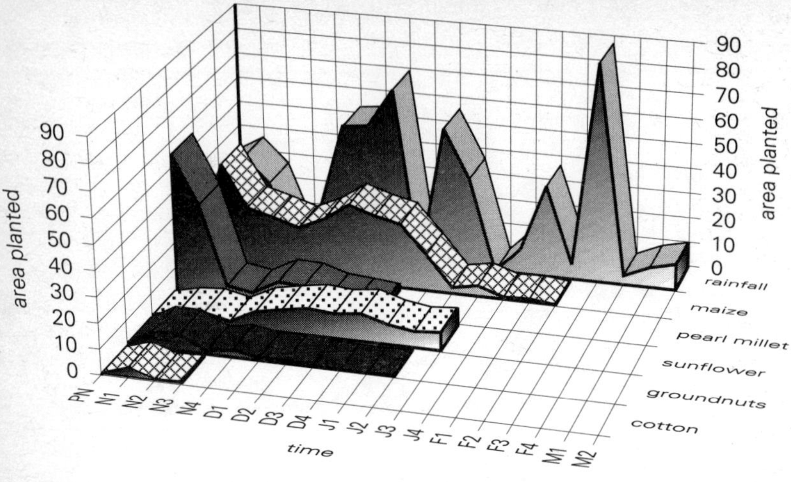

Figure 4.3 Planting patterns of selected crops in relation to rainfall, 1992–93 (pre-November, PN, to second week of March, M2)

ceiving the most attention. However, due to the lack of available hybrid seed and its escalating cost, many farmers were unable to plant maize until December. Locally available pearl millet seed was planted extensively early on, with around 40% of the pearl millet area being dry-planted. The whole pearl millet area was planted by late December, while the maize area was not fully planted until February. This uneven response, due to a combination of limiting production inputs, meant that crop planting was highly staggered. This meant that crops in farmers' fields were of varying degrees of maturity at any one time; this offset the impact of the mid-season dip in rainfall. Indeed, many of those who planted maize late in fact got the highest yields, as the maize matured during the later rains and did not tassel during the January drought.

The sequence of crop planting is thus dependent on a combination of the properties of different crops, their perceived value, availability of different soil types, access to labour and draught power and patterns of rainfall. Timing and responsiveness are key. Simple recommendations about planting dates, crop sequencing or crop combinations are largely irrelevant in dryland settings, as so many local contingencies intervene, making any sequence of activities on any farm in any year almost unique.

Weeding

Weeding soon follows ploughing and planting, and agricultural activities shift to keeping weeds at bay. Over 80% of the total ploughed area was weeded once during both 1990–91 and 1992–93. Second weedings were

Box 4.3 When is a weed a weed?

The labour involved in weeding crops is considerable, especially if you have a young family and your husband is working away like Mai D. As a consequence Mai D. thinks twice before following the recommendation to weed at least 3–4 times and to keep the crop area clean from ploughing until maturation. She recognises the need to weed early on in the season when the crops are young. Indeed during 1992–93 she hired some labourers to assist her in this task over the period of a week. This was because the weed infestation was particularly bad; hand hoeing, combined with a good rainy season, had resulted in a dense carpet of weeds. The weeding was repeated only once during February when the maize crop was approaching maturity. This was the last weeding as Mai D. reckons that the weed competition after this point is sufficiently low that it does not warrant the expenditure on further hiring of labour to carry out the task. The weeds thus cease to be weeds and may be used later for fodder, green manuring or compost. During the early part of the season (November–December), she was careful to leave certain species of plant growing in the field (eg. *rude*, *dererere* etc.) as these are important sources of green vegetables for the home. As the weeding progresses she collected sufficient for each day's meal, plucking the young leaves and letting others grow back. However, later in the season, on the second and final weeding, there was sufficient availability of these indigenous vegetables (weeds) in the bush and around the home that they were now weeded out, along with other 'weeds'.

done far more by non-draught owners, as these households owned smaller land areas and so invested more effort in weeding. In addition, very few practised any form of mechanical cultivation together or separate from weeding.

In both seasons, there were no differences in weeding between grain crops in the Chivi site; most received a weeding three weeks after planting. In many cases this was followed by a second weeding. In Takavarasha less attention was paid to weeding and most people only weeded once and at varying lengths of time after planting, reflecting the erratic rainfall pattern experienced. In Ngundu weeding was very punctual, around three weeks after planting. Those without access to draught power tended to weed their land areas quicker than those without draught, again reflecting the greater investment of labour in smaller land areas.

Patterns of weeding are affected in particular by the labour situation. Only a handful of the farm plots were weeded three times as recommended by agricultural extension, and most people weeded only once. Second weedings were concentrated on valued crops or when weed growth returned following rains after germination. What is a weed to a farmer will depend on the time in the season and the labour available, as the case study in Box 4.3 illustrates.

Harvest and storage

With such variation in planting dates, crop types and agronomic practice, harvesting tends to be a drawn-out affair in Chivi. Crops planted early in wetter, lower-lying land are harvested first. These may provide important 'hunger season' food prior to the main harvest or provide opportunities for exploiting scarcity prices. Green maize is often harvested during March or April and is eaten widely, as well as being sold at bus stops and along roadsides. At the same time, early groundnuts may be sold to traders, and the first heads of millet or sorghum may be plucked. This time is known as *shezha*, a time of plenty after a period of want. However, during 1990–91 there was very little harvest; small amounts were reaped but were insufficient for consumption needs. Virtually no grain was sold and only small amounts of sunflower made their way to market (Chapter 3). The 1993 harvest was different. Harvesting took place over several months, requiring major labour inputs. There was considerable hiring of casual labour, as well as sharing and hiring of scotch carts to transport crops from the fields.

Once crops have arrived at the homestead they are laid out for drying. Some crops are prepared for sale, with careful filling of bags to the appropriate amount. Other crops are prepared for storage. Winnowing of millets takes place later in the dry season and again involves considerable labour. During 1993, many people brewed beer and invited people to come for a work party to assist with the threshing and winnowing. When it was realised that the 1993 harvest was going to be successful, many had to rebuild their granaries, most of which had been empty for several years. Protection against pest damage is afforded by the granaries being raised from the ground and mud being packed around the walls, which are made from wooden poles. In addition, certain local plants or tree leaves are added to counteract the effect of weevils.

Draught power and labour sharing relationships

The ability to prepare land for planting is dependent on access to draught animals. The Chivi sample included 56.2% of households without draught access (two or fewer draught animals) during the 1990–91 season. Despite this, most were able to plough their land, and 80% of total available land was ploughed during the season. This figure did not differ significantly between those with and without draught animals. The timeliness of ploughing did not appear to be affected either. The cumulative area ploughed showed very similar patterns between the two groups, although those with draught access were able to winter-plough a greater area and were able to dry-plough and plant a larger area before the onset of the rains.

For many, the ability to plough is dependent on sharing relationships with others. These can be classified into three types. The first type of relationship is typified by the situation where an older male owns a number of draught animals and he lends them out to junior kin, neighbours or invalid relatives. In many cases this means that the 'big man' can draw on family labour from the 'client' households if particular tasks need doing. The second type of relationship is typified by the case where two households both have access to draught animals, but not enough to each establish a full ploughing span for the season. The third type of relationship is more informal and based on occasional linkages set up for particular circumstances. For most of the time, such households work alone. Very often draught arrangements will involve hiring of draught animals rather than receiving them free of charge under a loan agreement. Such households are typically in-migrant households without significant kin networks in the area. The distribution of households in these three categories within the household sample in 1992 is described in Table 4.1.

The contrasting patterns of linkage in the three study areas reflects the differing settlement history in the three areas (Chapter 2). In Takavarasha area a number of large families, who moved from the hills area, have maintained strong kin linkages over time as new families have established themselves in different areas of the plain. These families either share draught among themselves (exchange relationships) or stockless kin ('clients') are reliant on stock-owning relatives ('big men'). Both Chivi and Ngundu have a certain number of 'big men'–'client' relationships, but these are overshadowed by exchange relationships and loners. In Chivi area there are a few original settlers, plus quite a number of immigrants who have taken up the remaining land. Many of these people do not have close relatives in the area and so farm alone. Ngundu area has been settled much more recently. Clusters of families often settled together during the 1940s and 1950s, but the tradition of long-term, lineage-based production, as found in Chivi and Takavarasha, is by and large absent; hence there is a greater prevalence of exchange relationships.

Box 4.4 shows how a 'big man' relationship with close kin facilitates the ability to plough early. As this case illustrates, the negotiation of draught access is not without difficulties. Family disputes may spill over into sharing relationships, affecting the ability of particular households to plant on

Table 4.1 Linkage arrangements found in the Chivi sample

Linkage arrangement	Chivi (%)	Takavarasha (%)	Ngundu (%)
'Big man'	7.8	32.5	10.6
'Client'	17.6	32.5	19.1
Exchange	37.2	23.2	44.6
Loner	37.2	11.6	25.5

Box 4.4 Matye cluster, Mapuvire, Chivi – 1990–91

Mr Matye's position as headman means that he has a relatively large field that includes both sandy soil and clay soil plots. The different soil types mean that different agricultural practices must be applied, with different crops and different timing and intensity of operations in the different soils. The sandy soils are early-planted as they can respond quickly to relatively light rains. Maize does best here. The clay soils are planted later, after heavier rains, and this is where sunflower and pearl millet are planted. Finger millet and groundnuts are planted across all soil types. All the plots managed by Matye were ploughed and planted during November 1991 using his own span. Maize, groundnuts and finger millet were planted first in the two sandy soil plots around the home with the very first showers in the first week of November. The maize crop in the home field was weeded first in the last week of November. Other plots containing finger millet and sunflower received less attention, being only weeded once, between the third week of December and the second week of January. All but one of Matye's brother's seven plots were ploughed and planted during November. Tariro managed to join forces with Mr Matye using a combination of his own and his brother's animals to plough. Finger millet and sunflower were planted first, then maize was planted in the third week of November following rain. Bambarra nuts and groundnuts were planted in the last week of November. A final maize plot was planted following further rains in the third week of December. Matye's son, Stefan, works away from the area and the farm is managed by his wife. Mai Tawa managed to plant a plot of groundnuts in the first week of November with the help of her father-in-law, Mr Matye. Due to lack of draught power and insufficient rain, the remaining plots of maize and sunflower were not planted until the last week of December and the first week of January. One plot remained fallow throughout the season. Ebson, Matye's nephew, only managed to start planting in late November due to lack of draught power. In the past, Matye had shared cattle or donkeys with Ebson, but due to a rumbling dispute between the two these had been withdrawn. Two plots were planted with sunflower in the third and final weeks of November when a span was finally made available by Mr Matye. It was not until mid-December that the remaining land was ploughed and planted with maize, bambarra nuts, groundnuts and sunflower. Two portions of the field remained fallow throughout the season due to lack of labour and draught. Samuel, Ebson's brother, had planned to plant crops during 1990–91, but this was not realised. He is engaged in off-farm work and his wife was not in a position to mobilise labour and draught power for agriculture during the season. She instead relied on support from relatives and remittances from her husband.

time. In such cases, access to draught power may come late, as other arrangements have to be established.

The second case (Box 4.5) represents another arrangement. Here, a son's household with access to draught animals is able to help out an elderly and infirm mother. Although she produces from her field independ-

Box 4.5 Mai Edward

Mai Edward is a widow and so has little labour for agricultural activities. With few sources of other income, she has problems securing food. However, she is greatly assisted by her son's household. In 1990–91 she was loaned a span for ploughing and some of her grandchildren came to help. In all but two plots, Mai Edward plants maize. This is because it requires relatively little labour both for cultivation and processing. It also provides food early in the season, which is important for her as she usually has few stores. The remaining two plots were planted with small areas of groundnuts and finger millet, for peanut butter *(dovi)* and beer respectively, both of which provide important sources of income. Ploughing took place in 1990–91 on three separate occasions during November. The first ploughing in the first week of November resulted in the planting of groundnuts, finger millet and one portion of maize. Subsequent plantings, following rains in the next three weeks, resulted in maize plantings in the remaining three plots. Mai Edward's son's household is much less reliant on agriculture. Being teachers and shop-owners, the parents have other sources of income that are higher and more reliable than agriculture. The result is that farming must fit in with other activities off-farm. The resultant planting and weeding pattern showed a haphazard series of events, with some early- and some late-planted plots, some weeded, some unweeded. The field is planted mostly to low-intensity production of maize. This is later used in poultry production, which is linked to their shop enterprise at Chivi Office.

ently, she is assisted greatly by draught and inputs derived from her son's and daughter-in-law's off-farm income.

The third case (Box 4.6) demonstrates an exchange pattern of sharing. Two brothers, both with draught animals, exploit the opportunity of joining their draught animals to form a larger team. Sharing of labour also increases the aggregate productivity and their ability to fine-tune their responses to particular ecological circumstances. In this case, the contrasting agroecological properties of their two fields makes co-operative effort pay, as farm management responses differ in the low-lying and topland sites.

The final cases illustrate how, without effective social networks, farming can be a major struggle, and vulnerability to risks increases. This is particularly the case when illness or death strikes (Box 4.7).

These cases illustrate how agricultural practice is a product of social context. Networks and relationships form the basis on which social sharing and exchange arrangements are negotiated. But conditions change and such relationships are not static. The drought of 1991–92 dramatically reduced the availability of draught power, so requiring networks based on draught sharing relationships to be transformed (Chapter 10). However, social networks are critical components of people's livelihood strategies; understanding how relationships are formed beyond the household is thus

Box 4.6 Robson and Newton Zivhu

The two brothers work together when ploughing their land. The two fields are on different parts of the slope. Robson has a lower-slope, valley field with sandy soils that responds well to early and relatively light rains. Newton, by contrast, has a higher-slope field with heavier soils that requires several heavy downpours before planting, particularly of maize, can be considered. During 1990–91 they both owned spans and, when working together with another friend, could put together 3–4 spans to work simultaneously on a particular field. This meant that they could respond very quickly to rainfall events, ploughing and planting a whole field in a single day. Because of the different characteristics of the two brothers' fields, field operations tended to be separated in time. There was therefore no competition over labour and draught resources as cropping activities were out of phase in the two fields. Robson's land was ploughed first in the third week of November. He prefers to plant his land to maize all at one time, preferably in response to the first effective rains and following winter ploughing. There was no staggering, and first weedings were all concentrated in the second week of December and second weedings in the first week of January. This relatively high-risk strategy, involving a concentrated activity pattern, can be seen as a response to a combination of favourable field conditions and high availability of labour and draught inputs. By contrast, the first portion of Newton's field was planted in the first week of December. There was much more staggering of planting dates and, as a consequence, other activities were also separated in time. This staggered activity pattern provided a good response to the more risky agronomic conditions to be found in Newton's field.

critical in understanding people's differential ability to respond to the risks and uncertainties created by the vagaries of the environment.

Conclusion

Opportunistic farming requires that hazards are avoided and opportunities captured in the continuous struggle to make a living from the land. Farming in dryland environments is thus not a static process amenable to simple analysis and standardised recommendations, but a highly contingent affair, constrained by resource entitlements and always shaped by a wide range of risks and uncertainties. As Paul Richards (1989) notes, cultivation is a 'performance not a rehearsal'. Agricultural performance occurs through a rich variety of contingent responses, through the mixing of routines, through the combination of options and through the process of learning that is everyday practice. Farming is thus the result of improvisation, experimentation, innovation and creativity. This means that much planned activity is out of the question. This was recognised over 30 years ago by de Schlippe who commented: 'There are so many circumstances defeating

Box 4.7 Vulnerability without support networks

1. During late 1990 M. was seriously ill and had to spend some time in hospital. Mai R. tried to keep the farm going, but due to regular absences she found it most difficult. As a result a large area was left fallow and only a small portion was planted with maize. In early 1991, M. died. This meant that Mai R. now had to farm alone. Old age, and the lack of any relatives living nearby, meant life was very difficult. During the 1992–93 season she organised a work party (*humwe*) for field preparation. Recognising that she was in need, a number of women living nearby came to help and all five plots were hoed and planted.

2. A. settled in the area during 1989. He was granted a small field, but since he had no relatives living in the area he was unable to get any help with ploughing. The field was therefore prepared by hand during 1990, with the whole family working hard. However, due to ill-health, A. himself was unable to work much, and the burden had to be taken up by Mai P. and her children.

the foresight of the cultivator ... that he cannot be expected to make any plans. He must improvise his work from day to day' (1956: 206). The 'live' performance on farmers' fields is therefore not the same as the 'rehearsals' carried out on experimental stations or researcher-managed on-farm plots. Such activities are both 'out of time' and 'out of place', and bear little relation to the complexity of farmers' own practices (Richards, 1989). What we observe in farmers' fields is thus the outcome of a complex social activity, the cumulative result of responses to seasonally evolving events.

This suggests a more modest view of agricultural intervention and a reassessment of the role of agricultural experimentation and research. If farming practice is so complex, so deeply embedded in social, economic, political and institutional contexts and so highly dependent on uncertain events, then how can conventional research and extension, premissed as it is on assumptions about *planned* intervention, ever have an impact? Opportunities for a more flexible and adaptive approach to research and extension, attuned to the vagaries of the real world, are discussed in Chapter 8. First, however, further elements of farming practice are discussed with a look at crop choices (Chapter 5), farmers' use of slopes and space (Chapter 6) and soil fertility management practices (Chapter 7).

Note

1. The analysis presented in this chapter is based on a detailed study of farmers' practice on over 800 farm plots managed by 146 farm families. All farming activities were recorded for each plot between November and March during 1990–91 and 1992–93. These quantitative data are complemented by case studies illustrating and elaborating particular themes. Results of statistical tests are not reported here, but more details can be found in FSRU/IIED (1994).

CHAPTER FIVE

Risky decisions: dryland crop choices

What mix of crops is found in a field in any year is the result of a myriad of influences. As Chapter 4 has shown, responses to a range of contingencies emerge through a season. This may mean that decisions to replant, in-fill or abandon the plot may change the cropping pattern following initial planting. But what are the factors that influence the initial planting choices at the beginning of a season, and so determine broader crop patterns in dry areas such as Chivi?

In cases where the crop varieties are well known and the land being planted has been used for some time, farmers have a reasonable idea of the likely responses of different crops under different rainfall conditions. Although uncertainties impinge on farming practice, risks can, to some degree, be assessed and potential options gauged. Each crop has different risks associated, different resource requirements and different potential uses. This chapter asks what are the trade-offs made in the choice of crops by different farmers? Who takes risks and who avoids them?

The chapter uses data from four seasons between 1988–89 and 1992–93 (excluding the drought year 1991–92 when few crops were planted) to look at crop choices in over 800 plots covering around 600ha that made up the fields of the 146 farm households in the Chivi sample. Differences between the three study sites, between the characteristics of households and individuals, are considered, alongside differences due to wider economic, social and institutional conditions.

Choosing crops

Crop choices are influenced by risk and uncertainty in different ways. Different crops have different levels of susceptibility to drought, pest attack or poor soil conditions; different crops have different levels of input requirement, whether seed, fertiliser or labour for production or processing; different crops have different properties of taste or storage for home consumption, or market price and sale potential for cash income; and different crops have different socially defined roles and status levels. For instance, maize, which dominates the cropped area (Table 5.1), is highly susceptible to drought, has high seed costs, when hybrids are used, and stores poorly, but has relatively low labour requirements for production and processing, is widely preferred as the staple food, and can be easily sold. By contrast, small grains (pearl/finger millet, sorghum) are less susceptible to drought, can be dry-planted, seed is usually readily available, and grains can be stored for long periods. However, small grain porridge is generally not preferred and labour requirements for pest control and processing are high, although small grains, particularly finger millet, do have important roles in beer brewing for commercial and ritual purposes. Oilseed crops show similar trade-offs. Sunflower is preferred for late planting as it demands low inputs, is relatively drought-resistant and can be sold easily. Groundnuts are more susceptible to environmental conditions, but again can be sold or made into peanut butter. Cotton remains a specialist crop in Chivi; despite its hardiness, the input requirements (particularly fertiliser and pesticides) make it a poor choice for many.

Table 5.1 Choice of crop as percentage of cropped area

Crop	1988–89	1989–90	1990–91	1992–93
Cropped area (ha)	644.6	643.9	592.2	634.4
Bambarra nuts	2.3	1.3	4.6	0.7
Cotton	4.8	3.4	4.4	0.8
Finger millet	11.3	7.7	13.9	10.0
Groundnuts	7.9	8.6	10.8	3.4
Maize	35.3	40.5	35.0	39.7
Pearl millet	21.0	16.8	10.3	20.3
Sunflower	9.3	15.8	16.7	13.0
Sorghum	7.9	5.7	4.0	11.9

Source: Field surveys, Chivi

The crop mix has changed over time. Notable patterns include decreases in pearl millet and sorghum until the drought of 1991–92, followed by a revived interest in small grains following the drought. Sunflower areas have increased since the mid-1980s, reaching a plateau in the late 1980s when around 60% of households were planting at least some sunflower. Areas planted to cotton remained at a constant low level until after the drought when, because of lack of inputs, the area fell to a negligible level. Groundnut areas showed a similar pattern, with a constant level of 8–10% until the drought and then, because of lack of seed, a drop to 3.4% in the 1992–93 season. Finger millet and maize have remained more or less constant throughout the period. These localised patterns are reflected in national trends (Chapter 2).

Differences in cropping pattern are noticeable between the three study sites, particularly with respect to the ratio between maize and small grain planted (Table 5.2). Ngundu farmers have a significantly larger proportion of their land planted with maize. Takavarasha and Chivi farmers planted proportionately more small grains in all years. Both Takavarasha and Chivi farmers consistently plant more of their area with groundnuts, but less with cotton. Chivi area is also characterised by extensive fallow, which as a percentage of land area was significantly greater than the other areas in all years.

Table 5.2 Ratio of maize area to small grain area

Year	Overall	Chivi	Ngundu	Takavarasha
1988–89	0.88	0.84	2.83	0.35
1989–90	1.34	1.66	3.69	0.40
1990–91	1.74	1.71	4.13	0.38
1992–93	0.94	1.18	2.34	0.46

How can these patterns be explained? What factors influence people's choices? Table 5.3 summarises the results of two matrix scoring exercises with men and women,[1] illustrating the complexity of trade-offs involved in crop choice. The matrix demonstrates why maize is preferred over other grain crops, particularly by women, but also why other crops are included in the mix for different purposes.

The following sections examine crop choice trade-offs in detail, exploring the interaction of environmental, economic, social and institutional factors influencing farmers' decision-making under conditions of risk.[2]

Environmental variation

In Chivi, rainfall levels vary from year to year and from site to site (Chapter 1). As Chapter 4 has illustrated, people must respond through finely tuned timing in agricultural activities. However, between the study sites there are some more consistent patterns. In particular, due to its particular topographical setting, the Ngundu area usually receives more rainfall. With the risks of rainfall deficits lower than in Takavarasha, the more extensive planting of maize (Table 5.2) can be, at least in part, explained.

Spatial variation in soil quality is another important factor in determining crop choice. Again this differs between the study sites (Chapter 1). Land with high levels of available moisture (sands on the toplands and low-lying sites) can be expected to be planted with drought-susceptible crops, while those areas with low available moisture (heavier soils on the toplands and degraded sites) can be expected to be planted with drought-resistant crops. A measure of association between cropping area under a

Table 5.3 Matrix scoring of crop choice using informants' criteria (M = men; W = women; choice marked out of a total of ten; where criteria are not mentioned, the crop was not considered or the criterion was not relevant)

	Maize (R201)		Pearl millet		Finger millet		Sunflower		Groundnut	
	M	F	M	F	M	F	M	F	M	F
Easy to grow	7	8	8	7	5	6	8	8	–	3
Drought resistant	2	3	9	8	8	8	7	7	–	3
Pest-and-disease-resistant	6	5	4	2	5	3	8	7	–	4
Cost of seed low/access high	1	2	8	8	6	6	3	4	–	5
Storage good	2	1	10	10	10	10	2	2	–	3
Easy to process	–	8	–	3	–	2	–	–	–	6
Tastes good as *sadza*	8	9	7	6	2	2	–	–	–	–
Sales price high	7	–	6	–	8	–	8	–	–	–
Easy marketing	9	8	2	1	4	3	8	8	–	8
Use for rituals	–	–	–	–	10	–	–	–	–	–

Source: matrix scoring with a group of men and a group of women (mixed ages), Chivi

particular crop and the relative availability of a particular soil type is the preference index (PI). This is defined as:

$$PI = \frac{\text{\% of total area under crop } x \text{ planted on soil type } y}{\text{\% of total area available as soil type } y}$$

If PI > 1 then there is a preferred allocation of the crop to that soil type, if PI = 1 then the crop is allocated to that soil type in proportion to its availability and if PI < 1 then that soil type is avoided for that crop. The pattern of allocation for the 1990–91 season among all farm plots in the sample is shown in Table 5.4.

Table 5.4 Preference indices for crops and soil types (1990-91) for 842 farm plots in three areas, Chivi communal area

Crop/soil	Heavy clay (*chidaka*)	Loams (*dzvuku*)	Sands (*musheche*)	Mixed
Maize	1.70	0.83	1.04	0.82
Pearl millet	0.35	1.25	0.89	1.20
Sorghum	1.35	1.17	0.84	0.96
Finger millet	0.67	1.38	0.90	0.93
Bambarra nuts	0.00	0.44	1.32	1.40
Sunflower	0.78	1.18	0.74	1.34
Cotton	1.80	0.79	1.43	0.19
Groundnuts	0.13	0.79	1.26	1.12

The results show that maize is preferentially allocated to heavy clays (*chidaka*), particularly in wetter low-lying sites (Chapter 6). Cotton shows a similar pattern, with strong preferences for both heavy clays and sands. Pearl millet, finger millet and sorghum are preferentially allocated to loamy clay soils (*dzvuku*) and mixed (in the case of pearl millet) and heavy clays (in the case of sorghum). Bambarra nuts and groundnuts are preferentially allocated to sandy and mixed sandy soils, whilst sunflower is preferentially grown on mixed loams and sands.

Wealth differences

Crop choices are, of course, not only environmentally determined. Differences in resource access may be equally important in constraining options or providing opportunities. Households with draught access (broadly wealthier, asset-rich households) plant a greater proportion of their land with maize and a smaller proportion with pearl millet. Such households also plant a greater proportion of land with cotton and have proportionately less land left as fallow. These households also achieve higher yield levels, notably for maize and pearl millet. However, for other crops, the patterns across wealth groups is remarkably similar.

Wealthier households, with greater access to assets, thus plant larger areas and invest in high-return, relatively high-risk crops (e.g. maize rather than millet) and high-input, high-return cash crops (e.g. cotton rather than sunflower). Higher yields per unit area are achieved by this strategy, although wealth-related differences appear to be restricted to certain crops (notably maize) where most investment is applied. Yield levels are, however, very poorly correlated with total farm size for all crops, although the proportion of total area allocated to maize is negatively correlated with total farm size. Those with smaller farms thus appear to opt for a more diverse crop combination, spreading risks across a wider crop portfolio than those with bigger farms, who opt for a larger proportional commitment to maize production.

Gender relations and social networks

The choice of crops in a field is often hotly contested between men and women within households. Bargaining may be intense before trade-offs and compromises are reached. For instance, women regularly object to the planting of pearl millet because of the high processing labour demand (exclusively women's work) and may surreptitiously withdraw labour from farming the plot. In some cases, especially where the man is absent, women may refuse to plant millet and may always plant maize despite instructions. As one man complained, 'I always come back and find maize, but what can you do?' Both 'hidden' and more open opportunities for resistance are legion (cf. Scott, 1985). The data show how women opt for low labour-input (especially with respect to processing labour) crops, such as maize, as well as crops that can realise added value through local processing and marketing (groundnuts, bambarra nuts). By contrast, men focus on crops giving good cash returns (maize, sunflower, cotton) or good food security prospects (millets).

Just as intra-household relations are important, so too are networks, alliances and social relations between households. The ability to make use of a wider pool of assets, whether in the form of labour or access to draught power, is highly significant in determining the possibilities of agricultural practice in Chivi (Chapter 4). Social position within the wider community is thus critical in determining whether such relationships can be drawn upon. Those at the centre of lineage clusters, with a significant asset base, are clearly better off than those who must operate independently of others because they are recent in-migrants. The ability to take risks thus does not only relate to the wealth of an individual or household, but also to the position within wider networks.

Taste and preference

Patterns of preference relate to different people's experience, associated knowledge about different crops and tastes for them. Settlement histories have had an important influence over crop choice patterns in Chivi (Chapter 2). For instance, the Chivi central and Takavarasha areas have been settled for a long time and farmers have a long history of millet cultivation. By contrast, the Ngundu area has only been settled extensively relatively recently. Most settlers came from wetter areas further north and brought with them knowledge about maize farming, along with a strong preference for maize over small grains.

Prior to the maize revolution of the 1940s and 1950s (Chapters 2 and 8), small grains were much more widespread in Chivi. Older farmers know a lot about millet agronomy and varietal selection and are happy to eat millet porridge. Younger men and women are less keen, partly as the taste of maize is increasingly preferred, but also because they are more accustomed to the growing and processing of maize, finding it both easier and less labour-intensive. The data show how households with older heads consistently plant significantly more of their land to pearl millet.

Demographic status

Households with older heads are also more likely to have adult children sending remittances to rely on, as well as accumulated assets at the home. Middle-aged households are more likely to have young adults in the home available as a labour source, although they may have added school fee commitments and the husband may be working away. Younger households are most likely to be asset-poor, with young children and consequently a high dependency ratio. These different situations result in different cropping patterns, as concerns of income security (e.g. access to alternative income sources), food provisioning at the home (dependency) and labour availability (household size and age) come into play. Across all four years, older, larger households opted for more food-secure options (pearl and finger millet), while younger people planted fast-return, low labour-input crops, such as maize and sunflower.

Crop prices and market opportunities

Real prices of most crops have been eroded since the early 1980s, with exchange rate distortions providing disincentives for the production of tradeable commodities such as maize, cotton and tobacco (Jansen and Muir, 1994). With changes in the agricultural policy during the early 1990s some of these distortions were rectified. The producer price of maize was raised significantly and incentives were increased to plant cash crops for export sale. However, since most farmers in Chivi are net consumers of grain, consumer prices may have a greater impact on decisions (Jayne and Chisvo, 1991). Despite a variety of incentives against maize during the 1980s, farmers consistently grew large areas of the crop. Other factors, such as marketing opportunities, agronomic factors, storage and processing were probably more significant than price alone in guiding decisions.

The opportunities for crop marketing in Chivi have expanded enormously since Independence (Chapter 3). Although crop sales are few and far between, they are nevertheless important to the rural economy. Maize, and increasingly sunflower and cotton, are the major crops sold, and the opportunity to sell for cash represents a significant incentive to choose such crops. Changes in marketing through liberalisation have opened up new opportunities for some, particularly those with access to transport networks and with some capital base to engage in trading. Among the research sites, Ngundu has benefited most from these changes, with both large- and small-scale entrepreneurs (often women) taking advantage of regional and seasonal maize price differentials (Chapter 3). This has reinforced the incentive to invest in maize cropping in this area.

Different households balance cropping for cash or direct food production in different ways. Most do not sell any crops in most years (Chapter 3); however some do manage to sell maize, sunflower, groundnuts and cotton on a more regular basis. But farmers' concerns with ensuring food security mean that cash-cropping options are constrained. Among the household sample, outputs of groundnuts and sunflower were positively correlated with grain balance levels (storage net of consumption and sales) in all years (cf. Jayne, 1994), implying that such cash crops are only grown if grain supplies are assured. Because of the high costs of purchased food, particularly prior to the deregulation of milling, people who did not have regular surpluses of grain avoided growing significant amounts of sunflower or groundnuts as, even if they were sold, the ability to purchase food was limited.

Input markets have less of an influence on crop choice, as relatively low input levels are used. The use of fertilisers has proved uneconomic, even at high levels of subsidy (Chapter 6) and so they tend only to be used on specific crops, notably cotton, and in low amounts on specific areas of high-value crops, especially maize. Hybrid maize seed, by contrast, has been widely adopted, with virtually all farmers regularly planting at least some of their areas with purchased hybrid maize seed since the 1980s. Availability of hybrid maize seed has largely been good, although escalating costs mean that some farmers are thinking again about the value of hybrids (Chapter 8).

Alternative income sources

The attraction of alternative income-earning opportunities also affects crop choice. For instance, some people work for others during peak periods of work, such as weeding or harvesting (Chapter 3). Although wage rates are low, younger women or men who have been unable to find work in towns, who are recent immigrants with limited or no land (e.g. refugees from Mozambique), or whose own farming enterprise has collapsed, due to lack of capital or assets, may divert labour from their own farm. Wage employment outside the communal areas, however, offers much higher returns (Chapter 3). This largely attracts men for whom the incentives to abandon farm work and move to town in search of employment are high, especially when the low and uncertain returns to farming are considered. Access to cash remittances allows a higher level of investment in farm inputs and capital assets. Despite the withdrawal of (largely male) labour, there was no significant difference in the proportional area of crops planted between remittance earners and others for all years studied. However, maize yields were significantly higher in some years. Households with absent males sending remittances thus do not appear to shift crop choice significantly, but focus investments (notably fertilisers, hired labour etc.) on yield increases of maize.

External influences

Influences on crop choice stretch beyond the immediate farm setting to external influences, including extension recommendations, incentives provided by development projects, and legal constraints. The state and development agencies, through extension agents and projects, have established ideas about what is appropriate. These, in turn, influence the way people choose crops on their farms.

The agricultural extension system in Zimbabwe (Agritex), encourages a set of practices based around a series of regional recommendations, each approved by the research wing of the ministry. However, the promotion of standardised recommendations is of limited utility in a highly variable environment. Some recommendations are rejected outright as being inappropriate, others are adapted to suit local circumstances. The social pressure to conform with formal recommendations is reinforced by the Master Farmer training scheme (Chapter 6). Officially promulgated ideas of good farming may not, however, be coincident with what farmers believe to be appropriate. But the passing of Master Farmer training and attendance at extension groups ensures prestige, extension advice (which is valued, despite inadequacies) and sometimes preferential access to credit and inputs.

A range of development projects are active in Chivi, promoting various forms of agricultural or resource management – from conservation tillage to agroforestry to grazing schemes. Farmers in Chivi have become accustomed to the process of rural development. They see the Land Cruisers arriving and hear about the benefits accruing to people in other areas. Involvement in, or at least compliance with, development projects may result in free inputs (fencing, seedlings, breed animals, food aid etc.) that can be acquired individually or as a group. In addition, exposure to what are perceived to be 'modern', 'European' ideas promoted by development agencies may also shift attitudes and affect practice. Following the rhetoric of much development and extension work, normative value may be attached to the benefits of modern ways, with 'traditional' practices being rejected.

Such normative views on what is appropriate may be reinforced by legislation. For instance, legislation regulating land use has an important impact on crop choice options. In Zimbabwe, it remains illegal to cultivate wetland areas or sites close to riverbanks (Chapter 6). This prevents a wetland/dryland cropping strategy, restricting field crop cultivation to dry upland areas. Maize and other crops more suited to a wetter, lowland environmental niche thus must be grown in unsuitable, dry areas. A flexible, adaptive use of diverse landscapes is thus constrained by legal statute and bureaucratic interference.

This does not mean that external influences are not contested and resisted. Local views about what is appropriate practice may directly contradict the official line. For instance, the revival of 'traditional' values during the drought period (Chapter 10) resulted in the active promotion of indigenous grain varieties by spiritual and lineage leaders in some parts of Chivi, with extension recommendations involving the use of 'modern' technologies being explicitly blamed for the drought. Resistance may also be less direct. For instance, people may be ashamed to carry out intercropping, it being deemed untidy and unproductive by extension workers; thus intercrops may be concealed in the centre of the field, with a pristine monocrop exposed to extension workers and other passers-by.

Conclusion

As the data presented in this chapter amply show, there is an immense range of influences on crop choice, from environmental factors, to economic circumstances, to social and institutional contexts. It is thus very difficult to disentangle the influences on particular choice trade-offs. Simple decision models that try to describe such detail will almost inevitably fail due to specification problems. Instead, analysis more rooted in people's own perceptions of decision trade-offs is required. Rather than inferring risk attitudes through the difference between actual practice and a modelled outcome or through direct elicitation procedures (Chapter 1), a more direct assessment of trade-offs, using people's own criteria, is more illuminating (cf. Table 5.3).

Whilst much farming practice may be the result of unplanned 'performance', responses to uncertainty and unexpected contingency (Chapter 4; Richards, 1989), trade-offs between options with different risks and where different, known environmental, economic and social conditions pertain also imply a degree of planning (Batterbury, 1993). But since so many factors are influential there is no optimal crop choice or combination for an area. This makes extension recommendations highly problematic. Instead of promoting particular choices, a more appropriate strategy would be to invest effort in supporting farmers' risk management strategies, encouraging diversification and flexibility. This theme is pursued further in the next chapter, with a consideration of the spatial dimensions of managing risk in dryland areas.

Notes

1. The matrix scoring was carried out separately with a group of men and women, with ages ranging from 25 to 60. Criteria were identified through discussion; scoring, using beans, was carried out with maximum scores for a box chosen as ten. Much discussion resulted before the group decided on the appropriate score (see Maxwell and Bart [1995] for more discussion on the methodology).

2. Various comparisons are made in the following sections. The following definitions were adopted for the purposes of statistical comparison between groups: wealth comparisons were based on draught ownership as a proxy (Chapter 1); female-headed households refer to those households where elder males are absent permanently or for long periods; major decision takers within the household were determined for each plot (named individuals grouped as men or women for this analysis); household size comparisons were based on above- and below-sample average (7); age comparisons were based on age of named household head above and below sample median (40 years). Details of statistical tests are given in FSRU/IIED (1994).

CHAPTER SIX

Making the most of spatial variation: adaptive use of slopes and space

Agriculture has an important spatial dimension. In southern Zimbabwe farming is carried out in a variety of niches at different spatial scales. Different possibilities are realised with the contrasting agroecologies of upland fields, lowland riverbank gardens and *dambo* plots. Spatial variation also occurs at the field level, with variations in soil types, topography, erosion and water flow dynamics, making a complex mosaic of different opportunities. Individual crops may use space in a multitude of ways, with a variety of crop combinations, agroforestry practices and plant spacing adding further dimensions to spatial complexity.

This chapter is about how spatial variation, at a variety of scales, is made use of. The chapter does not dwell on static classifications of resource types, but instead focuses on adaptive use: on how landscapes, fields and individual plots are shaped and sometimes transformed by human agency. This dynamic view of spatial variability shows how the agricultural landscapes we see today are products of long histories of interaction, manipulation and change. Spatial variability is thus the result of both biological potential and social context, both of which change over time.

Spatial variability is sometimes seen as a major stumbling block to generalisation in farming systems research, where site specificity in findings limits the transferability of technology recommendations (Carter *et al.*, 1994). But all sites are inevitably different, and generalised recommendation domains are, by and large, a myth: a product of our eagerness to impose static categories on dynamic process. A detailed study of spatial variability in dryland farming systems instead offers an alternative perspective. This chapter shows how understanding access to and control over resources at different spatial scales offers insights into agricultural management. The chapter also shows how key spatial patterns can be recognised only once critical processes managed by farmers are identified. This provides an opportunity for generalisation – not in terms of spatially mapped recommendation domains, but in terms of the links between spatial process, resource entitlement and agricultural management.

Patterns of use at different scales

Spatial patterns and processes change over time. Dynamic responses at different spatial scales, from landscape to field to crop, occur at different rates and may be subject to different levels of manipulation and intervention by the farmer.

At the landscape scale, changes in catchments occur over relatively long periods. Over the last century, landscapes in Chivi have changed dramatically (Chapter 2). In the early part of this century, much farming was largely restricted to small, high-potential patches close to rivers. This was complemented by areas used for dryland cultivation. Over time these areas have expanded. A combination of population expansion through natural growth and in-migration and technological change (notably the introduction of the plough) has resulted in the clearance of large areas of woodland for fields. This pattern was accelerated by the imposition of land-use policies that encouraged upland farming and banned wetland and riverbank cultivation. The result has been a conversion of watersheds from woodland to farmland.

This has had a number of consequences for the pattern and quality of spatial niches for agriculture. Extensive upland arable sites are generally of relatively poor quality. Soil erosion, soil leaching and extended use have reduced the quality of many of these soils. In order for them to give effective returns, careful management of soil and water must be carried out. With reduced woodland cover in the catchment, the transport of soil and water down slopes has inevitably increased, both in scale and speed. The result is that low-lying sites that act as soil and water sinks or transition zones have increased in value relative to upland sites. Thus as landscapes change, the relative importance of different patches within them also changes. Today, lowland key resource patches are at a high premium, while many upland sites are exhausted and in need of intensive investment and skilful management for successful agriculture.

Patterns of change at the field level occur over a shorter time span. The micro-topography of a field changes both within and between seasons, as soil and water properties of particular areas alter through erosion, deposition or cultivation. Detailed observation of such changes is part of everyday farming practice. Such observations are the basis on which crop allocation or agronomic management decisions can be made. Farmers can also manipulate such changes: changing slopes through ploughing in a particular direction over time, encouraging channelled water flows by the construction of ridges or bunds, moving and mixing different soil types or building pits or troughs to harvest water and soil. All these practices can affect the direction, velocity and level of soil and water flows. They may have both positive and negative effects. Sudden increases in water flows, causing the breaching of bunds or ridges, may result in flooding, gully erosion or siltation of areas. However, experimentation and adaptive change allow farmers to develop local solutions appropriate to their own fields.

The management of space at the crop scale must be even more responsive. As a season unfolds, farmers may choose different crop combinations, different types of intercropping, different sequences or relays of crop types or different plant spacing and weeding regimes (Chapter 4). The choice of agronomic practice cannot be defined beforehand; there is no universal recommendation for any portion of land. It is more a matter of adaptive response to particular and uncertain circumstance. Over time these responses have changed. With greater pressure on land today, available land must be used more intensively. Most intensification, for instance more complex relay and intercropping systems, have occurred in high-potential sites (gardens, *dambo* fields) or in those portions of dryland fields that receive most attention (home fields as opposed to out-fields).

Resource entitlements, socially differentiated use and tenure

The use of different portions of the farm landscape, the type of field management and the degree of cropping complexity are also socially differentiated. High-value patches are highly contested. *Dambos*, for instance, are often the centre of intense local political claims and counter-claims. Securing farming rights over such resources clearly has major material benefits, and lineage leaders – or other more powerful political figures (largely older men) – do their utmost to assert authority and ensure access. Similar advantages derive from access to riverbank garden sites. These are established by gardening groups (mostly women) or by individuals (men and women). Such rights to farm may be contested by the state. In Zimbabwe, the barrage of anachronistic conservation laws (Chapter 2) officially prevents the cultivation of wetlands and riverbank areas within 30m of the stream course.

With such spatial variation in the value of different resources in the agricultural landscape and with different people having different entitlements to these resources, a complex tenurial system arises whereby different landscape niches are controlled by different groups of people (Nhira and Fortmann, 1993). Higher-value resources, such as wetland sites, have more tightly defined and exclusive tenure rules, whereas access to lower-value resources, such as dryland rough grazing, is less well defined and a more diffuse set of overlapping rights may exist (cf. Behnke, 1994). This spatial patterning of tenure regimes is replicated at the field level, where some arable areas, particularly home fields and gardens, are exclusively owned and often fenced, whereas dryland fields and the trees within them are exclusively managed during the cropping season, but they revert to common property in the dry season.

Field-level management varies between different actors. Resource-poor farmers with small fields must make good use of limited space and typically have intensively managed farms with a range of diverse cropping patterns. Richer farmers, by contrast, may have greater access to labour for the construction of more elaborate soil- and water-harvesting structures. Many women sow intercrops among main field crops – pumpkins, melons or sweet sorghum may be sown and particular 'weeds' retained as vegetables. Such practices may come into conflict with husbands, whose main production concern is the dominant grain crop. However, these patterns are by no means clear-cut. Sometimes it is down to interest, enthusiasm and motivation. Some farmers are fascinated by the potentials of water management, others obsessed by issues of soil conservation, others determined experimenters with plant spacing or intercrop combinations.

The following sections offer data from the Chivi sample households and case studies to illustrate the patterns of spatial management that occur at different scales, from landscape to field to crop.

Landscape-level spatial management

This section illustrates various aspects of spatial management used for coping with uncertainty at a landscape level. The case studies highlight the different investment strategies and roles of different actors in production in cropping fields and garden plots, home fields and out-fields, wet fields and dry fields. Each case emphasises the need to take a spatially differentiated view of production patterns in order to understand the complex spatial trade-offs involved in agricultural production in dry areas.

Cropping field and garden plot

Most cropping fields are owned by men, although women do have access to plots, sometimes for their own exclusive use. Women's agricultural space is largely confined to dry-season garden areas. These are usually located near a river, stream or *dambo*. In the past these have often been outlawed by environmental legislation, but despite this, women still develop them, although they are increasingly part of authorised group gardening activities (Box 6.1).

Within the Chivi sample, 38% of households have members who have access to gardens. Virtually all of these are managed by women. The pattern of gardening differs between the study sites. Gardening is most prevalent in the Takavarasha area, where 80% of households are involved. This is partly because of the low yield potential of the cropping land and the need to compensate through dry-season production activities. It is also due to the close proximity of the Runde river and the lack of other dry-season income-earning opportunities for women in the area. Fewer

Box 6.1 Gardening

Mai Tawanda has her own small garden by the riverbank, along with many other women from her village. Water is collected from sand holes (*mifuku*) in the riverbed during the dry season for watering of the vegetables. This gardening provides a regular source of green vegetables during the dry season, and some independent income through sales. The local extension worker says that the gardens are too close to the river and must be moved. He is trying to encourage women to form group gardens at designated sites. Mai Tawanda and friends are planning to join together to form a garden group, as they hope that they can then get access to better seeds, pest control chemicals and maybe even some water pumping equipment from an NGO working in the area.

households are engaged in gardening in the Ngundu area (only 17%), as the major rivers are far from the homesteads, and the available *dambo* sites are all fully occupied. Also, women in this area can make more money from trading (often in vegetables purchased elsewhere), than in production. The Chivi situation is intermediate, with 29% of households involved. Vegetable producers in this area have a good market due to the presence of the Chivi Office. However, the availability of good gardening sites is limited.

Home field and out-field

Most households have one field portion close to the homestead and another further away: the home field and the out-field. The home field represents nearly 19% of the total cultivable area in the full sample. Both the cropping pattern and the intensity of investment differ between these sites. Home fields are usually planted with maize, and ploughed and planted earlier; they are winter-ploughed more frequently and receive more of the fertility inputs than out-fields (Chapter 4). The intensity of management is assisted by the proximity to the home and the opportunity for labour to be employed easily. Men and women often take charge of separate plots on the home plot, with women concentrating on groundnut and bambarra nut production (and sometimes vegetables) and men on maize production. During the 1990–91 and 1992–93 seasons, around 50% of home fields were planted with maize, representing about one quarter of all maize planted (Table 6.1).

Wet fields and dry fields

Another dimension of landscape heterogeneity is the contrast between dry upland fields and wetter low-lying fields. There are relatively few

Table 6.1 Home field cropping patterns, 1990–91 and 1992–93

Crop	% of home field as crop *x*		Crop *x* in home field as proportion of total farm area under crop *x*	
	1990–91	1992–93	1990–91	1992–93
Maize	50.3	49.4	24.2	24.6
Sunflower	14.1	4.4	14.2	6.6
Finger millet	11.7	16.5	14.2	32.5
Groundnuts	10.8	2.9	16.8	16.8
Sorghum	5.1	7.6	21.5	12.6
Bambarra nuts	4.9	0.2	17.6	4.6
Pearl millet	3.3	14.8	5.3	14.4
Cotton	0.0	1.6	0.0	36.9
Cow pea	0.0	0.0	0.0	0.0
Fallow	0.0	0.0	0.0	0.0

farmers with access to valley-bottom *dambo* farming land within the sample. This is due to a number of factors. First, none of the three sample sites are found in the valley areas of the *miombo* hills areas with extensive *dambos*. Second, *dambo* areas constitute only around 5% of the total area (Whitlow, 1985); many are in grazing areas, others are heavily waterlogged and are unsuitable for agriculture. Third, it remains illegal to cultivate *dambos* in Zimbabwe (Bell *et al.*, 1987; Scoones and Cousins, 1994). Legislative protection for stream banks and *dambo* sites thus provides a strong disincentive for cultivation, so that most arable lands are allocated away from valley areas and *dambo* sites (Chapter 2). Despite these factors, some farmers are able to make use of the contrasting properties of wetland and dryland farming areas. The case study in Box 6.2 gives details of such a farmer.

Field-level spatial management

Managing the spatial variability of soil and water flows at field level provides a further set of opportunities for avoiding the hazards of a highly variable environment. Capturing, redirecting and harvesting soil and water allow farmers to expand their repertoire of cropping patterns, to increase the range of crops and trees grown, and to increase yields. The case studies in Box 6.3 illustrate two different strategies for field-level spatial management. In the first case, the farmer makes use of existing slopes, contours and micro-topography, along with the varied soil types found in the field, to direct flows of water to particular sites. These sink areas thus become important microenvironments within the field, supporting different crops with higher production potentials. The second case study documents more direct intervention – the construction of

Box 6.2 *Dambo* farming

Mr Tichaona Benji has the good fortune to own a portion of swampy low-lying *dambo* land as part of his farm. The lowest part of his farm runs along the edge of the *dambo*, with the central portion reserved for communal grazing, a few gardens and the village well. The farm traverses the catena from the *dambo* through the *dambo* edge to the dryland above. Each part of this catenal variation can be used in a different way, exploiting the variation in soil and water properties of the land across the slope. In the waterlogged portion, Mr Benji intercrops maize and rice alongside a number of raised beds for vegetables. In the slightly higher (and less wet) area, maize is planted alone. In the next plot there is finger millet and above that pearl millet, adjacent to the rocky outcrop where Mr Benji's house is. This variation, over a small distance of 100m or so, allows Mr Benji to cultivate a wide diversity of crops. The wet portion of his land also allows a seasonal extension of cropping activities compared to dryland farmers. The *dambo* is ideal for the cultivation of winter vegetables. He and his wife make use of his field land, along with a small garden on the other side of the *dambo*. In the field area a second (and sometimes third) crop of maize can be planted; this is sometimes combined with winter wheat. In a wet year like 1992–93 the wet and dry fields provide important complementarity, allowing the growing of different crops and the use of different seasonal niches, spreading labour while ensuring high output. In a dry year, such as 1990–91, the wetter *dambo* portion became critical as this was the only part of the farm that yielded anything. Although the rice crop largely failed due to lack of water, maize did reasonably. This was in stark contrast to the surrounding dry fields. But the *dambo* is unable to cope with the most extreme droughts; in 1991–92, even the *dambo* area dried up.

infiltration pits. These also harvest water and soil, but in this case an artificial microenvironment is created that can support tree growing.

Farmers regularly make use of natural ecological patterns and processes in the management of agricultural lands. For instance, various species of termite are important components of savanna ecosystems in Zimbabwe, and termite mounds are common features of the agricultural landscape. Farmers can make use of termites to further transform their farms by using the soil from termite mounds or by encouraging termites into areas with hard soils so that infiltration rates are increased by water penetrating along the channels dug by termites. In wetter areas, increasing the rate of organic matter breakdown is facilitated by attracting termites to grass or crop residue piles.

When fields are cleared from natural woodland, certain species are retained (Campbell, 1987).[1] Selective maintenance of key tree species allows some of the benefits of the natural woodland to be drawn upon. Trees that are maintained include a variety of fruit trees, as well as species that provide good shade or leaf litter. The improvement of poor sandy soils

Box 6.3 Field management

Manipulating slopes, contours and local topography

Mr Shanduka has a sloping field made up of largely sandy soils. The two clay soil plots are planted irregularly with pearl or finger millet because they do not yield well under drought conditions. The remaining plots have been planted to a mix of pearl millet, finger millet, sunflower and maize. Mr Shanduka makes maximum use of the water flows on his field. Water flows from a sodic soil run-off patch at the top end, down a waterway towards the stream at the bottom of his field. At the other end a large, low termite mound provides a similar run-off surface. The water is channelled along contour ridges, but the ridge running along the highest ground has been unable to discharge all the water into the waterway and has breached, spilling water into a dense patch of sunflowers and out into a gully forming along the path running up the waterway. Mr Shanduka has plans to extend the top bund to avoid the breaching problem and to deepen the remaining bunds in order to increase slow seepage into lower portions of the field. At the moment, water flows are directed to two patches in the lower part of the field just above the stream. Water thus flows into depressions that are already rich in humus and other soil deposits. During 1992–93 these sites were planted to maize and sunflower and both plots yielded very well. A similar pattern of water harvesting and management is seen around the home. Here, water running off the home area's yard is captured in a deep-ploughed depression that holds water due to a sodic soil bank that surrounds it. This is a very productive patch and during 1992-93 produced a very good crop of finger millet. In the maize field that surrounds the home, great care has been taken to conserve soil and water to avoid the risk of maize failure. This involved the deepening of contour ridge drains and the construction of extra earth bunds to attempt to spread water, rather than allowing it to flow with the probable result of bad leaching from the already nutrient-poor sands.

Water management: infiltration pits

Water flows from a small granite rock surface (*ruware*) are captured around Mutoworera's home and diverted towards a series of infiltration pits. The pits are between 50cm and 1m deep and are dug into clay soils adjacent to rocks. The pits temporarily store water following a storm and then subsequently release it to lower-lying areas. This increases the infiltration into the clay soils and reduced wasteful and sometimes damaging run-off from the soil surface. The infiltration pits have allowed the establishment of a number of fruit trees that had previously proved very difficult to plant in this dry area.

through the deposition of leaf litter, or the attraction of livestock (and so dung) to a field with a fine shade tree, allows farmers to increase the fertility levels of field patches at low cost.

The manipulation of weed and pest ecology may equally have benefits. The conversion of woodland areas to farmland inevitably changes the ecological conditions, encouraging the expansion of species able rapidly to colonise open land and cropped areas. Some species may inflict unacceptable economic damage and so need to be controlled. However, other species may offer new opportunities and be encouraged. For instance, in most years mice populations in field areas can be controlled and the benefits of catching mice for eating or sale probably outweigh the potential costs of their elimination. Similarly, many fast-colonising plant species are nutritious food sources and important vegetable supplements to the diet (Wilson, 1990).

Crop-level spatial management

Spatial management also happens at a more micro scale, involving the manipulation of crop–soil–water interactions through plant spacing, intercropping or relay cropping. The case studies in Box 6.4 highlight different aspects of this micro-management. The first case illustrates why standard plant spacing recommendations do not make sense in highly variable environments. Different soil and water conditions exist over relatively short spaces and at different times. To maximise returns thus requires good judgement, based on experience, observation and experimentation. The second case study illustrates the now-common case of farmers having to make use of a very limited area to maximum advantage. This requires a whole range of innovations that would conventionally fall outside recommended practice, yet represent sensible responses to a difficult situation.

Intercropping is an important strategy for crop-level spatial management. Major crops, such as maize or millets, are intercropped with sweet sorghum, pumpkins, water melons, bambarra nuts or cow peas. More often than not, farmers have more than one intercrop in any field. Table 6.2 shows the patterns of intercropping among sample farmers in two seasons. Intercropping is most prevalent in pearl millet and maize fields

Table 6.2 Patterns of intercropping – areas intercropped with one or two species

	Intercrop (% area): 1990–91	Intercrop (% area): 1992–93
Bambarra nuts	61.0	77.7
Cotton	30.8	0.0
Finger millet	42.5	85.8
Groundnuts	69.0	71.4
Maize	74.7	83.9
Pearl millet	83.8	65.0
Sunflower	24.5	37.5
Sorghum	42.5	63.4

Box 6.4 Arranging crops

Plant spacing in maize

Plant spacing in maize varies in Mr Vurayayi's field depending on the soil and water conditions at a particular site. At the dry end of the field, where sandy soils predominate, a wide spacing is used, with rows separated by a medium stride and plants in rows sufficiently far apart so that you can walk between them. However, in other parts of the same field a much more dense plant population is feasible. For instance, where water flows from an anthill to a sink area or where surplus borehole water is channelled into a small garden, plants can be planted at almost double the density without any yield reduction. Plant spacing also changes according to soil type. The sandy soils, with good infiltration, can cope with a higher plant spacing than the clay or anthill soils where large amounts of water are required to get good crops.

Making use of a limited area

Antonio has a small field of only a single plot. As an in-migrant to the area, he is unable to increase the land size. But together with his family he is struggling to get the most out of a very small area. Every portion of the land is planted – even rocky outcrops have been seeded with pearl or finger millet in the hope of yielding something. The main field, however, is almost exclusively maize. The eldest son explains that it is necessary to plant maize, even at the risk of it failing, because maize provides easy food. Maize is the staple crop, it requires relatively little labour in cultivation and processing, and suffers fewer pest attacks (particularly birds) than millet. The maize has been planted in two phases. Household ash, together with some other plant detritus, has been applied to different portions of the plot each year. In those areas where maize has failed, finger millet was transplanted from the rocky sites into the spaces. This transplanting process took place at a number of sites and at a number of times during the 1992–93 season. In other years, replanting of maize would have been attempted, but there was no available seed. Around the house intercropping of water melons and pumpkins is particularly evident. These provide both leaf material for relish and fruits. Wild foods are also harvested from the plot. These include wild fruits from the *Sclerocarya birrea (mupfura)* tree, which are transformed into *mukumbi* beer and *shomwe* nuts, and a variety of green vegetables (e.g. *derere, rude*) that are collected from the field edges while weeding.

and least common in sunflower and cotton fields. Also intercropping is more prevalent in women's fields, as many of the characteristic intercrops are used by women for preparing relish or providing snacks for themselves or their children.

Three contrasting case studies on intercropping are presented in Box 6.5. They highlight the different incentives and disincentives to carry out complex intercropping and the experiments farmers carry out to see how intercrops affect main crops and vice versa.

Box 6.5 Intercropping

1. Mai Nelly, in common with most farmers in the area, regards intercropping as a good practice. On a small field, returns are maximised and, if the right combinations and the appropriate planting sequences are used, there are limited yield reductions on either crop. In most of Mai Nelly's field, pumpkins (*mananga* of several varieties), water melons and sweet sorghum are growing together with maize, sorghum and finger millet. She received a mixed bag of seed from a friend living nearby which she broadcast liberally over several plots in her field. The same applied to the area around the homestead, where such intercrops are planted even more densely. These intercrops do not have an effect on the main crop. But the intercrops' yield may go down if planted in very dense pearl millet or sorghum. The same applies to cow peas, which are planted between the rows of maize and amongst the finger millet on her farm. Cow peas, if harvested regularly and if planted in relatively widely spaced maize or finger millet, do not suffer.

2. By contrast, Mrs Zivhu does not have any intercrops in her field, except a line of sweet sorghum that got there 'by mistake'. This is because she is a Master Farmer trainee, and the Agritex extension recommendations discourage intercropping. Passing of the Master Farmer certificate means that the standard practice of intercropping must be concealed in the middle of the field away from the extension workers' eyes!

3. Intercropping may be a response to poor germination or seed shortage. Tafirei has in-filled his maize field with sorghum, groundnuts and sunflower in different areas. Since he does not have enough money to purchase more maize seed, and he has some other seed left over, he has decided to opt for a complex cropping pattern in the one plot where maize failed to germinate effectively.

Integrated spatial management for successful farming

It is rare to find farmers who integrate the range of spatial considerations discussed above in the design of their farm. Most farmers are unable, due to constraints of labour or capital, to develop their farms to their full potential. Others are simply not interested, preferring to pursue other livelihood options rather than invest too much in the complex craft of farming in a dryland area.

However, there are some farmers who, together with their families, have truly made the most of spatial variation. One such farmer is Mr Phiri of Msipane area, near Zvishavane. Mr Phiri's farm of 2.5ha consists of a mixture of rock outcrop around the homestead, dryland sandy soils and a small patch of wetland at the bottom of the slope (Figure 6.1). This

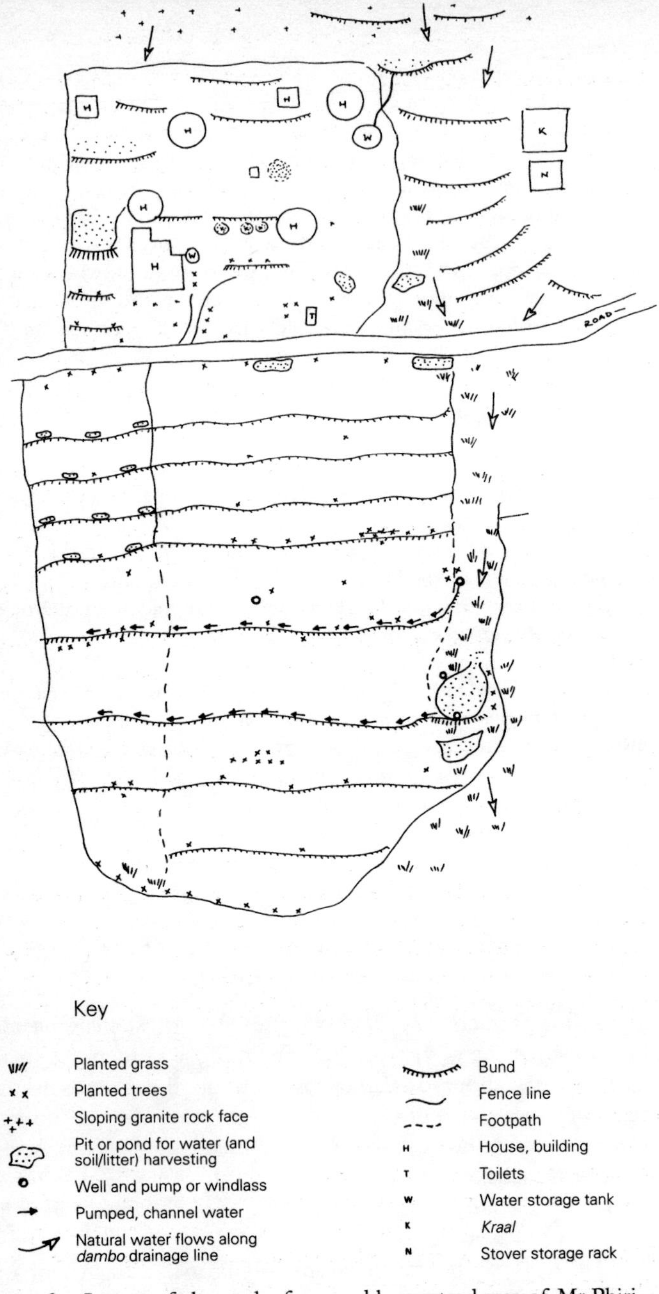

Figure 6.1 Layout of the 2.5 ha farm and homestead area of Mr Phiri, Msipane, Zvishavane, in November 1994

Box 6.6 Making the most of spatial variation

Water flow management, rock catchments and bunds. Water is captured, diverted and stored even before it reaches the field area on Mr Phiri's farm. Above the home a large, granite rock face is used as a catchment surface. Water falling here is directed by a series of bunds towards pits and storage basins dug into the soil at the bottom of the hill and around the home. Through a process of water recharge at all points along the slope, soil moisture is increased in all cultivated areas. As Mr Phiri puts it, 'no water escapes my farm ... I must plant the water before the crops.' Water storage is enhanced in the farm with the construction of a pond in the upper part of a small wetland patch (*dambo*). This retains water through most of the dry season, with slow seepage extending the period of wetness in areas adjacent to the pond. Pond water and a series of *dambo* wells open up possibilities of small-scale irrigation through canals to drier areas of the farm.

Slope and field surface management. Natural changes in soil moisture and nutrient availability across the farm's slope are further manipulated by the construction of earth bunds and soil pits. Soil bunds along the contour increase the conservation of water and soil, while field ridges may act to divert surface flow or decrease waterlogging effects in wetter areas. Pits are dug into the contour bund in order to increase infiltration. By changing the function of the contour bund from one primarily designed for preventing soil erosion and so draining water away from the field, Mr Phiri has redesigned them in order that they fulfil a water harvesting function.

Soil management. In the central wetland area, heavier soils, with high nutrient and organic matter content, exist. These soils retain water and provide the best sites for dry-season and drought cropping. High-density maize stands are planted; these may provide a double crop in good seasons. Limited fertility inputs are required in these areas. In areas further away from the central wetland, the drier, sandier soils have a lower nutrient content. These are suited to groundnut, sorghum and millet planting. Additions of manure and termite soil are concentrated here. Mr Phiri makes use of no inorganic fertiliser as he says it destroys the soil. Instead, he uses a range of techniques to improve soil fertility. Continuous ridging helps the build-up of soil organic matter in the ridges. The same effect is achieved by ploughing in crop residues, grass matter and specially grown green manures and alley crops (Chapter 7). Deep ploughing is practised on all plots in order to avoid the development of an impermeable plough pan.

Space management. During the cropping season of 1988–89, 23 different crop species, 26 different tree species, plus bees, fish, reeds and grass fodder were harvested from Mr Phiri's 2.5ha plot. The identification and creation of spatial niches to maintain diversity are important parts of his strategy. Complex intercropping and relay cropping systems are employed which exploit the environmental heterogeneity of the area.

Box 6.6 (*cont.*)

Temporal variation. Micro-management varies seasonally; the complex patterning of crops, trees and grasses is a result of a set of sequential management decisions that emerge through the season. The *dambo* area is used differently between seasons. In drier years, there is less sequential cropping, less rice and less maize planted. In wetter years, multiple cropping of a greater diversity of annual crops is possible, although waterlogging may occur in some parts of the farm.

Source: visits to Mr Phiri's home since 1985 (see also Maseko *et al.*, 1987; Scoones, 1991)

range of available environmental resources is exploited by managing water flows, manipulating field slopes and surfaces, improving soil structure and fertility, and making the most of limited available space (Box 6.6). A mixture of detailed planning and adaptive performance is the key to success.

Mr Phiri's home has become an example for farmers around to follow. Although his neighbours do not try out the whole range of practices, they often come and observe, trying and testing different options on their own land. This process of farmer-to-farmer sharing of ideas and on-farm adaptation has always been the way new practices have spread. However, the formal extension system has, in the past at least, been a constraint to the spread of innovation (Chapter 8). Many of the practices that are so well exemplified in Mr Phiri's farm are not part of the standard set of extension recommendations. Indeed, those following the extension service's Master Farming training used to be actively dissuaded from following some of the practices so central to Mr Phiri's success. For instance, removing trees from fields used to be a requirement of attaining a Master Farmer certificate (Wilson, 1989). Equally, pitting techniques, particularly those that disturb the design of the standard contour ridge, were seriously frowned on. Other practices are in fact illegal, such as the cultivation or the digging of small dams in the *dambo* area. Prior to Independence, Mr Phiri had successfully won a series of court battles with the Department of Natural Resources and had been granted permission to make use of the wetland area. However, others are more cautious about taking on authority, fearing the consequences of apprehension, fines or even arrest.

Fortunately, there is an increasing recognition among the extension services that the initiatives of people like Mr Phiri are useful opportunities for spreading ideas. As part of the work of the Zvishavane Water Projects which Mr Phiri established in 1987, large numbers of extension workers from all over the country now visit his farm, along with farmers from different areas. Following linkages made between Mr Phiri and farmer groups supported by Intermediate Technology, a number of innovations, including infiltration pits, shallow wells and rock dams, are beginning to spread in nearby Chivi (Hagmann and Murwirwa, 1994)

Conclusion

Making use of a wide range of agricultural management options, differentiated in space at different scales, is a vital component of farmers' strategies. Spreading risk across slopes, between different sites and exploiting a range of microenvironments allow a diverse response to uncertain events and the contrasting dynamics of different parts of the landscape. This is combined with detailed management of field-level soil and water processes and plant–soil–water interactions. The art of dryland farming always makes the most of this spatial complexity. In a dry area, the manipulation of spatial processes to increase the availability of water is central. Through a variety of techniques farmers are able to reshape their landscapes, fields and plots to increase water availability for crops and so reduce the production risks of dryland agriculture. The ability to do so depends on access to and control over land resources, capital and labour.

In order to increase the diversity of options available to farmers, research and extension approaches that encourage local experimentation and farmer-to-farmer sharing are the only way an adaptive approach to agricultural resource management can be encouraged at a broad scale. Because of spatial heterogeneity, simple generalisations about site-specific solutions are impossible. Instead, generalisations about processes are more appropriate, both in terms of key agroecological processes of significance to dryland survival and in terms of the processes by which experimentation, innovation and sharing can be encouraged. These themes are pursued further in the next two chapters.

Note

1. The fifteen most common trees retained in fields in nearby Mazvihwa communal area are (in order of occurrence frequency): *Sclerocarya birrea, Azanza garkeana, Diospyros mespiliformis, Lannea stuhlmanni, Strychnos madagascarensis, Berchemia discolor, Strychnos spinosa, Colophospermum mopane, Gardenia spatufolia, Combretum imberbe, Afzelia quanzensis, Kigelia africana, Lonchocarpus capassa* and *Kirkia acuminata* (Gumbo *et al.*, 1990).

CHAPTER SEVEN

Managing soil fertility

Savannas are characterised by highly variable patterns of soil fertility, ranging from nutrient-poor dystrophic savannas, typical of sandy soils, to the relatively nutrient-rich eutrophic savannas (Frost *et al.*, 1986; Scholes and Walker, 1993). When rainfall is higher, or when irrigation water is provided, available soil nutrients may become the major constraint to production. However, when rainfall is low, soil moisture may be the primary constraint. In the highly variable environments that typify the dryland farming systems of Zimbabwe's communal areas, this fundamental interaction between soil nutrients and rainfall is central to the dynamic potentials and risk responses within farming systems (Chapter 1). This chapter describes the variety of strategies used by farmers to maintain and improve soil fertility. These strategies must respond to the immense variation in soil types, the changing constraints of soil-available moisture and nutrients and the socio-economic conditions facing farmers. It is this complexity – matching soils with fertility inputs, choosing the appropriate combination of soil amendments, trading off input levels with yield returns over time – that makes up farmers' decision-making. All aspects, as will be seen below, are characterised by risk and uncertainty.

Box 7.1 highlights the dilemmas of fertility management for a relatively wealthy farmer in Chivi. He has a large field, is a local lineage leader and is the chairperson of a local farmers' club.

Soils and fertility management

The soils of the study area can be broadly categorised into two clusters – low infiltration rate, relatively high fertility clays; and high infiltration rate, relatively low fertility sands. The clays are either alluvial clays or derived from dolerite outcrops, and the sands are derived primarily from granite. Within and between these broad types, there are numerous intergradations. For instance, local classifications, which broadly parallel technical soil classifications (Bennett, 1985), identify at least eleven different types (Table 7.1).

Soil types are not evenly distributed across the study area. There is a predominance of heavy clay soils in the Takavarasha site, while sands dominate the Chivi central area. Ngundu shows an intermediate position,

Box 7.1 Soil fertility management practice is complex

Mr Mawarire has a large field of over 20 plots, with a total area of 15.3ha. The field is a mix of sandy and clay soils. All fertility inputs are applied to the six plots around the homestead; four other regularly used plots in the main field do not receive any inputs at all. The remainder have remained fallow for some years. The home field plot, which has sandy soils, had a rotation of maize, groundnuts and bambarra nuts over the past three years. The whole field received some fertility inputs over this period, with an alternate application of manure and inorganic fertiliser. Neither are applied at rates recommended by the extension service, but are concentrated on particular sites of low fertility or on particular crops. Within each home field plot there is immense variation in background fertility levels, the result of local soil variation, past fertility management history, and topographical variability resulting in changes in soil and water characteristics over short distances. For instance, during 1992–93 one plot was planted to maize, bambarra nuts and pearl millet. The maize was planted in the area where manure was applied to the maize crop during the previous year, the bambarra nuts were planted in the remaining portion, with pearl millet filled in late in the season in the remaining area, both beneath the *musuma* (*Dyospyros mespiliformis*) tree and along one edge of the plot. Nearby, a plot of finger millet showed a highly varied response to fertility conditions. In one portion the crop was lush and deep green. This was where there had been deposition of silt eroding from a ridge created from many years of continuous ploughing. Just adjacent, the crop looked much less healthy, as the same erosion process had resulted in leaching and water stress. In another portion of the same plot, a healthy circle of finger millet stood in among yellowing plants. This was because this was the site of a goat *kraal* abandoned nearly 25 years ago. In other portions of the same plot variations are due to the removal of soil for building, changing the infiltration properties of the surface layer; the impact of a *musuma* fruit tree on soil with the deposition of leaf litter, and the decrease in surface soil water loss.

with a mixture of both. Over the whole sample (c. 700ha over 800 plots), the distribution of soils in farmers' fields shows sandy soils (*musheche*) being the most common (57.4%), followed by red clays (*dzvuku*) (27.4%) and heavy black clays (*chidaka*) (15.3%). A mixed category covers 36.8% of the field area.

To fertilise, or not to fertilise

There are a range of fertility inputs available to farmers in Chivi. These include: inorganic fertiliser (basal and top dressing), manure, ash and household compost, termitaria and leaf litter. These may be combined with a variety of management options that potentially increase soil fertility; these include: fallowing, crop rotation and the use of leguminous crops.

Attention to soil fertility management has long been part of farming

Table 7.1 Soil types in Chivi – local names and descriptions

Local soil name	Soil description
Chidhaka	Black clay
Chishava/zungu/ga'na	Red, hard clay
Dzvuku	Red clay
Chinamwe	Grey, heavy clay
Guvi/matoro	Black loam/clay
Rumhamhare	Sodic soil
Rujekese	Stony soil
Musheche mukobvu	Grey sandy loam
Musheche mushava	Red sand
Musheche muchena	White sand
Musheche weguvi	Pale sand

Source: FSRU (1993)

practice in Chivi. In the days when land was plentiful and policy allowed the cultivation of the most fertile strips along the riverine fringes and in the *dambos* (Chapter 6), there were few problems faced with declining soil fertility. With increasing land pressure and changes brought about by government policy interventions, increasing needs to manage soil fertility were felt. During the 1920s farmers were reluctant to invest the large amounts of labour required in head-loading manure in baskets to their fields and increasing the intensity of weeding due to manuring. However, with the increased availability of scotch cart transport from the 1940s and the growing incentives to intensify production, manuring increased (Chapter 2).

Inorganic fertiliser first became available during the 1950s, but was barely used in the communal areas. Due to limited distribution networks and high prices, this remained the case until the 1980s when consumption increased significantly. This was associated with shifts towards fertility-demanding crops, such as cotton and hybrid maize, as well as support for inorganic fertiliser use in credit packs widely distributed in the mid-1980s. Vigorous promotion of inorganic fertiliser use by extension agents has been a feature of training programmes for many years.

However, today most farm plots in Chivi are not fertilised. Between 75% and 90% of the total area remains unfertilised by any source in any one year (Table 7.2). For instance, in 1990–91 only 13% of the total land area was fertilised: 6% with inorganic basal fertiliser, 6% with manure and the remainder with a mix of ash, compost and inorganic top dressing. In all years the largest proportion of each fertility input type was applied to low-fertility, sandy soil areas.

The level of fertilisation is decreasing over time. This absence of fertility

Table 7.2 Percentage of total area fertilised, and inputs applied as percentage of fertilised area

Year	Total area (%) unfertilised	Basal fertiliser	Top dressing	Manure	Ash and compost
1988–89	81.4	42.8	2.3	53.0	1.8
1989–90	82.4	37.9	4.2	54.2	3.6
1990–91	87.2	47.6	2.4	46.7	3.3
1992–93	90.9	60.1	5.1	29.9	4.8

Source: Chivi field surveys, 1990–93

input is due to a number of factors including: the lack of available cash for inputs such as inorganic fertiliser, as well as the lack of effective supply (marketing and transport constraints); low and uncertain returns to fertiliser inputs; lack of manure available due to limited livestock in relation to arable area; and labour constraints on leaf litter collection, composting etc. The pros and cons of different fertility inputs were discussed with farmers in Chivi, who highlighted the trade-offs between different options (Table 7.3).

Inorganic fertilisers

Most fertility management research in Zimbabwe has focused on the application of inorganic fertilisers (top dressing and basal applications) to dryland maize. This is despite the widely reported observation that, particularly in dryland areas, farmers do not apply fertiliser in any quantities and that recommended fertiliser applications are uneconomic. A number of studies have shown how returns to fertiliser inputs are highly risky, illustrating why farmers' responses are justified and why extension recommendations based simply on yield reponses are inappropriate (e.g. Bratton and Truscott, 1985; Whingwiri *et al.*, 1987; Ashworth, 1990).

A net benefits analysis of fertiliser yield responses derived from trial data between 1983 and 1986 showed that extension recommendations of 200kg Compound D and 200kg AN were excessive. On average 25% of recommended levels gave the best economic return during this period (Whingwiri *et al.*, 1987). On-farm data from Chivi suggest even greater caution. Data from the period 1984–85 to 1989–90 showed that yield responses were minimal, especially on the red soils, and the economic returns decline with increasing fertiliser applications. According to this data, economically optimal application levels would be close to zero (Mudhara, 1991). National-level data confirm these conclusions (Ashworth, 1990). All studies show that yield response is highly variable, depending on local soil conditions and rainfall patterns. In general, net returns from

Table 7.3 Fertility input alternatives – farmers' views

Fertility input	Rank A	Rank B	Rank C	Advantages	Disadvantages
Manure	1	2	1	Good moisture retention, increased germination and yield, residual effect, improves structure	Needs large *kraal*, crops may burn, encourages weeds
Termitaria	2	4	4	Reduces waterlogging, 2–3 years residual effect	First-year application not effective; overapplication kills crop, labour needed
Leaf litter	3	3	2	Increases crop growth, improves soil structure, reduces salinity	Crop may burn if little water; labour for collection
Ash compost	5	5	5	Crop growth increases, good for vegetables	Needs plenty of moisture
Inorganic fertiliser	3	1	2	Crop growth high	Yearly application, needs high rainfall, expensive

Notes: A: Rank of actual use; B: Rank of preference under good rainfall; C: Rank of preference under poor rainfall conditions

Source: FSRU (1993)

fertiliser application decline in poor rainfall years and on relatively nutrient-rich soils. Economic returns to fertiliser application are affected by the relative prices of inputs and outputs. With the removal of subsidies on fertilisers their price has increased dramatically (Figure 7.1). This increase has not been compensated by increases in crop prices. The consequence is that today blanket fertiliser application is even more uneconomic.

Chemical fertiliser response is directly related to the soil condition. Very poor soils (low organic matter, low cation exchange capacity), typical of many in the communal lands, are subject to extensive leaching and so poor fertiliser response. The consequence is that most fertiliser is applied in small quantities with specific timing. Very little research effort has been invested in exploring the consequences of the finely tuned application strategies (spot applications, split dressings, fertility input mixes etc.) that dominate farmer practice (Box 7.2).

Selective application of limited amounts of inorganic fertiliser offers opportunities for boosts in economic returns. However, there remain a number of factors preventing this strategy for fertiliser use in the communal areas. First, research has focused on blanket application yield

Box 7.2 Fertiliser applications

Unlike many other farmers in the area, Mr and Mrs Kwanisai are convinced that inorganic fertiliser application pays. Mrs Kwanisai notes that it is particularly important for their key crops – cotton and maize. However, they apply fertiliser with a lot of care, realising that in order to get effective returns from their investment, they must be very disciplined in the process of application, applying just the right amount at just the right time. For instance, during 1992–93 Compound D fertiliser was applied in a line at planting in the maize field. This was followed by some selected spot applications to individual plants in areas of very low fertility at weeding. This was followed by a top dressing (a mix of AN and Compound D) later on, but only when the rains were very heavy and coincided with the growth phase of the maize. A similar pattern was followed with the cotton crop, although Compound L was used instead. No fertiliser was applied to groundnuts, as they missed the opportunity of the last rains due to the occurence of a mourning period after a funeral in the area. Manure is the favoured fertiliser, although they have never tried ash, anthill or leaf litter on their land. Mrs Kwanisai has noted the difference in maize plant growth and yield response on plots that have been manured (especially over a period) and those with only Compound D applied. Manure is thus preferentially applied to maize plots, allowing the cultivation of maize on the same area for several years after application. In previous years, manure was applied in rotation around the field and the crop rotation followed this. In 1992–93, due to the death of most of the cattle, the amount of manure was much diminished and the small amount extracted from the *kraal* was applied to the maize area around the homestead.

response relationships, with virtually no attention being paid to economic factors and issues of placement and timing. This in turn has an impact on extension recommendations, which remain inappropriate due to lack of appropriate research on alternatives. Second, fertiliser pricing and marketing affects supply to farmers. This is particularly important if low-input application approaches, relying heavily on precise timing, are to be adopted. In the past, fertiliser prices have been controlled by government. Through the 1980s, patterns of fertiliser price change were stepped with periods of price stability and then sudden rises. This introduced risks to both consumers and producers, as no one was able to predict what the season price was going to be until negotiations between the industry and government were complete (World Bank, 1991). With the removal of subsidies and price controls in the 1990s, prices have risen steeply in real terms (Figure 7.1). The industry is controlled by two raw material suppliers (Sable Chemicals and Zimbabwe Phosphate Industries) and two retail companies (Zimbabwe Fertiliser Corporation and Windmill), resulting in real dangers of monopsonistic control. Fertiliser distribution in the communal areas relies on a network of rural retailers and, in some areas

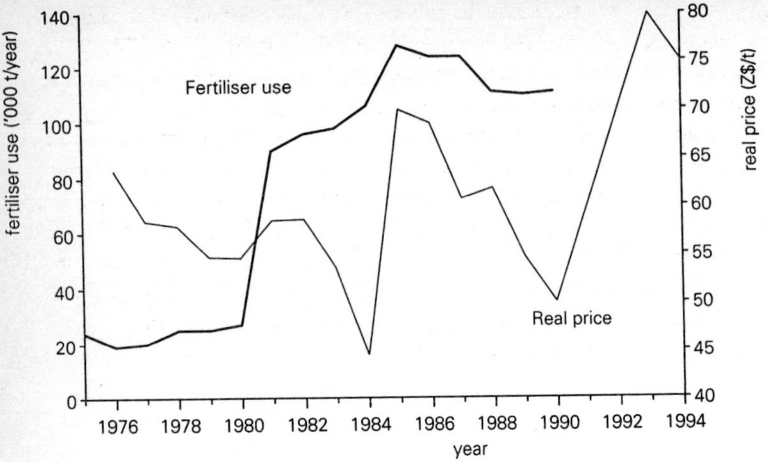

Note: prices are for 50% Compound D and 50% AN (deflated with CPI base = 100 in 1960)

Figure 7.1 Fertiliser use in the communal areas and real price, 1975–94

although not Chivi, sales representatives of the major fertiliser companies. Poor distribution networks and lack of storage facilities in the communal areas are other constraints to effective supply (FSRU/IIED, 1991).

Manure

Most farmers rely on some form of organic fertility input. Cattle manure is the most common source of organic fertiliser. Manure improves nutrient content, texture, cation exchange capacity and water holding capacity. It is particularly significant on sandy soils, where both structure and nutrient levels are poor. However, most *kraal* manures in the communal lands are of poor quality, with high sand fractions and low N and P contents (Mugwira and Mukurumbira, 1984). Despite this, manure is highly valued and applied to particular fields in rotation. Manure application (as with other fertility inputs) is concentrated in maize fields, usually home sites and gardens (Table 7.4).

Manure may be applied together with other sources of fertility. For instance, crop residues, grass and other mulch may be mixed in with *kraal* manure to produce a richer compost. Manure may also be applied in conjunction with inorganic fertiliser, with the manure acting as a basal fertiliser, with long residual effects, and the inorganic fertiliser acting as top dressing with carefully timed spot applications reducing the quantities applied to a minimum. Unfortunately, research on various forms of manuring and composting has been very limited in Zimbabwe. A reasonable amount is known about the chemical properties of manures, some research has been carried out on crop responses in sandy soils (Mugwira and Shumba, 1986), but virtually nothing has been done on the consequences of complex management practices (Campbell *et al.*, 1993a).

The opportunity to use manure extensively is limited by access to cattle. Between 25% and 40% of households own no cattle; many own only a few (Chapter 11). The quantity of available manure is severely limiting. This is particularly a problem on sandy soils where returns from manure application is highest. On clay soils, by contrast, manure is applied less frequently due to the higher inherent fertility of the soils. In clay soil areas, manure may be offered to non-cattle-owning households for application to gardens or fields (Scoones, 1990).

Ash, compost and leaf litter

For those without access to either inorganic fertilisers or manure the options are limited. A number of households in the Chivi sample (Table 7.2) made use of household wastes (ash and compost) as a fertility input to home fields. However, the overall area that this is applied to is extremely limited.

A number of studies show that leaf litter is used more extensively in higher rainfall areas where decomposition and nutrient cycling is faster. Several studies report that between 100% and 38% of households make use of leaf litter on their fields (Campbell *et al.*, 1993b). This study did not find such a prevalence of leaf litter collection. In terms of area covered, leaf litter was not significant. Most farmers indicated that it was too laborious to collect leaf litter from distant hills, that the effects were slow and that they preferred to rely on natural litter fall from trees in fields (e.g. *Parinaria curatellifolia*, *Ficus spp.*, *Sclerocarya birrea*) which provide localised inputs of rich humus (Campbell, 1987; Wilson, 1989). Leaf litter appears only to be collected by a few farmers without any access to other fertility sources. It is applied to small patches of particularly low fertility or to gardens or fields where vegetables or other high-value crops are being grown.

Termitaria

Termitaria represent an important source of concentrated nutrients. Termite mounds have higher Ca, Mg, N, K and clay content than surrounding sandy soils (Watson, 1977). Termitaria are often applied to sandy soils in combination with manure, as they have complementary nutrient release and water-holding capacity properties. The digging of termite mounds is an immensely labour-intensive process and so the extent to which termitaria soil can be spread to poor sandy soil areas of a field is limited. However, yearly movement of some termite soil to particular patches

Box 7.3 Use of termitaria

Mr Muzondiwa makes extensive use of termite soil in his farm. His soils are poor and sandy and he has found that yields significantly improve if he adds termite soil. Within his field he has one termite mound, but this has almost all been dug out. Nowadays he must travel into the grazing area and bring the termite soil to the field by cart. This is hard work, and he is helped by his sons and his wives. But he reckons it is worth it, as he argues that the termite soil both increases fertility and the 'strength' of the soil, so that it holds water better.

does gradually improve the soil's water-holding and nutrient properties and is carried out by some farmers with fields in sandy soil areas (Box 7.3).

Fertility mixtures and focused applications

Most fertility inputs are placed in particular areas and focused on particular crops. For dryland fields, fertility inputs are concentrated in home fields (c. 20% of total cropped area) and on maize (c. 35% of total cropped area) (Table 7.4). For wetland or garden areas, inputs are concentrated in riverbank gardens and on vegetables.

Table 7.4 Percentage of total area of treatment where either home field or maize area

Input	Home field area		Maize area	
	1990–91	1992–93	1990–91	1992–93
No input	16.8	26.6	26.0	28.8
Ash compost	79.6	90.6	47.6	69.8
Basal fertiliser	14.2	10.6	33.2	52.9
Manure	45.7	26.1	67.9	36.9
Top dressing	45.8	51.2	100.0	24.0

Rather than following extension recommendations that promote blanket applications, farmers follow a low-input nutrient conservation strategy that makes best use of limited available nutrients on-farm. Most fertility inputs are combined in mixtures of two or more and much effort is invested in increasing the efficiency of use. Box 7.4 contains a variety of farmer practices which allow for low external input, high-efficiency fertility management.

Fields and fallows

Fertility inputs are only one component of fertility management. Rotations and fallowing offer alternative ways of boosting fertility on farmers' fields.

Box 7.4 Low external-input agriculture: fertility management options

Green manuring is practised by a few farmers when space allows. Cow peas are the favoured crop and these are ploughed under to increase soil organic matter. However, because land holdings are small, most farmers practise green manuring only inadvertently when an early crop fails and has to be ploughed in before replanting.

Agroforestry has been widely promoted by extension agents and development projects, but the tree species and tree–crop combinations have not found favour among farmers. This is because the packages being promoted were designed for higher-rainfall zones where water competition is less of a constraint. For this reason, alley cropping systems designed for soil fertility improvement have been largely rejected, although some farmers are testing pigeon peas along field boundaries and bunds. Instead, most farmers prefer to use indigenous agroforestry practices for improving soil fertility in their fields, including the retention of key species (such as *Parinari curatellifolia*, *Ficus spp.*) in fields for the provision of litter.

Manure treatment is commonly practised by farmers. Treatment of manure through adding crop residues or other vegetable matter to the livestock *kraal* is common practice. Some farmers also make slurries by adding water to the *kraal* prior to digging out. This allows the manure to be spread over a wide area. Others, by contrast, prefer to have concentrated manure for focused application to particular sites. Urine conservation is carried out by a few farmers, who add dry grass to the cattle *kraal* in order to prevent urine leaching into the sub-soil or draining away.

Compost is mostly applied to gardens and small plots around the homestead. Household wastes, sometimes combined with livestock dung, are mixed together, placed in a pit and left for a period. Due to the high labour requirements of composting and the limited volume of composted materials produced, application to dry fields is rare.

Early concern with the impacts of low fertility input mono-cropping of maize on commercial farms in Zimbabwe prompted extensive research on rotational systems for different agroecological regions (Chapter 8). A general set of guidelines for sustainable maize cropping was evolved for the large-scale commercial sector. Recommendations for the communal lands were based on an ideal, four-course rotation. This was promoted by Alvord and the early agricultural demonstrators from the 1930s and remains the basis of extension advice today. The levels of manure application and the length of rotations are, however, impractical for most farmers, who must rely on maize or other grain crops planted in small farm areas.

During the three-year study period the most common crop sequence on a single plot was mono-cropped maize. This represented the cropping sequence of 13.8% of all plots; another 15% of the plots had at least two years in the previous three when maize was planted. Overall, the cropping sequence was dominated by cereals with a continuous cereal monocrop over three years on over 30% of the plot area (Table 7.5).

Agricultural extension recommends rotation with legumes to improve soil fertility. Groundnuts are the most commonly grown legume, yet most crops do not follow groundnuts in the cropping pattern. Indeed, only 15% of all farm plots included in the study were planted with groundnuts between 1988–89 and 1990–91. Pearl millet, cotton and sunflower had a relatively high proportion of their area in 1989–90 and 1990–91 preceded by groundnuts in the previous year. Since these crops are usually regarded as a low-priority crop for fertility inputs, this is surprising. It appears that the choice of site for planting has less to do with desired rotation and more to do with what is feasible to do under highly constrained circumstances. Although farmers are almost all aware of the desirability of legume-based rotations, data on actual practice show that reality does not match desired goals.

Fallowing offers another potential option for improving soil fertility. However, this is not open to many. The proportion of the total field area that was left fallow was only 8% in 1988–89 and 1989–90, rising to 16% in 1990–91. Fallowing is rarely intentionally used as a fertility management method. Fallow land remains uncultivated due to lack of labour or draught and is found most on farms owned by very land-rich farmers (usually local lineage leaders) or on farms owned by resource-poor farmers, especially those homes without access to draught power. Fallow land is particularly concentrated in the Chivi central area, where long-term residents have resisted local in-migration and have retained large fields. In this area the percentage of the total area left fallow is significantly higher than in either of the other study sites. Fallow land, as a percentage of

Table 7.5 Crop rotations over three years (1988–89 to 1990–91)

Rotation	% of area
C–C–C	31.77
F–F–F	4.37
O–O–O	1.08
L–L–L	0.30
2C-plus F/O/L	33.90
2O-plus C/F/L	9.21
2F-plus O/C/L	4.60
2L-plus C/O/F	5.61
Three different	9.72

Note: C = cereal; F = fallow; O = oilseed; L = legume (total area = 750ha in 842 plots).

total farm area, is also significantly higher among those households without draught access in the sample as a whole.

Conclusion

The management of soil fertility inputs is a complex task. Small inputs are applied to small areas and particular crops at specific times. Bulk and blanket applications are rarely carried out. Scarcity of fertility inputs necessitates a low-input, fine-tuned management strategy. Farmer practice thus contrasts dramatically with extension recommendations, which emphasise the agronomic ideal, rather than the practical and economic reality (Appendix 2). The challenge remains to design research and extension appropriate to local conditions and adapted to existing management practices. This is the subject of the next chapter.

CHAPTER EIGHT

Exploring experimentation: challenges for research and extension

Experimentation lies at the heart of science; it is also central to the day-to-day practice of farmers. This chapter asks: how do scientists and farmers learn about the world and improve upon it through experimentation? Farming in dryland agroecosystems cannot be understood simply as a mechanistic, designed and planned activity (Chapters 4–7). Farming is more of a 'performance', a continuous, elaborate response to contingent events (Richards, 1989). Farmers' agricultural knowledge is often in their action, implicitly part of the everyday activities of farming. But knowledge about everyday practice may remain hidden and unexpressed. When outsiders ask farmers about their agricultural practice, reference may be made to 'traditional' practices ('we have always done it this way') or to 'official' versions, such as half-remembered recitals of extension advice ('we follow a four-course rotation with legumes' or 'we prefer not to intercrop in maize'). Significant areas of agricultural knowledge are not (or cannot) be simply and openly expressed. As Fabian (1990: 6) points out, 'this sort of knowledge can be represented – made present – only through enactment or performance'. Understanding agricultural knowledges becomes a complex task of unravelling challenging, sometimes hidden, interactions. These observations present important methodological challenges to the agricultural scientist (Fairhead, 1993).

Uncertainty pervades practice and is intimately bound up with farmers' construction of agricultural knowledge. This presents problems for scientific investigation, because, as Brian Wynne comments in relation to industrial risks, 'Ordinary social life, which often takes contingency and uncertainty as normal and adaptation to uncontrolled factors as a routine necessity, is in fundamental tension with the basic culture of science, which is premissed on assumptions of manipulation and control' (Wynne, 1991: 120).

The parallels with agricultural development are clear. Agricultural science attempts to control, standardise and aggregate in order to reduce 'unexplained variability' or 'eliminate human error'. The result is packages, messages and recommendations derived from controlled experimentation managed by researchers. The experience of this scientific endeavour when applied to the complex and variable dryland environments of Zimbabwe (as elsewhere) can only be described as disappointing. Why is this? Some would argue that the search for the right technologies has not been going on long enough, that it is only a matter of time before breakthroughs are made. This chapter argues that the problem runs somewhat deeper. It lies more in the conceptualisation and methodological approach of the scientific project.

Comprehending complexity: challenges for experimental methods

Experimentation may take different forms: from conventional controlled, statistical comparison of fixed treatments to adaptive, performative, exploratory experiments judged on outputs, resilience or adaptability. These differences parallel different perspectives on variability, uncertainty and risk (Chapter 1). In conventional agricultural experimentation, uncertainty and variability can be effectively eliminated through controls (standardised plots with varying slope, soil type or fertility applications). Conventional statistical applications require this in order to pick up treatment effects that might be obscured by the noise of the real world. Uncertainty and variability are thus removed from consideration or reduced to probabilistic risk, which is amenable to mathematical simulation or normal statistical analysis. What is lost by this approach to experimentation is the performative nature of farming: the regular response to unfolding circumstances, the dealing with uncertainties as part of routine.

In fact, formal experimentation invariably does involve this type of performance, but the pretence of scientific method keeps it hidden. On most research stations and many on-farm settings, labourers are sent out to deal with a pest attack, crops are given supplementary watering, fertilisers are applied in sequence according to the rainfall pattern. Indeed, without this attention the crops would inevitably die. But in the artifical write-ups of agricultural science journals and reports, these experimental actors, the research technicians and labourers, remain invisible and a misleading presentation of objective factual comparison of predefined treatments is given. This presents a problem, as farmers are expected to follow the scientist's protocol if the improved technology treatment out-performs the control with due statistical consistency. Very often the hidden performance of the experimental station is so expensive (in terms of labour, inputs and so on) or so unrealistic (flat land, uniform soils), that farming in the real world cannot match expectations. The technology is 'perfected yet rejected' (cf. Starkey, 1987). The catalogue of such experiences in Zimbabwe is extensive, from fertiliser packages to herbicide treatments to breed livestock to hybrid varieties to soil ridgers. This is not to say that there have not been successes. Hybrid maize from SR52 to R201 is of course the classic case. More recently, the small grain releases of PMV1 and 2 and SV1 and 2 have equally been well received by many farmers.

There is, however, a need for a re-evaluation of the process of agricultural experimentation, particularly as applied to small-scale farming. There is a need to emphasise process not only output, sequential learning instead of predefined design, performance rather than plan (Richards, 1989). If farming is seen more as a sequential response to uncertain events, rather than a fixed, deterministic and planned activity, then experimentation must reflect this. This presents some basic challenges. Experimental design must be more open-ended, farmers must be engaged and intervene in the experimental process, adaptation must be inherently part of experimentation and open learning must be encouraged. This reconceptualisation of experimentation as an adaptive learning process requires fundamental shifts in conventional views of scientific knowledge and practice.

What is experimentation?

Just as there is no single scientific method, there is also no single experimental method. In its most general sense, to experiment is 'to create, produce, refine and stabilise phenomena' (Hacking, 1983). There are broadly two forms of experimental inquiry, coincident with long-established distinctions in the philosophy of science. The first is an inductive approach to exploring the world: seeing what happens. This involves the progressive accumulation of observation through experiential play, such that theories or interpretations can be induced (Medawar, 1982: 94). The second approach is deductive: testing a pre-specified claim or hypothesis. In this case, a hypothesis is suggested, based on some prior theory, and then experimentation is carried out in order to falsify the claim. Through this sequential process of theoretical conjecture and experimental refutation, new understandings emerge (Popper, 1975).

Of course, scientific endeavour in practice involves a combination of deduction and induction, but the current rhetoric of modern science claims adherence to the rigour of the hypothetico-deductive approach and the primacy of theory over empiricism (Hacking, 1983). Rampant empiricism is regarded as somewhat illicit, while theoretically informed experimentation is definitely proper practice. The emergence of probabilistic statistics in the mid-1800s helped to establish this trend. Frequency-based statistical analysis provided an objective order to chaotic chance or subjective inference based on degrees of belief (Hacking, 1975; 1990). Quantitative measurement and statistical analysis have thus come to dominate experimental science over the last 150 years (Chapter 1). With appropriate sampling and statistical treatments, usually involving heroic assumptions about the population distribution of observed phenomena, the randomness of the natural world is contained and 'objective' statements about reality are made. This is the origin of the classic agronomic experimental design – for instance, randomised blocks with replications amenable to 'simple' statistical tests. But a number of myths have grown up around experimentation. These are problematic, especially when we are wanting to explore complex phenomena with high degrees of variability in on-farm settings. Four prevalent myths can be identified.

Measurement must be as complete and detailed as possible. The 'fetish for measurement and accuracy' (Hacking, 1990) is very prevalent in experimental science. This is driven in part by the increased availability of measuring instruments and computing power, combined with the competition among scientific peers and in scientific journals. But it is also driven by a false belief that more measurement means better results. This is untrue. More sophisticated measurement means more complex analysis and so means greater difficulty in interpretation. Medawar (1982) comments: 'A "good" experiment is precisely that which spares us the exertion of thinking: the better it is, the less we have to worry about its interpretation, about what it really means.' Simple, elegant designs with measurements that speak for themselves are the 'best' experiments.

Normal statistics are the only way of establishing validity. The dominance of frequency-based statistics, founded on assumptions about population distributions (usually the normal distribution), cannot be doubted. Examine any basic textbook designed to train agricultural scientists and the prevalence of this form of analysis is clear. Because scientists are often not trained to use other forms of test (e.g. qualitative analysis, non-parametric statistics, statistics for high spatial and temporal variability etc.), experimental designs are very often driven by the requirements of normal statistics, rather than in response to a particular problem or question. This is bad science. It presents a particular problem in three instances: first, where important problems are not investigated because they cannot be forced into the prespecified experimental design; second, when experiments are abandoned because the results cannot be analysed ('too much variability', or 'no signficant results'); and finally when the results that emerge from an experiment are not conducive to conventional statistical analysis, but are nevertheless massaged to fit (e.g. through the use of such seemingly dubious, but apparently acceptable, techniques as 'smoothing' or 'removal of outliers').

Good experimental results show stability and constancy. The aim of so many experimental programmes is to repeat experiments year after year in order to (at some unspecified point in time) 'prove' something. This is a hopeless enterprise. First, experiments are never the same, they always evolve. Experimenters striving to seek a stable response will manipulate the treatments in various ways. It is virtually impossible to find a stable treatment sequence in long-term experiments; the temptation has always been too great to fiddle something. This of course is what learning is about; it is progressive and cumulative and requires both strategic intervention and creative, imaginative and adaptive play. Trying to (or at least pretending to) maintain constancy and stolidly repeat an experiment for scientific credibility is self-deceiving: no one does it. Very often, new insights come not from endless repetition, but through the discovery of 'esoteric differences' (Hacking, 1983: 244); through being imaginative and noticing the unusual; and through indulging in 'speculative adventure and excursions into the unknown' (Medawar, 1982: 32).

The experimenter is independent of the experiment. The simplistic, positivist view that the scientist is somehow a rational and independent actor who has no influence on the outcome of an experiment, beyond the functional execution of 'the scientific method' is, of course, not the case either. There has been an extensive critique of the positivist view of science from both realist and idealist perspectives (e.g. Latour, 1987; Hesse, 1980; Sayer, 1992). Without diverting into this philosophical quagmire, a few examples will illustrate the point. Most plant breeders (in Zimbabwe as elsewhere) want to work on hybrids, rather than on open-pollinated variety improvement (see below). The range of experiments designed reflects this bias. This is reinforced by the social and professional pressures imposed that define how breeders get on in their careers. In this way the social setting of crop breeding affects the experiments. Similarly, when an experiment comes to be established in a field, the experimenter also has an influence through the levelling of the plot, the manipulation of the soil, the direction of the planting rows, the level of supplementary irrigation and so on. All these decisions, extraneous to experimental design, have an effect on the experimental output. Bias is everywhere: it must not be ignored, but recognised and embraced.

The history of agricultural experimentation in Zimbabwe

The history of experimentation by agricultural scientists in Zimbabwe is illuminating in several important respects. Since 1900 there have been significant changes in the way the research agenda is defined, with a notable shift from a demand-led approach, where farmers (in this case European commercial farmers) identified research problems, to a supply-led approach where scientists took over this role. The period has also seen a shift in experimental approach, from simple to increasingly complex designs, with a greater emphasis on measurement, quantification and statistical analysis. There has also been a changing emphasis on solutions to agricultural production problems, with shifts between concerns for low external-input solutions to high-input, technology-transfer solutions. Finally, there has been a shift in the way results are reported, from simple direct interaction between researchers and farmers and publication through farmers' journals to a more indirect linkage through an institutionalised extension service.

An exploration of the history of experimental practice offers lessons for the future, particularly in the context of finding solutions for resource-poor farmers operating in highly risk-prone environments. From this perspective, not all that is old is bad and not all that is new is good. Important lessons, in terms of experimental approach and organisational relationships, can be learned from past practice. Four phases of cropping research in Zimbabwe can be discerned over the period from 1900 to the present (a similar history of livestock interventions is observed, although the chronology is different; Scoones, 1990). These are of course not distinct, but a reading of research station reports and the results of experiments published in the *Zimbabwe* (formerly *Rhodesia*) *Agricultural Journal* shows some definite patterns (see also Wienmann, 1972; 1975). These are reviewed briefly below.

The early years: learning to live in a new environment

European farmers arriving to settle in Rhodesia usually did not have any skills of farming in the tropics; many had no experience of farming at all. Research stations were established initially in the prime agricultural zones of the country, the first being the Salisbury (now Harare) Experimental Research Station. Research results were published in the *Rhodesia Agricultural Journal*, which had its first issue in 1903. In the early years of colonisation, research was geared to exploring the options for settler agriculture. A huge variety of experiments was carried out – everything was tried. In 1915, for instance, 28 different crops were being tested on the Salisbury station (Walters, 1915) in the quest for 'new crops for Rhodesia'. This was a period of joint learning between farmers and scientists. Scientists had very limited resources, were unable to travel extensively, and had few experimental sites. Scientists, also recent immigrants themselves, equally did not know what was appropriate for the area, although some ideas could be borrowed from South Africa or the USA. An open, adventurous approach to inquiry was essential if the hopes of the new settlers were to be fulfilled. This required forging partnerships with farmers and opening new channels of communication.

The submissions to the *Rhodesia Agricultural Journal* in the first decades of the century were down-to-earth and practical. Scientists tested ideas on their research stations, while at the same time farmers were trying out similar options. The results were reported in the journal, often with practical suggestions by the research scientists as to what farmers might try out. The following is a typical excerpt from this period: 'The following experiment is one of simple and practical character which any farmer can repeat for himself with such modifications as he may desire to suit his own circumstances, and learn much that is of real practical use' (Nobbs, 1915: 747). The journal was thus a vital tool of communication, produced regularly and read by farmers. Other channels of informal communication also existed between farmers and scientists. Ideas for experimental research were often suggested by farmers in correspondence or through meetings with researchers forged by the emergent farmer groups in the country.

Clearly the political and institutional setting for research was dramatically different from contemporary Zimbabwe: the clients of research were a relatively small group of European farmers with broadly similar levels of resource access and farming objectives, and the farming groups were well organised and accessible. Later the Commercial Farmers' Union (CFU) became a formidable lobbying group with great political clout (Herbst, 1990). Today, research must serve a very diverse group of farmers, living in a range of environmental conditions and holding very different objectives. Clearly, making research client-oriented and demand-led, as was obviously the case in the early years with European settlers, is a much more difficult task. However, despite these differences some important lessons can be learned from this historical experience. We will return to these later.

Sustainability concerns

Early concerns were expressed about the sustainability of settler agriculture, particularly the effect of maize mono-cropping on soil fertility. From 1913 until the mid-1950s an impressive series of rotation and fertility amendment experiments was instigated in response to this. The first long-term rotation experiment was established in Salisbury for the 1913–14 season, with new ones added in 1919, 1926 and 1939. From the 1920s, the rotation experiments were extended to other regional research stations (e.g. Matopos, near Bulawayo). The experiments were changed as new information arose and new demands from farmers became recognised; they were adaptive experiments in which cumulative learning took place. Until the mid-1950s the experiments concentrated on low external-input treatments (mulching, fallowing, green manuring, cover crops, manuring etc.). By 1950 around 15 treatments were in place on the experiment started in 1913 (Rattray, 1950). The long-term rotation experiments ran until the 1960s, but increasingly became transformed as the hybrid maize revolution took hold.

Other agronomic experiments showed that there was an evident interest in sustainability issues among both researchers and farmers from the mid-1910s until the 1940s. There are numerous reports of experiments exploring the management of soil fertility in this period. Compared to the simple fertiliser response curve trials that superseded them, these trials were quite sophisticated: mixed dressings, complex amendment combinations and between-year treatments were tried. Yet, especially in the early period, *Rhodesia Agricultural Journal* reports always remained simple and straightforward, and often included suggestions made for farmers' own trials or comments on the results of farmers' trials sent in by farmers themselves (e.g. Morkel, 1925).

Technological breakthroughs: the hybrid maize revolution

Rhodesian agricultural science was transformed after 1945 when significant breakthroughs in hybrid maize breeding took place (Mashingaidze, 1994). This was a period of great excitement, and not a little (white) nationalist pride as Rhodesian maize yields rocketed, out-competing the mid-West Americans. The statistics are impressive. When the first commercial hybrid maize variety entered the market in 1949, it represented 22% of the maize planted on European commercial land and yielded 7.96 bags/acre, significantly out-yielding its open-pollinated competitor. By the 1957–58 season, hybrid maize made up 83% of the maize area, was yielding 11.16 bags/acre, nearly double the average yield of open-pollinated varieties that year (Anon, 1959).

This dramatic technological success was achieved through committed, persistent scientific endeavour. Great care was taken to ensure that the new breeds fitted the conditions of the local environment. Attempts at using breeding stock from the USA were rejected, and the new hybrids were derived from locally adapted white dent open-pollinated varieties (Rattray, 1951). This was a technological revolution based on indigenous materials. In addition, the breeding programme involved farmers in pre-testing varieties in a huge number of locations. This supplemented the systematic testing at up to eleven experimental sites around the country. The technological revolution was thus participatory in nature, with farmers very directly involved. The fit between the new technology and farmers' needs was excellent; the result was a dramatic spread of hybrid maize. By the early 1960s nearly all commercial farmland was planted to maize and a high proportion of communal land farms had newly released, locally bred hybrid maize planted.

Keeping going, but getting stuck

The hybrid maize revolution of the 1950s was a watershed in agricultural research in Zimbabwe. This period saw the transition from exploratory adaptive research, usually using limited external inputs, to technology-driven research requiring higher levels of inputs, particularly of chemical fertiliser. The success of hybrid maize breeding instilled a certain confidence into the crop research establishment. The struggle to find joint solutions to problems that characterised the earlier era had gone, and research scientists turned to refining the technical gains of previous breakthroughs.

Prior to Independence, white commercial farmers had enjoyed a major influence over the direction of national agricultural research. Through the CFU and the various commodity producer organisations, research priorities were influenced. This cosy relationship was upset at Independence when the new government announced a major shift in focus for agricultural research, away from the large-scale sector towards the problems faced by communal area farmers. The commercial farm sector increasingly relied on privately funded research and consultancy support. Although the national system has notionally changed direction since 1980, the transition has not been wholly effective. Many inappropriate assumptions, developed for the large-scale farming context, have been transferred to the addressing of the problems of small-scale farming, with the consequence that research has been poorly targeted with limited impact. Without a coherent and representative organisation to lobby for their interests, communal area farmers have been poorly served.

The period from the 1960s to the present has seen no major agricultural research breakthroughs. Undoubtedly quality research has been carried out: new hybrids have been released, new yield response curves have been defined, new permutations of spacing, planting dates etc. have been explored for an increasing number of crop varieties. But nothing spectacular has happened. The dynamism, the urgency and the commitment to applied problems has, it seems, gone. There has been a tendency towards uniformity and regulation, with the implicit message that science and scientists know best. For instance, regulation has beset the crop breeding process, with elaborate forms of seed certification, prohibition on pre-release and limited farmer involvement in the breeding process (Friis-Hansen, 1990), resulting in centrally directed, unresponsive breeding research. Uniformity has also arisen in the form of extension recommendations emerging from research. These have become agronomic recommendations of optimal practice based on research station findings. They are scientifically accurate, but often practically useless. This contrasts with the earlier tendency to offer ranges, conditions, acceptance of uncertainty and economic analyses of options useful to farmers. For instance, both Holborrow and Blackshaw (both 1915) report on fertiliser experiments by giving a series of tables of costs and returns of different options. With an institutionalised extension service, this is now supposed to be the role of extension: research is not supposed to dirty itself with the applied complications of its results. The *Rhodesia Agricultural Journal*, and its post-Independence successor, thus became a scientific journal in the classic mould: complex, dense, inaccessible, with the contents judged not by farmers but by scientific peers and international reviewers.

Maybe this inertia is the inevitable consequence of the maturing of a research system, with the humdrum exploration of the interstices of 'normal' science (cf. Kuhn, 1962) becoming the bread-and-butter function of national research scientists. Maybe it is to do with the difficult times faced by agricultural research in Zimbabwe since the 1970s: first civil war and the exodus of (largely white) research professionals, then the turbulence of the early Independence era and the need to redirect research attention to focus on communal area problems, and now the difficulties of maintaining morale and commitment with a young research staff with a high turnover and a research budget allocation cut by one quarter in real terms in the ten years from 1980.

Agricultural research in Zimbabwe appears to have been seduced by scientific credibility and lost its way. It is not that the research that is currently being carried out is irrelevant or that, within its own boundaries, it is poorly done, it is just that the research, supposedly focused on farmers' priorities and needs, does not attempt to relate to farmers' daily realities. We offer two examples to support this claim (Box 8.1), before moving to a more constructive discussion of how things might change.

Box 8.1 Inappropriate science?

Case 1 Breeding for who?

Hybrid maize breeding in Zimbabwe is currently carried out by a number of private and public concerns. But most crop breeding programmes remain geared towards the concerns of the large-scale commercial farmers and breeding for dry and low-input conditions is barely considered. The assumption behind the breeding strategy is that selection should occur in conditions where genetic potential is fully realised. Unfortunately these conditions (intensive pest and disease control, supplementary irrigation etc.) do not replicate communal area farmers' fields in Zimbabwe at all. This breeding strategy may result in the rejection of genetic material adapted to poorer conditions, resulting in the selection of a variety that does not perform well across all environmental conditions (Simmonds, 1990). The selection criteria used are chosen by the breeders. These are yield-dominated; the competition for maximum yield levels set in motion by the hybrid maize revolution of the 1950s is still in place among Zimbabwean breeders. Competition to enter the so-called ten-tonne club (yield levels of 10t/ha) is intense. Although other criteria such as season length are relevant to the dry areas, there is no attempt to involve communal area farmers in on-station assessment or early on-farm testing of new varieties as happens in other breeding programmes (e.g. Maurya *et al.*, 1988; Haugerud and Collinson, 1991; Sperling *et al.*, 1993).

With the rising cost of hybrid seed, farmers are increasingly demanding low-cost maize seed and the supply of good open-pollinated varieties that can be reused and undergo localised selection. This is frowned upon by hybrid maize breeders. This is in part for commercial reasons, as the seed industry in Zimbabwe has profited significantly from their effective monopoly over maize seed instituted through the tripartite and bipartite agreements established since 1970 and 1981 respectively (Tattersfield and Havazvidi, 1994). As a result of these agreements, all open-pollinated maize seed produced in the country is exported and it is effectively illegal to sell such seed within Zimbabwe. But also the disapproval of open-pollinated maize varieties relates to a sense that this would involve 'going back to the past' – to the period prior to the halcyon

Box 8.1 (*cont.*)

days of the Zimbabwean hybrid maize revolution. This is unfortunate, as the current economic reality of farmers in Chivi is that they cannot afford hybrid seed. Instead, they are forced to reuse hybrid seed, with dramatic losses in yield. They would prefer to have a mixture: some hybrids to be planted on the relatively wet or well-fertilised patches and good-quality open-pollinated maize to be planted elsewhere. At the moment, the scientific establishment, in alliance with the commercial breeding companies, is restricting this vision.

Case 2 Farming Systems Research off the mark

The FSRU regularly carries out on-farm trials on farmers' fields in Chivi communal land. The subjects these trials deal with are undoubtedly questions of interest to Chivi farmers. Since 1990 the following trials have been established each year: crop variety trials (maize, pearl millet, sorghum, sunflower, groundnuts, cowpea), crop management trials (fertiliser application on maize, investigation of die-back in sunflower and sorghum), risk aversion trials (crop staggering and varietal mixes). No one could deny the importance of these issues, but the trials have revealed virtually nothing that can be related to farmer practice. Despite being physically on-farm, they more closely resemble classic research station experiments. The experiments are designed by scientists based in Harare, without treatments resembling what happens in a farmer's field. Research hosts were relatively rich farmers with large land areas and access to draught animals; sites for on-farm trials were chosen on flat, uniform land and the trials were carried out using hired labour.

Just how off the mark these trials are is illustrated by the example of one farmer, Mr Matye, who both hosted a FSRU trial and was part of a monitoring study. During 1990–91 Mr Matye had one of his large sandy soil plots devoted to FSRU researcher-managed trials of maize, pearl millet, sunflower and finger millet. These trials included crops not normally planted there and with fertility levels (both basal and top-dressing inorganics) never contemplated by Mr Matye. Mr Matye has relatively fertile soils, even on the sands, and so rarely uses fertiliser or manure. He claims that fertilisation is too risky in such a dry place and prefers to rely on residual fertility and rotation practices. The crops in the research trial plot were weeded four times in the period between the second week of December and the fourth week of February. This level of weeding is not possible for Mr Matye as he has a large field and relatively little labour as most of his children are now grown up. He usually weeds only once, except for maize which sometimes gets a second weeding. The experiments did not replicate even Mr Matye's relatively well-endowed farming situation, let alone the situation of the larger portion of people with less income, no draught animals and smaller fields.

Farmers' experiments

Farmers' experimentation is a mixture of rigorous comparison and creative play, much like conventional science is in reality. Comparisons may be carried out with controls adjacent to treatment plots or with controls 'in the head', reinforced by memories of how the plot performed in years past. Farmers' experiments tend to happen in sites where regular observation is possible: around the homestead or in the home field or garden. Plots dedicated to experiments shift depending on the nature of inquiry, but they are usually small in size, reducing the risk of failure of any experimental innovation. Replications tend to be limited within years, but may occur between a number of years. Adjustments of treatments also occur over time, as progressive learning takes place. Assessment criteria are complex and usually relate to a range of agronomic, economic, cultural and other indicators. As farmer experimentation is so bound up in agricultural practice, hypothesis formulation, testing and evaluation tend to be part of a continuous process of exploration and learning.

All farmers experiment in some way, but different farmers experiment in different ways. For instance, men and women, old and young, and rich and poor farmers have different curiosities, different problems, different needs for technology adaptation and meet different fortuitous circumstances in their farming activities. As a result, they design different experiments. This diversity is important as it reminds us that farming societies are highly differentiated and one standard experimental design may not answer the type of questions pertinent to the full range of people.

Some individuals are particularly keen on experimentation. This may be out of interest, to satisfy an enquiring mind, or out of necessity. There are many experimental enthusiasts in Chivi. Very often they concentrate their experimentation on particular themes: some on soil conservation, some on water management, others on particular crops. These local experts are important in local networks for sharing information. Those who must experiment out of necessity tend to be marginal to the society: recent in-migrants, widows, people with very small plots of land or exceptionally poor soils, those without draught power and so on. Agricultural strategies employed by the majority do not apply and learning to cope under very constrained conditions is necessary.

Three broad types of farmer experimentation can be identified which are based on organised testing of options (Rhoades and Bebbington, 1988). These are: curiosity experiments, problem solving experiments and adaptation experiments. In addition, fortuitous experimentation may arise because of unforeseen circumstance, where farmers must respond to events and improvise.

Curiosity experiments

Very often learning arises through curiosity. Farmers may try something out just to see what happens (see Box 8.2).

Box 8.2 An unexpected discovery – a new old crop

Mutoworera discovered some unfamiliar seed stored in the eaves of his late father's hut and decided to see if they germinated. Although they were certainly more than ten years old, they germinated without any problem. The crop is *zengeza* or *tirigwe*, a grain crop similar to finger millet that used to be planted widely in the area. It has since died out completely. Over several seasons Mutoworera has been building up some seed stores and this season he has planted out a small portion around his home. His assessment is that it is an exceptionally drought-resistant crop, it is able to survive in poor soils and rocky conditions, and it can store for a long time. However, it has drawbacks. First, farmers do not know it, so weeding is very problematic, because in its early stages it looks like other types of grass. Second, processing is incredibly laborious. The consequence is that the crop is good for growing for long-term storage for extreme drought occasions, but not for regular planting on the farm.

Problem-solving experiments

Farmers continuously face problems. Very often these are specific to their farm, dependent on such factors as local soil fertility or moisture conditions, pest or disease incidence or labour availability. Experiments are often designed in order to tackle these. Box 8.3 provides cases of experimental responses to problems. The first is an example where germination and die-back problems in sunflower were faced. A variety of solutions were tested, but in this case to no avail. The second case illustrates the responses to seed shortage following the drought of 1991–92.

Box 8.3 Responding to problems

Problems with sunflowers

Rugare is a very industrious farmer. She is a divorcee and lives alone at the homestead of her late parents. Her crops, particularly the maize and pearl millet around the home, are impressive and are visibly in better shape than those of her neighbours. But she has failed to solve the problem of sunflower germination. Over the last few years, she has designed experiments that test sunflowers on different soils, with different water regimes, with different planting strategies, but she still cannot seem to get good germination. And if there is germination, then there is a pronounced die-back.

Box 8.3 (*cont.*)

Seed shortage

Sophie Zivhu has experienced changes in the availability of sorghum varieties over the past years. In the past, there were a number of important sorghum types in the area. These included *rudende*, *chifumbata*, *bedyane* and *tsveta*. *Bedyane* was the best, providing the highest yield and the best *sadza* from the grain, but it needed a lot of rainfall to grow well. With the recurrent droughts in the area, these varieties have now died out. *Rudende*, *chifumbata* and *bedyane* disappeared in the serious droughts of the early 1980s, and *tsveta* has disappeared in the last few years. This year Mrs Zivhu has had to experiment with unfamiliar sorghum varieties. She has tried three types this year. The first is SV2, a short-season variety that she transplanted from a research plot nearby in 1990–91 and had retained some seed of. Next, she managed to get some seed of *chidade* from her sister who stays in Mberengwa. This is a more traditional, longer-season variety. She has mixed these with a Shangaan variety brought by a friend from Mwenezi, which appears to be similar to the short SV2 type. Following harvest, Mrs Zivhu selects and stores her favoured varieties for following seasons.

Adaptation experiments

Farmers may adapt new technologies to known environments or known technologies to new environments. A classic case is the testing of crop varieties. Box 8.4 gives an example of a farmer regularly testing new

Box 8.4 Experimenting with millet varieties

Over the years Mapuvire has been trying out different millet varieties on his land. When experimenting with new varieties he usually allocates a strip of land within a plot where his usual variety is planted. He will plant at the same time and apply the same management practices across the plot. During recent years he has compared the local small grain crop types or landraces (distinct plant types) of pearl and finger millet (*rushambo/jimukoro* and *chikumbo*) with introduced varieties (PMV1 and *garindi*). He has acquired new varieties either from friends who are members of the same farming club, or from the Farming Systems Research team who used to have trial plots on his field. He was not impressed by the introduced finger millet variety and has since rejected it. However, the good tillering abilities, early maturation and drought resistance of the introduced pearl millet has resulted in him selecting seed for planting. This is despite his observation that PMV1 is not as good as local varieties for beer and has problems with pest attack, particularly because it is early-maturing. When selecting seed for the next season's planting, he has a number of selection criteria. The most important of these are plant tillering ability and the size and hardness of the seed. Other criteria include the length of seed head and the size and strength of the plant.

varieties according to his own criteria, using a system of plot-based comparison.

Fortuitous experiments

Experimentation may happen by chance. Events may dictate changes in practice that result in new learning experiences. Box 8.5 gives an example of a farmer who learned a lot about transplanting sorghum and finger millet during the 1992–93 season as a result of disruption of planting by a mid-season drought and a funeral.

Box 8.5 Learning through agricultural performance: transplanting of small grains

In the course of the 1992–93 agricultural season, Tichaona made use of the good February rains to transplant sorghum into patches where it had previously failed. Because of the intermittent early rains he avoided field-planting finger millet altogether and planted in small nurseries, so that the whole crop was transplanted. Under controlled conditions near the house, the nurseries do not suffer the same variable soil and water conditions in the field and germination is usually very high. Other reasons may prompt the need for transplanting. For instance, in mid-February he was transplanting a large portion of pearl millet. This was because a death in the village and subsequent funeral a few weeks before had prevented him planting the whole plot at that time. The small portion that he had planted had germinated well and he was transplanting plants from this area into another. As a result of the unforeseen circumstances Tichaona unexpectedly learned a lot during the year about transplanting options for small grains. This he says will stand him in good stead in future years. He may even preferentially establish nursery sites and plan in future years for transplanting by heavier sowing in more favourable spots.

Farmers' experimentation is very similar to that of scientists: there is a variety of ways of going about experimenting, there is a range of different ways of testing validity, and the process of experimentation is part of a continuous and progressive learning experience conditioned by social forces and cultural norms. Thus farmers carry out both exploratory, inductive experiments and deductive, hypothesis-testing experiments (Johnson, 1972; Richards, 1986; Stolzenbach, 1994). But the objectives and actual practice of experimentation often differ. Scientists must come up with generalisable statements and rules, with rewards based on peer acclaim and publication records. Farmers, by contrast, have a primary responsibility towards their own agricultural production. Success and failure are judged by immediate, short-term outputs. The practice of experimentation is also, in some respects, different. Experimentation is bound up with action and implementation is part of the process of inquiry. As Donald Schön (1983: 49) notes:

> When we go about the spontaneous intuitive performance of the actions of everyday life, we show ourselves to be knowledgeable in a special way. Our knowledge is ordinarily tacit, implicit in our patterns of action and in our feel for the stuff with which we are dealing. Knowledge is *in* our action.

Farmers gain knowledge through this process of 'reflection-in-action'. Unlike in the formal descriptions of science, theory and practice are not separated. As Arthur Stolzenbach (1994) points out:

> The management of a farm can be seen as a continuous series of experiments, by which, through the labour itself, the agricultural performance improves. It therefore becomes difficult to talk of an 'experiment' as a special action, separated from activities. What we can do is to concentrate on 'experimenting' as a continuous and innovative element in the craft of farming.

This performative interpretation of experimentation, where learning is bound up with action, is an important departure from experimentation as usually described by research scientists.

Sharing information: farmer-to-farmer learning

Learning about the results of farmers' experiments occurs through interaction within social networks. Social interaction may both encourage and inhibit sharing of agricultural innovation. Information on agriculture is shared among farmers in Chivi in a variety of ways. Knowledge may be gained inadvertently by walking along a footpath through someone's field or by passing fields or gardens on a road. More covert activities are also known, where people may secretly enter someone's field without permission (this, however, carries serious risks). Social networks of kin and friends are particularly important. Married women's paternal homes are usually some distance from their husband's home and visits may be an important occasion for picking up new crop varieties or cultivation tips from relatives. Older women, particularly those married into large polygamous households, remember the days when there was an incredible network of sharing of smallgrain varieties among wives and their relatives (Box 8.6).

Zimbabwe's migrant labour economy, with seasonal and more long-term migration to towns, exposes men, and sometimes their wives, to a range of different people from different parts of the country. Exchanges in town are thus an important source of innovation for the rural areas of Zimbabwe. Social and work gatherings in the rural areas are also good occasions for discussions about agriculture. Beer parties, weddings, funerals, church services and other meetings, related or unrelated to agriculture, may provide occasions for such discussions. Similarly work parties (*humwe*)

Box 8.6 Sharing knowledge

Ambuya Kunjani was born in the early part of this century. She was married into central Chivi as a young and favoured wife of the old man Mukamuri. He was an important traditional healer (*n'anga*) in the area and travelled widely. Ambuya Kunjani often accompanied him during his travels, and in this way was exposed to a wide range of areas, both within Chivi and far beyond. During these journeys, she developed a keen interest in crop varieties, and she would avidly collect new finger millet, pearl millet and sorghum varieties for testing at home. Mukamuri himself was also a keen experimenter, particularly with finger millet, a crop that was important for traditional beer and ceremonies he had to perform at home. In a wide-ranging study of indigenous crop resources in southern Zimbabwe, Ken Wilson (1987) found that Ambuya Kunjani knew of nearly all the varieties named by informants from a number of different communal areas, amounting to several hundred small grain crop types or landraces.

also provide good opportunities for both discussion about and observation of people's fields. Women also have similar group activities in group vegetable gardens where talk about vegetable production may extend into other spheres of agricultural production.

Institutionalised opportunities for sharing also exist in Chivi. The extension service, Agritex, holds field days at its demonstration plots, as does the Farming Systems Research Unit at field trial sites. Although such occasions tend to be oriented towards lecturing of farmers in the design of 'proper practice', the social event itself often provides occasion for wider discussion, even if not formally planned for. The same applies to the extension service's extension group meetings. Although designed for the delivery of technical messages, such farmer group meetings (admittedly dominated by the local elites) often have lively discussions about a range of issues. Opportunities for organised exchange visits sometimes occur. One NGO, Intermediate Technology, operating in Chivi has established a regular system of farmer-to-farmer exchanges, visits to research stations and seed fairs (Hagmann and Murwirwa, 1994). This has provided much impetus to local development activities.

There are a variety of ways in which extension workers can help facilitate information exchange, so enhancing the existing process of farmer-to-farmer extension. Some of these are listed in Box 8.7.

Despite all the opportunities for information sharing, there are significant barriers. One such barrier is the fear of witchcraft. Some people fear showing success publicly for fear of rivalry, jealousy and social competition, particularly from relatives, resulting in their being bewitched. A safer strategy is thus to conceal success and keep innovations secret. Another related barrier concerns access to others' fields. Those who wish ill on

Box 8.7 Facilitating information sharing

Organisations

Village research/extension groups
Farmer extension leaders

Information exchange

Farmer-to-farmer exchanges
Technology fairs, e.g. seed fairs
Technology tours
Farm walks
Field days
Innovators' workshops

Media

Songs, theatre, dance media
Newsletters, radio programmes, booklets, journals

Institutional linkages

Links with other groups (traditional leaders, church groups, savings associations etc.)

someone can destroy yields through pests, diseases or the striking of lightning by placing medicine in a field. Allowing people unrestricted access to fields during the growing season is thus viewed as highly risky, as opening oneself to the potentials of crop failure.

Lack of confidence in the efficacy of local knowledge in the face of a dominant Western scientific view of agriculture is another significant barrier. Many farmers exclaim to the visiting researcher: 'I don't know anything, I need your advice,' and then show him or her round a field packed with experimentation and innovation. A history of intensive external intervention has characterised Zimbabwe's communal areas, resulting in local knowledge being devalued not only by science, but also by farmers themselves.

The nature of agricultural research and extension itself provides another barrier to local-level communication and sharing. As already described, conventional research tends to adopt an arrogant attitude ('we know best'), with limited farmer participation in the design and running of trials either on-farm or on-station. This is reflected in the extension system. The system is designed to offer packages and messages to farmers off the research–extension conveyor belt. Many extension approaches, including the Training and Visit system promoted by the World Bank, do not attempt to incorporate farmers' insights or knowledge; they are simply a technology delivery system, based on a set of simple management rules (Moris, 1991; Röling, 1994). Admittedly, many extension workers do not follow the system by rote; they adapt and change the messages to suit the local setting, they encourage discussion among farmer leaders and follower groups, and they introduce new elements to Master Farmer training. However, this is left to the individual's initiative; it is not part of the formal system, which still remains an institutionalised barrier (Drinkwater, 1991).

Working together: challenges for research and extension

Interaction between research carried out by farmers and by scientists is increasingly being encouraged. This interaction may take a number of forms, involving farmers and research scientists working directly together, involving farmers learning from scientists' experimentation and vice versa. The banner of 'participation' has become so all-encompassing that a disaggregated analysis of methodological approaches is needed. Stephen Biggs (1989a) describes four approaches to farmer participation that have emerged from the experience of the last decade:

- contractual – role of farmer is minimal, merely providing resources for scientists to experiment on
- consultative – farmers define the problem, researchers develop solutions
- collaborative – joint participation at various stages
- collegiate – scientists work together with farmers to strengthen the informal research and development capacities of farmers.

Much of conventional Farming Systems Research (FSR) is in the contractual and consultative mode. However, Farmer Participatory Research (FPR) attempts to deepen and widen the engagement, to more collaborative and collegiate interactions (Cornwall *et al.*, 1994; Okali *et al.*, 1994).

In Zimbabwe, the Farming Systems Research Unit was established in the Department of Research and Specialist Services in 1982. The model adopted featured the classic hallmarks of the FSR approach, including the formation of a multi-disciplinary team, a mixture of formal and informal survey work to define problem areas and recommendation domains, and on-farm testing and adaptation of technologies derived from research stations (Collinson, 1982; Mombeshora, 1987; Avila *et al.*, 1989). While the approach had many advantages over a purely technical, commodity focus for research, a number of limitations were evident. The lack of attention to issues of variability, risk and uncertainty characterise many of the problems faced.

Recommendation domains and technology packages. Conventional FSR assumes that simple recommendation domains can be defined according to a combination of agroecological and socio-economic criteria and that technology packages can be extended to certain groups of farmers. This is based on a number of faulty assumptions, particularly in dryland environments characterised by high levels of variability. In such settings, neat recommendation domains cannot exist as so many factors impinge to make most individual farmers' situations different. Focused packages are therefore unlikely to be effective, as only very few people are likely to find the package suitable to their situation at any one time.

Reliance on off-the-shelf technology. One assumption of the early FSR approach that has been found wanting is that there is a wide range of technologies just sitting around waiting to be tested, adapted and used. Unfortunately this is rarely the case, especially in dryland settings. In the case of Zimbabwe, pre-Independence agricultural research had failed to address the issues of communal area agriculture, and this has remained largely true today. Simply transferring, or marginally adapting, the existing repertoire of technological or management options designed for capital-intensive, high-input systems is inadequate and a more fundamental rethink of technology design is necessary.

Farm and agriculture focus. Farming may be only one component of people's livelihoods. Most people are engaged in non-farm work of various kinds; in migrant labour economies, such as are found in Southern Africa, the importance of remittance incomes may overshadow the returns from on-farm labour. FSR that ignores this fails to assist farmers. A livelihood or food systems focus that includes factors such as alternative employment options, product marketing and the impacts of economic policy offers opportunities for expanding the horizons of FSR (Baker, 1992; Pottier, 1993; Bebbington, 1994).

Lack of farmer participation. Despite the many feedback loops incorporated into the classic diagrammatic representations of FSR (e.g. Norman *et al.*, 1994: 11), there is often very limited farmer participation in FSR. The linear approach of the conventional formulation tends to move from diagnosis and problem definition to on-farm testing very quickly, without allowing for a more continuous process of diagnosis involving farmers. Methodological innovation, such as the use of Participatory Rural Appraisal (PRA) techniques (Chambers, 1992), has encouraged increased farmer participation in the diagnostic phases of FSR, but this has often been overshadowed by a heavy reliance on researcher-designed and managed on-farm trials, which often involve complex designs and exclude farmers from analysis and evaluation.

Poor linkages with other actors. The institutionalisation of FSR has been plagued by poor linkages with the key actors in agricultural research and extension. Poor linkages with farmer clients through inadequate attention to participatory processes is perhaps the most fundamental failing. This is exacerbated by failures to link research with extension and the maintenance of an artificial separation between the two. Another linkage that has been poorly developed is that between government and NGO actors. Mounting evidence suggests that there are major potentials for com-

Table 8.1 Transforming Farming Systems Research: challenges for future

Theme	Conventional FSR	FSR for the future?
Focus	Component agricultural technologies for farming households.	Improving livelihoods, including intra- and inter-household, non-farm and policy issues.
Activities	On-farm technology adaptation and testing.	Systems analysis in action-research framework, ranging from on-farm trials to policy analysis workshops.
Outputs	Problems identified and technology packages developed, focused on specified recommendation domains.	Options and choices that may trigger change; a range of technology, management and policy choices offered recognising heterogeneity, diversity, risk and uncertainty.
Evaluation and assessment	Objective criteria (e.g. rates of technology adoption) measured by outsiders (e.g. external consultants) at end of an activity.	Evaluation by farmers according to their criteria; qualitative and quantitative assessments of process through continuous feedback and reflection; iterative improvements in design.
Role of FSR team	Outside the system – objective analysts who implement diagnostic surveys and on-farm trials.	Part of the system – engaged in participatory research with farmers and establishing relationships between farmers and research, extension and policy actors.
Skills required	Multidisciplinary sectoral skills (agronomy, livestock science, economics, sociology/anthropology).	Interdisciplinary analysis, process design, facilitation, networking, conflict negotiation, adult learning and workshopping skills.
Role of farmers	Relatively passive implementors.	Active co-learners in design and implementation of trials, analysis of diagnostic surveys, peer review and monitoring of FSR process.
Organisation	Individual 'co-operating farmers' supported by a research team.	Farmer research groups – self-forming and flexible – part of co-researching networks of farmers and researchers.
Research–extension linkages	Outputs of on-farm testing offered to extension for dissemination to farmers – technology transfer.	Research–extension distinction breaks down, as all actors are involved as co-learners in an action-research process.

Sources: for conventional FSR see Norman, 1980; Byerlee *et al.*, 1982 and others; for FSR for the future, see Scoones and Thompson, 1994; Okali *et al.*, 1994; Drinkwater and McEwan, 1994; Webber and Ison, 1995

plementary activity between the NGO and government research and development communities in the field of agricultural technology development (Farrington *et al.*, 1993; Wellard and Copestake, 1993).

The mid-1990s offer some exciting challenges for the farming systems approach. The original formulation has been found wanting in a number of respects, but recent field experience suggests that a new role for FSR, founded on a combination of methodological innovation and new organisational arrangements and linkages, offers the potential for an exciting future. Some of the major shifts required for this transformation are outlined in Table 8.1. This envisages a shift from a technology transfer mode, where problems are identified by researchers and science is assumed to be able to provide solutions, to a facilitation mode, where research and action are linked, multiple perspectives and interpretations are respected, and collegial interactions are encouraged. FSR thus shifts from a hard systems approach, where models are formulated, solutions designed and the process is controlled by researchers, to a soft systems or co-learning approach, where boundaries and conditions are negotiated among actors, where action and reflection become part of an ongoing cycle, and where the political implications of encounters are made explicit (cf. Bawden, 1992; Long and Long, 1992; Scoones and Thompson, 1994).

The beginnings of this transition have been occurring in Zimbabwe, and the last few seasons have seen important new innovations in the on-farm research approach in Chivi. The FSRU has developed a farmer-led process of research that allows problems identified by farmers to be tackled with simple trials designed and managed by farmers. Box 8.8 discusses the

Box 8.8 Experimentation with soil fertility issues in Chivi

During the 1993–94 season a series of trials were established in southern Chivi. These followed from discussions held as part of a Rapid Rural Appraisal exercise in the area (FSRU, 1993). The RRA identified a range of soil fertility problems in the area. Subsequent meetings with farmers resolved to tackle these with some simple trials. The farmers formed themselves into groups and someone within the group offered a portion of their land for a trial. A discussion meeting was held to which the farmers came with the treatments they proposed to tackle each of the problems. At the same meeting, the FSRU team also offered one solution. These treatments became the basis for the trials at each site. The FSR team assisted the farmer groups in establishing a simple plot comparison trial and the rest of the work was carried out by the farmers. During the season, meetings were facilitated by the FSR team at each research site to discuss progress. At harvest, comparisons between the treatments were carried out using both simple measurements of yield as well as more complex ranking exercises carried out by the farmers using their own criteria. The trials implemented during the 1993–94 season by two farmer research groups were as follows:

Box 8.8 (*cont.*)

Dare group: Fertility treatments for groundnuts on sandy soils (identified by women members). Treatments chosen include gypsum (researcher treatment), termitaria, leaf litter, mixture (farmers' treatments), control. The pest *striga* was mentioned as a serious problem by the men in this group. The farmers had no ideas as to test treatments to apply beyond their normal practice of planting pearl millet in a rotation. All the researchers' treatment suggestions (e.g. underplanting with sunhemp for a year, chemical treatment) were rejected as unrealistic (even if they worked). As a consequence, this trial was not attempted.

Museva group: Improvement practices for problem soils: *rumambare* (sodic soil), *rujekese* (gravel), *chinamwe* (sticky clay). All these soils are usually avoided by on-farm research, yet make up a significant portion of arable land in this area. The treatments for the sodic soil were: lime/gypsum mix (researchers), river sand, leaf litter, ash (farmers), and control, with sorghum as the test crop.

Source: Farming Systems Research Unit, Chivi

Box 8.9 Farmer research on water management

Farmer groups in Ward 20, Chivi, have been experimenting extensively with water management techniques. Ideas for testing have arisen as a result of visits to Chiredzi research station and farmers in neighbouring Zvishavane district. These visits were facilitated by the ITDG. From these visits the farmer groups decided that they would experiment with a variety of technologies that they had observed. The dryland farmers' groups designed experiments to look at ridging techniques (seen at Chiredzi research station) and soil moisture conservation pits (seen at Mr Phiri's farm in Runde communal area – see Chapter 6). The women's gardening groups decided to investigate the effect of underground clay piping for improving irrigation efficiency.

During the 1992–93 season, Mr Chiuswa was carrying out ridging experiments in one long plot in his field. He had designed a complex trial that compared ridges of different spaces and different tie frequencies. These were contrasted using five different crops, separated in different portions along the plot. Thus the design allowed comparison of yield per area between different treatment plots. In addition, Mr Chiuswa had been trying out different options in particular sites with peculiar local conditions. For instance, in an area with greater localised run-off due to a rock outcrop nearby, he had increased the frequency of cross-ridge ties. While this disrupted the neatness of the overall experimental design, he used this opportunity to learn more about particular microenvironmental conditions.

Source: Discussions with Mr Chiuswa, Chorumuvati, Chivi and Kudakwashe Murwirwa, ITDG-Zimbabwe

soil fertility management research being carried out with farmers in southern Chivi. In other parts of the district, farmer groups have chosen different themes to investigate.

Similarly, NGO groups are also developing participatory research approaches (Box 8.9). It is hoped that the pilot work initiated in Chivi will have a wider impact on government research and extension services, as the returns from a more participatory research approach become apparent.

A major challenge is to encourage scientists to learn from farmers' experimentation, to realise that all research questions cannot necessarily be reduced to simple plot designs, and that farmers have a lot to offer to the process of inquiry. There remain many professional biases against such shifts in perspective (Chambers, 1993); these include the pressure to publish, the need for regular 'results', and the limitations set by conventional analytical techniques. However, there are encouraging signs of a growing recognitition of farmers' experimentation, combined with a greater openness and willingness to learn within mainstream agricultural institutions. This trend needs to be reinforced.

Effective interaction between researchers and scientists need not be only one-way. In fact, farmers profit greatly from learning from scientists' approaches to experimentation. A variety of activities encourage this form of linkage including: field days where on-farm work carried out by researchers is explained and discussed with farmers; research station visits where farmers are invited to research stations to discuss researchers' trials,

Table 8.2 Contrasting approaches to extension

Theme	Transfer of technology	Facilitation
Focus	Technology adoption; making use of external knowledge.	Problem ownership; increased capacity for adaptive response and learning.
Assumptions	Communication and diffusion approaches.	Farming as a social process; farmers as actors/adult learners within social, political and economic contexts.
Extension worker activities	Group meetings, lectures, message or package delivery, demonstration, contact farmer training.	Networking, skill-sharing, farmer-to-farmer linkages and exchanges, problem-solving workshops, organisational development, capacity building, conflict resolution.
Farmers' roles	Adopter, target, beneficiary, client, group member, trainee.	Actor with expertise, co-learner, part of social networks.

Note: after Chambers *et al.*, 1989; Moris, 1991; Röling, 1994

to explore new ways of collaborating and to share new ideas and technologies; and involvement in early screening and testing of new crop varieties involving on-station assessment groups where farmers are part of variety assessment committees.

All this suggests a new brief for extension. Rather than being the conduits for technical messages, extensionists need increasingly to become catalysts of local activity, facilitators of information exchange and brokers between formal agricultural knowledge and local insights (Moris, 1991; Pretty and Chambers, 1994; Farrington, 1994). A shift from a transfer of technology approach (typified by the Training and Visit system) will require some major shifts in extension approach. These are summarised in Table 8.2.

Conclusion

Farmers and scientists need to explore new ways of working together in productive partnership. Researchers must provide farmers with a basket of technology and management choices that they can pick, choose and adapt to their diverse, risk-prone farming environments and individually contingent social and economic settings. The process of technology testing and adaptation must therefore be one that involves all parties, making use of the evident benefits and skills of both research scientists and farmers. A new role for extension is suggested that does not focus on pushing particular solutions as pre-defined packages or messages, but rather engages, together with farmers, in the more complex function of diagnosing problems, searching for solutions, and ensuring sharing and spread. These new challenges for research and extension will require new skills, new professionalism and new institutional and policy settings to make change possible (Pretty and Chambers, 1994). But unless these new challenges are met, adequate responses to risk and uncertainty in dryland farming systems will remain elusive.

PART THREE

Drought

CHAPTER NINE

Multiple actors, multiple perspectives: risk perception and drought in dryland Zimbabwe

Individuals – farmers, research scientists, extension workers, development aid personel, politicians – see the hazards of the everyday world through different eyes. The way that such risks are perceived and responded to is based on educational background, gender, age, historical and personal experience, attitudes and behaviours derived from peers, friends, family and so on. Everyone is different and there is no 'right' or 'wrong' way of seeing the world. What people perceive as undesirable and the way people react to a hazardous environment are not solely based on a positivist assessment of outcome probabilities. Instead, responses to all types of risk and uncertainty are based on values and preferences (Chapter 1).

Uncertainty has important political and social consequences. Increased uncertainty implies decreased control. This may occur at a personal level, with uncertainty provoking a sense of helplessness and lack of control over future destiny. At a wider level, uncertainty may result in a loss of control in a political or social sense: those with power losing it through their inability to determine or influence the course of events. Narratives on drought in rural Zimbabwe are embedded in these personal, social and political contexts.

The realisation that risk perceptions are socially framed has important implications for public policy. If there is no 'right' way of deciding what appropriate action should be; if the standard techniques of risk assessment provide only one view of risk, then what should policy towards risk be? How can multiple perspectives and multiple perceptions be taken into account in public policy formulation? This chapter examines how farmers perceive drought. A variety of causal explanations are offered; although most do not provide a 'rational' explanation in a scientific sense, they nevertheless offer a means of explanation, a way of ascribing blames and a route to coping with the situation. Coping with risk and uncertainty in dryland areas is as much about dealing with the personal, religious and political ramifications of drought impacts as the material issues of food provisioning and survival.

Perceptions of drought – different actors, different perspectives

Perceptions of drought are complex and responses are often unpredictable. People do not view drought in a simple, unified way. Farmers do not have one overriding scientific model of cause, effect and response; they have multiple perceptions and so multiple responses. In order to understand the diversity of coping strategies (Chapter 10), it is necessary to explore the social framing of risk and ask: how do different people explain the causes of drought? What are the social, political and institutional factors that provide contexts for these individual perceptions? How do these affect different people's varied responses?

Farmers' perceptions of drought attempt to reduce the fears of uncertainty and the perils associated with losing control, both political and personal. Thus causes are attributed and blame for misfortune or disaster is ascribed. Drought is therefore not perceived as a chance event, but explained in terms of particular cause–effect relationships. Different people offer different interpretations, but all attempt to derive order from apparent chaos. Such perceptions offer a way of coping with the stresses and uncertainties of a crisis. The form of argument offered depends both on the type of person and the type of drought. Different explanations are offered for causes of drought of different magnitudes: from local-level crop failure on an individual's field, to wider impacts at local, regional and national levels. The type of explanation offered depends on how someone's perceptions are derived. Influences range from religious affiliations, educational background, party political allegiance, social and political status and historical experience. Perceptions are not static; they may shift over time or be expressed under altering circumstances. For instance, differing perceptions may be held by one individual at the same time, a product of living within different social, political or religious networks.

A series of discussions held in Chivi at the height of the drought (May–June 1992) provides insights into the local debates about the causes of drought.[1] The following sections group some of the reasons given into various categories of 'cause', ranging from the local-level to regional and national levels. Each section contains a series of (anonymous) quotes culled from the full transcripts of these discussions.

Moral decline and lack of respect

The most frequent reason given for the cause of drought was general moral decline. Prostitution, in particular, was singled out by many. Lack of respect and changes in the moral order were seen to result in retribution from God or the ancestors.

> The causes of drought are the drinking rate of beer. One might see a girl of 17 years drinking beer in public, sharing love and jokes with elders. There is no respect. Now God and the ancestral spirits are angry with the situation.
>
> People are sinful; that's why we are not getting rainfall. Young girls and boys are doing evil things ... even old people too! You will find an old man of 80 years being a 'sugar daddy'. And you will find a small boy with a 'sugar mamu'.
>
> Drought was brought by prostitution. Young people have now resorted to prostitution. Even the married ones are practising it This is why no rainfall has fallen.
>
> Prostitution is the leading Olympic Games in Africa. People do not care if it is day or night, they just go anywhere. Every bush has a durex behind it. Remember God hates sins and God is everywhere. People think they are in a free Zimbabwe and forget God.

Many people noted that 'modernity' had brought changes in values. Perceived shifts in the social relationships between young and old and men and women were highlighted as factors resulting in disquiet amongst the ancestors, the arbiters of the 'traditional' order. The modern state was also accused of encouraging these detrimental shifts in values, thus adding to the problems faced by society. An older woman commented thus: 'The young no longer offer respect to the elders, they just call them by any name.' And one (male) commentator argued that 'The government is supporting women rather than men. Most of the workers in government departments are women. That is why the forefathers are not giving us rainfall as they are angry.'

The cleansing of the land and the respect for those who died during the liberation war was another recurring theme in the discussions held. The need for appropriate respect, proper burial and appeasement of the spirits of the dead was seen as paramount. Without this, angry spirits would continue to trouble the country, bringing drought and disaster.

> Drought is caused by President Mugabe. During the liberation struggle many people died, including ones from foreign lands. Instead of taking the bodies to their own land, the bones were left in the area. Then rainfall cannot fall because the relatives and ancestors are angry. The president was supposed to brew beer and cleanse the bloodshed of the liberation struggle.
>
> The government has moved the bones of some ancestors from their resting places, such as at Great Zimbabwe. They are moving them to Hero's Acre where there are electric lights. The government must reconsider.
>
> The government leaders loved the ancestors when they were fighting the war. But from the day the ancestors gave them this country they have abandoned the spirits. The angry spirits do not let the rain come because the government officials are troubling the children of Zimbabwe.

Local politics, local religion

Many people, both old and young, noted how those in charge of 'traditional' ceremonies, particularly those responsible for rain-making, were not following the appropriate customs of the past. For instance, sexually active women were now involved in brewing beer; rain messengers (*nyusa*) sent to the Matonjeni shrine of the Mwari cult in the Matopos (*Zame*) travelled by bus rather than on foot; people no longer obeyed the strictures of rest days (*chisi*) which ban people from working in the fields on one day a week; and the appropriate sequence of propitiation was no longer being followed by modern chiefs and their followers, now influenced by town life and European ways. The result was poor rainfall caused by the displeasure of the ancestral spirits.

> Our grandparents were carrying out rain-making ceremonies which were successful. Every year people asked what to do from the rain-maker. Then he would go to Matopos on foot. He was given instructions and when the *nyusa* was back ... the old women and some very young girls without knowledge of boyfriends would brew beer. At the ceremony the chief would forward thanks to the ancestors. What causes drought is that the new generation is destroying all this. They are not following their customary laws; although they are doing the rain-making ceremony, they are not doing it in the proper way.
>
> If the government can allow the chiefs to lead the ritual ceremony, using the proper African cultural system, then the country will be receiving rain and enough yields for the country and the people.
>
> Ian Smith [the Rhodesian Front leader of the UDI government from 1965–79] was very clever. He used to call all the chiefs and tell them to go home to do the ceremonies. All this resulted in the country having much rain. But today the chiefs have been thrown away by the educated but blind leaders.
>
> The modern ways have taught chiefs and headmen to travel on buses when going to *Zame*, instead of going on foot as it was long ago.
>
> People are no longer going to *Zame* at Matopos where we used to ask for rain. If only this was done I am sure the rain would soon come.
>
> People are working in the fields on sacred days (*chisi*), so God decided to punish the whole country. Even the innocent ones are dying.

The drought of 1992 saw a revival of 'traditional' religion in some parts of Chivi, particularly in the Takavarasha area, one of the worst-hit parts of Chivi. During the height of the drought, a female *nyusa* (rain messenger), Ambuya Juliana, arrived in the area, sent from the Matonjeni shrine in the Matopos hills. She claimed to have been sent on a mission that started at birth to resurrect lost traditions and to bring rain back to the country. She was said to have studied the ancient traditions over three full years while living as a water sprite (*njuzu*) in the mud at the bottom of one of the great rivers of Zimbabwe. She travelled on foot and was accompanied by a small group of old women past child-bearing age. Through contacts with local headmen and chiefs, she managed to encourage a revival of interest in following the strict traditions of Shona custom. During a series of meetings she relayed to the population the requirements for successful rain making. These included a strict observation of *chisi*, a proper following of the rain-making (*mitoro)* ceremony, the planting of millets (*mhunga* and *rukweza*) for beer, and respect for the environment, particularly sacred trees, wetlands and mountains. This discourse about appropriate practice was quickly seized by lineage leaders in the area who became the local hosts of Ambuya Juliana. Her powerful message attracted much attention and her meetings were well attended by people of all ages. She set up a base in nearby Mazvihwa where buildings were built with voluntary contributions. Major ceremonies were accompanied by the slaughtering of several black oxen, purchased through offerings made across the community. The scale of her following had not been seen for many years; although it parallels, in many ways, earlier traditional revivals in other parts of the country.

This period saw an interesting set of new political alliances prompted by the drought. Ambuya Juliana, a young woman aged around 30, as a representative of a regional rain cult was able to link up with older male lineage leaders in need of reasserting their authority in the area. This event has to be seen within the context of wider changes in the local polity during the past decade (Chapter 2). The abandonment of the 'old ways' and the lack of respect for ancestors is very much associated with the marginalisation of lineage leaders as the key political force in the rural areas and the emergence of a new generation of younger, more political actors who are active in the new agendas of development. The hostility of the post-Independence government towards chiefs and 'traditional' leaders and the attempts, at least in the early 1980s, to supplant these leaders by party-dominated politics in the rural areas were seen by traditionalists to result in ineffective rain-making ceremonies and discontent amongst the ancestors. However, local shifting allegiances, the decline in party politics in the rural areas and an increasing accommodation of chiefs and traditional leaders by the government have led, in recent years, to a reassertion of power by the chiefs and lineage leaders over the councillors and village development committees (VIDCOs), or, in some cases, to the fusing of the two groups, who for so long had remained opposed. This dynamic was further reinforced by the experience of the drought and the widespread belief that the lack of rainfall was due to the lack of attention to the traditional ways. As a middle-aged man commented:

> Our government leaders have condemned our culture. They no longer follow the traditional customs. They want to rule by themselves and forget the chiefs,

headmen and spirit mediums. Instead, we have the councillors and VIDCOs. These people come from other areas and don't know the rules of the area. Also the chiefs are now younger people of 30–40 years. They went to school and now want town life, so they are not worried about the rain.

Local discussions were thus dominated by elaborations of the 'correct' way of doing things. Such issues are political. Blaming drought on incorrect behaviour by lineage leaders, rain messengers or local political officials provides an explanation for the drought and other problems in the area. Local perceptions of drought are thus initimately bound up in the complex negotiations of local politics. The success of the *nyusa*, Ambuya Juliana, is a case in point. By 1993 her impact had resulted in a shift in political power in favour of the 'traditional' leaders and the strict enforcement of a series of rules that were widely being followed in some parts of Chivi and Mazvihwa communal areas. These were further asserted by a series of ceremonies designed to ensure the continuation of good rains through the season. However, there were distinct variations in her impact across Chivi. Her influence was most felt in areas where traditional lineage leadership was relatively strong, despite the arrival of the councillors and VIDCOs in the 1980s. This was particularly so in Takavarasha and to a slightly lesser extent in central Chivi. However, in Ngundu, where immigrant populations dominate local politics, she was largely dismissed. Gossip and rumour that she was embezzling money or travelling on buses were rife, and her influence never took hold. With the arrival of the rains in 1993, the crisis appeared to be over and in most areas discussion about Ambuya Juliana decreased. By 1994 she had been forgotten by many, others had a range of explanations for her disappearance. Some said she had been arrested for stealing money; others said she had got married; and still others said that she was being pursued by the angry spirit of one of the people she had caused to die. However, her legacy, in terms of a reassertion of traditional practices, supported by shifts in political power, remained in some areas.

Religious activity

The proliferation of small churches in Zimbabwe over the past decade meant that there were people available for comment from every denominational perspective. Most church-goers, however, agreed that the drought was the consequence of God's displeasure and the drought was punishment for sins and misdemeanors of various sorts. Various sections of the bible were quoted at length in support of this view. Several people also commented that divisions within the Christian community were a source of some of the problems. For instance, some argued that the expansion of the number of churches resulted in unnecessary divisions in the spreading of the word of God and that, as a result, too many small churches existed with leaders out for financial advantage, rather than the spiritual renewal required to end the scourge of drought.

> The churches have divided into many, many, because each individual wants to lead and get money. They always want gifts of money from the church-goers. God does not like this and is punishing the people.

> We need to pray and nothing else. God is the only source of better life. Everything that we are seeing now was already said in the Bible. We should not be shocked by what is happening.

Throughout the drought, both the churches and traditional religious leaders made great play of their social role. This was widely reported in the Zimbabwean press.[2] In January 1992, the *Bulawayo Chronicle* reported a call by the heads of the churches in Zimbabwe for people to join them in a week of prayer for rain (17 January 1992) and hundreds of Christians gathered in Masvingo. The *Herald* reported that 'preacher after preacher extolled the virtues of Christianity and castigated the vices of promiscuity, drug-abuse and adultery that they felt may have had the Almighty frowning upon the province' (*Herald*, 20 January 1992). By September the heads of denominations in Matabeleland had joined together to send a delegation to petition the president on problems of drought (*Bulawayo Chronicle*, 23 September 1992).

Practitioners of traditional religion were equally active during the drought. The president of the Zimbabwe National Traditional Healers Association (ZINATHA), Dr Gordon Chavanduka (also pro-Vice Chancellor of the University of Zimbabwe) attacked the government in January 1992 and blamed it for erratic rains on the grounds that: 'they removed powers from the chiefs who had always played an important role in rain-making ceremonies' (*Bulawayo Chronicle*, 16 January 1992). The *Herald* reported a story of Comrade Mutassa from Manicaland who 'possessed the power to make rain'. He had approached the Minister for Water Resources, Herbert Ushewokunze, who commented, 'at this stage I will try anything'. Comrade Mutassa claimed there was a lot of rain in the skies, but before this fell, a 'cleansing' ceremony to remove the blood spilt during the liberation struggle had to be held (*Herald*, 24 February 1992). Traditional healers also gathered together to assist in rain-making. In October the *Herald* reported a gathering of over 500 healers from all over Zimbabwe at the Matonjeni shrine in the Matopos hills (17 October 1992).

The argument that drought was retribution for societal failure in upholding traditional, moral values pervaded all the discussions. Social institutions – the churches, village leaders, the government – could be blamed. In some cases this recognition encouraged a resurgence of interest in following the 'proper' way. As well as the revival of traditional religion in some parts of Chivi, the drought also resulted in increased attendance at church. Religion and ritual in whatever form, whether 'traditional' or Christian, played an important part in providing some form of hope and certainty in an uncertain world.

Ecological control

The association between the 'correct' use of the environment, particularly in relation to sacred aspects of the environment (wetlands, pools, trees, mountains, particular animals), and rainfall is very strong in local mythology (Schoffeleers, 1978; Mukamuri, 1988). A number of commentaries argued that disturbance of sacred aspects of nature resulted in the displeasure of the ancestors leading to drought.

> The country is bare as people have cut down the largest trees where the ancestors used to rest and discuss. We used to use these trees as places for traditional ceremonies. But now the whole country is covered with very small bushes.
>
> Some sacred pools are being used for gold panning by those who do not want to farm. The ancestors are angry with this destruction.
>
> Some people are selling fruits such as *musuma* [*Diospyros mespilliformis*], *matobwe* [*Azanza garkeana*] and others. These should not be sold and should only be for consumption.
>
> Today when people cross the mountains they do not pay respect. They do not put a stick on the *chisororo* heap of firewood, which would burn when the rains were approaching.
>
> People no longer plant *rapoko* and *mhunga* [finger and pearl millet] which are best for our ancestors' beer.

This discourse of environmental religion is manipulated by local lineage leaders to assert local political power over people and resources. The threat of drought is a strong disincentive to disobey regulations of use set down by the local lineage elite.

Directed misfortune: witches and witchcraft

In most years, in most villages in Chivi, there are some accusations that witchcraft has impeded crop production. Usual accusations of witchcraft relate to the misfortunes of one family or the failure of one field. The perception is that localised crop failure is the result of medicine *(muti)* being applied to the field or lightning being made to strike, thus destroying the growing, harvested or stored crop. Such misfortune is deemed to be directed, the result of malicious intent; often by someone who is closely related. The exposure of witches may occur through divination by a *n'anga* (traditional doctor) who may identify the witch. Public occasions may also be held to expose witches where suspects are expected to drink some medicine which in turn exposes the guilty party.

A few ascribed the failure of their crops to ongoing misfortune perceived as due to witchcraft. Others observed the hopelessness of the drought situation. Its widespread nature meant that normal recourse to the *n'anga* was ineffective and despair set in. Some adherents to Christian churches pointed to their perception that excessive practice of witchcraft was now being punished by God.

> People have bewitched our fields. There is no chance of any crops. Everything is lost.

> The *n'anga*s cannot do anything; the witches are too powerful in this drought.

> People have been using lightning, *muti* and other methods to kill others, so God has decided to bring drought into the country to stop these practices.

As with other perceived causes, witchcraft provides a route to ascribing blame for misfortune. Perceptions of drought are thus deeply embedded in such beliefs. However, during 1992 there was relatively little discussion of witchcraft. In the face of such a widespread impact, affecting everyone, not just the unfortunate few, wider reasons of a more global nature (local politics and religion, societal behaviour and morals, government misdemeanors etc.) were generally put forward, as highly personalised malevolence through witchcraft was deemed insufficient to explain such widespread calamity. This contrasted with the following year, when the tensions surrounding getting a harvest following drought gave rise to a range of accusations (Chapter 10).

Failed government: unfulfilled promises and corruption

The widespread nature of the drought meant that local-level explanations were insufficient for the calamity that was clearly facing the whole country. Wider problems of weak, ineffective and unreliable government authority became the subject of blame. The widely felt displeasure with the conduct of the government and the ruling party dominated nearly all the discussions held. Politicians' loss of control over the economy, over corruption and over food supplies reflected their paralysis in doing anything about the drought. By mid-1992, the long association between the rural voters and the ruling party that has sustained ZANU–PF in power since 1980 seemed to have been shattered by a lack of confidence in the government's policies and increasing evidence of high-level corruption. In stark contrast to the muted political debates of only a few years previously, people were not in a mood to mince their words. Few kind words were reserved for the former Minister of Agriculture, Witness Mangwende, who was blamed in large part for the mismanagement of the food stock situation over the previous few years. The resounding advice to government was to change course and listen to what the rural people have to say. Amongst all this criticism there was a widespread acknowledgement that the government (usually President Mugabe was referred to rather than the government, now tainted by ministerial incompetence and corruption) had saved lives in its efficient delivery of food aid. Maybe the contract between the party and the rural poor will be held together, as it has in the past, through the subsidy of food in rough times.

> They [the ministers] are misusing the money; that's why they are talking of ESAP. They have already stolen the money. Some of these ministers are stealing the maize and selling it to other countries for their own benefit. Some of them steal tonnes and tonnes of maize and sell it in their own shops for a profit.
>
> God is not in favour of this ruling party. The ministers are stealing the money of the country aiming at their future life, because they know that they are no longer going to be voted in during the next general election.
>
> We are being led by sinners. The councillors fill their granaries before handing the relief maize to the poor people and the ministers are stealing the country's wealth.
>
> The government told us many things from 1980 up to now and nothing they said has happened. God and the ancestors hate people who tell lies. The government should be changed.
>
> The ministers say things they cannot do, like 'everyone will be employed by the end of the year'. This causes problems in the country.
>
> The drought was caused by the Minister of Agriculture. He said we had stocked plenty of maize and then people decided to grow less. Now we have none in the country.
>
> The government doesn't look at the poor people's views. It thinks that when one is poor in money one is poor in mind. But it is the poor people that know most about rainfall.
>
> Mugabe will not let the people of Zimbabwe starve. The government has done a good job in getting food to the people. We are thankful for this.

The government's economic strategy came under particular scrutiny in a number of discussions. The Structural Adjustment Programme is hitting hard and affecting the livelihoods of many in the rural areas (Chapter 3). Everyone has a view on ESAP and the way the economy is going. Interpretations of the acronym abound, ranging from 'Economics for Starving African Peoples' to 'Satan ari pano' (Satan is here). Typical commentaries on the economic ramifications of drought included the following:

> Bernard Chidzero [Minister of Finance and Economic Planning] is the problem. He studied in America on economics for rich countries, not poor countries in Africa.

> The government ignored the advice to build more dams in the country. Instead they built luxury things like the National Sports Stadium.

> The people of Zimbabwe are the problem. Each and every worker is aiming high and for a better life, yet the money in the country is too little.

> ESAP is a programme that means the death of people. How can they introduce it in a year of drought when there are no crops?

Coping with uncertainty: differentiated views

A striking feature of the commentaries was the consistency of themes. Whether the discussions were held with a group of older men at a rural beer party, with government officials in the district growth point, with a group of women at a riverbank garden, or with people of different religious denominations, the same themes arose. They may have been presented differently; for instance, Christians associated the link between drought and moral decline with the wrath of God, while traditionalists associated it with ancestral displeasure. But the same point was made in each case – societal misdemeanor results in supernatural intervention in the form of drought. The national-level political commentaries were almost universal amongst all groups; even a local party official present at one of the discussions was forced to admit (under pressure admittedly) to some aspects of government incompetence.

The starker differences were generational and related to local political position or educational exposure. Older people tended to reiterate the issues of moral decline more regularly, blaming 'modern' ways and the youth of today – a familiar retort the world over. However, this was not an exclusive concern of the older generation. Many younger people, particularly committed Christians, followed a similar line of argument. Arguments about local political responsibility for the drought were divided between those who blamed the local lineage leaders for inappropriate practice and those who blamed in-migrants for not following the 'proper' ways. Not surprisingly, one group blamed the other, part of the ongoing political contest over rights and responsibilities in all rural areas in Zimbabwe. Education had a certain impact on the style of people's arguments. There were some who offered a 'scientific' view of the problem (referring obliquely to such factors as global warming, desertification and the El Niño effect), when information derived from formal schooling, newspapers or radio/TV was employed. While some denounced outright the 'backward', 'ill-informed' or 'nonsense' interpretations of traditional or religious views (notably some stridently agnostic teachers), others presented 'scientific' interpretations alongside others. Depending on the context, individuals were seen to hold different, sometimes conflicting, views simultaneously.

People must attempt to explain uncertainty in order to cope with it to offer some provisional certitude in order to provide some basis for action rather than despair. Drought has personal, emotional impacts, as well as material ones; the anxiety, fear and distress experienced by many suffering hardships in Chivi during 1991–92 were very real. Explanations are, of course, varied, but all rely on the assumption that the drought was somehow predictable if only we knew more, or took more notice of the signs. People in Chivi were convinced that the world was not totally uncertain, soley determined by chance and beyond control and intervention. They were sure, as Albert Einstein was, that 'God does not play dice' (Einstein, 1971: 91).

What people's perceptions try to do is to offer some hints of order in what appears to be a frighteningly uncertain world. Defining a single reality, a unitary truth about a risk or hazard is well beyond our grasp. Complex narratives of assumed cause and effect suggest a multiple range of 'truths' and 'realities'. People's perceptions of drought, or of any other risk or hazard, are made up of just these. Taking people's perceptions seriously is vital. There are a number of very practical reasons why this is important. It is widely recognised that technicians, scientists and policy-makers do not have all the answers and that local understandings are important. The ways in which farmers and scientists deal with an uncertain world are in many respects similar. Michael Jackson compares the approaches of science and traditional diviners:

> When we examine the great variety of ways in which science and divination alike introduce a semblance of order and system into an uncertain universe, it begins to look as if establishing the 'truth' of science or of divination in terms of some notion that systems *correspond* to external reality is not necessary in order for these systems to help us cope with life and make it meaningful. (Jackson, 1989: 66)

For policies dealing with drought to be effective they must be believed and the implementors must be trusted. Taking cogniscance of people's risk perceptions is thus key, as people will respond according to what *they* believe to be the case, rather than to what scientists think should happen (Chapter 10). The local responses, discussed in the next two chapters, are conditioned and mediated by perceptions of risk; understanding these are important when interpreting the nature of local coping strategies.

Notes

1. In all, 21 interviews/discussions were carried out usually in discussion forums at the following venues: the GMB depot drought relief point, Chivi; Magwizi wholesale shop, Chivi; Madhlangove beer hall, Chivi; Magwati dam food-for-work site; District Administrator's officers' club; Maregere *kraal*; Gwamuti beer party; Methodist church; Dikondo party, Chivi South; Mbaimbai borehole; Ngundu maize ration point; Tokwe river gold panners; Takavarasha beer hall; *humwe* (work party), Mazvihwa; various individuals' homes.

2. Press reports are derived from clippings collected during 1991 and 1992, combined with the Britain Zimbabwe Society Review of the Press compiled by Terrence Ranger.

CHAPTER TEN

Coping with drought: strategies and responses in southern Zimbabwe

The drought of 1991–92 was the worst in living memory. The rivers and wells ran dry, all crops failed, people's food stores were consumed and cattle perished in large numbers. But drought is not a rare phenomenon in Chivi communal area: rainfall deficits resulting in crop failure occur on a regular basis. Pessimists argue that the communal areas in the dry parts of Zimbabwe are so agriculturally marginal, so over-populated and environmentally degraded, that there is little hope for anything but continued subsidy. Subsidy is simply the price the government – and the aid community – must pay for failing to address the land question seriously and resettle people to areas where they can successfully make a living. An alternative view suggests that livelihoods in such areas are viable, if given the appropriate support. Rather than spend money on continuous relief, these resources would be better spent investing in rural production and ensuring sustainable livelihoods.

This chapter explores both the context of the drought and people's responses to it, setting the events of 1991–92 in Chivi within the wider changes occurring in the rural and national economy. The chapter addresses what has been termed the 'paradox of food insecurity' in post-Independence Zimbabwe (Mudimu *et al.*, 1990; Jayne and Chisvo, 1991). In a country that regularly produces a food surplus and has massively increased output in the small-scale farming sector, there remains large-scale, largely hidden, food insecurity in certain areas and amongst certain sections of the population. Chivi communal area is one such place and a close examination of drought coping strategies there offers important insights. Drawing from this experience, the chapter examines policy options for coping with drought.

Drought: a regular occurrence

The history of Chivi and surrounding areas is a history of recurring drought. In the 78 years between 1914 and 1992, over one in five years can be classified as having severe or very severe droughts according to a simple drought index (Parry *et al.*, 1988) (normalized with a mean of zero and a standard deviation of one), where DI is calculated as:

$$DI = \frac{P - X}{S}$$

and where:

P = annual precipitation; X = long-term mean; S = standard deviation.

In Southern Africa, rainfall deficits do not appear to be totally random events. Various researchers have noted rainfall cycles with 13–19-year periodicity in Southern Africa (Tyson, 1986). This may be related to the El Niño effect, as recent research has shown a strong correlation between sea surface temperatures in the eastern equatorial Pacific and maize yields in Zimbabwe (Cane *et al.*, 1994). Table 10.1 examines the type of season experienced between 1980–81 and 1991–92 for Chivi using the drought index, divided into different degrees of drought severity.

Table 10.1 Deviations from mean annual rainfall for Chivi

Year	% Deviation from mean	Drought Index (DI)
1980–81	22.2	
1981–82	−21.6	**
1982–83	−74.6	****
1983–84	−30.1	***
1984–85	49.3	
1985–86	−19.6	**
1986–87	−40.5	***
1987–88	30.0	
1988–89	−10.1	*
1989–90	16.2	
1990–91	−31.0	***
1991–92	−72.6	****

Notes: Figures are based on rainfall data between 1914 and 1992 (mean annual rainfall = 548mm (37% CV)). Light drought (*) DI = < −0.2; moderate drought (**) DI = < −0.5; severe drought (***) DI = < −0.8; very severe drought (****) DI = < −1.3

The relationship between meteorological drought (as defined by a rainfall-related index) and impact on agricultural or livestock production is not always clear. Equally, responses change. Under different economic conditions, affected by such factors as changing availability of off-farm income, intensity of trading operations and scope of government intervention, responses differ. Thus, defining agricultural drought solely by rainfall is clearly inadequate. Stephen Sandford (1979) offers an economic definition of drought where drought is defined as a 'rainfall induced shortage of an economic good'. By this definition, drought depends not only on rainfall levels, but also on changes in other demand and supply factors influenced by prices, market conditions, levels of infrastructure and so on. Thus, every drought is different; some affect people through food shortages, some affect livestock, some affect both.

Famine and feast: a brief history of drought in Chivi

A brief historical sketch of previous drought periods provides an insight into the varied drought coping responses employed over time. This is drawn from archival sources and historical interviews from Chivi and surrounding areas. A schematic chronology is drawn up in Table 10.2, showing how impacts and responses have changed over time.

Droughts during the pre-colonial period were characterised by local responses involving exchanges for grain, collection of wild foods, and migration. Major food crises were exacerbated by warfare and disease. For instance, during the so-called Swazi invasions of the mid-1800s, the disruption of production was combined with a smallpox epidemic resulting in significant mortality (Iliffe, 1990). The drought of 1861 is relatively well documented. A missionary observed the situation in Matabeleland:

> We see them going by scores about the country gathering various wild fruits, on which, for the most part, they are subsisting, and must do so until the harvest around April. Many of them travel 80 or 100 miles on foot with a few beans in their hand to buy a bushel or less of corn, from people who are more highly favoured with rains. [Sykes to Tidman, September 1861, quoted by Iliffe, 1990: 18]

The period of the colonial invasion in 1896 combined with a major outbreak of rinderpest and resulted in widespread food scarcity. The lack of saleable livestock reduced the ability to exchange cattle for grain. This was combined with insecurity in many parts of the country, particularly in Matabeleland. The Chief Native Commissioner distributed food to several thousand people a day in Bulawayo until February 1897 when he claimed that there was sufficient wild produce to keep people alive (Iliffe, 1990: 27).

Droughts in the early part of the twentieth century followed a similar pattern as those in the pre-colonial era. Localised production failures were offset through the exchange of livestock assets for grain and the collection of wild products. The Native Commissioner for Chivi notes in 1903 how the Shangaan population in the southern part of the district had to move some distance in search of food, while those living closer to the main administrative centre were able to get food from traders (NC Chibi, 1903).

Drought struck again in 1912, this time with greater severity. Although

Table 10.2 Chronology of droughts in Chivi

Year	Severity (DI)	Impacts	Response
c. 1861	nd	Crop failure	Use of wild resources; cattle exchange
1896	nd	Crop failure, rinderpest die-off of cattle	Food relief in Matabeleland; wild foods
1903	nd	Crop failure	Cattle-for-grain exchange; migration; wild food use
1911	*	Crop failure	Local cattle-for-grain exchanges
1916	**	Crop failure and food shortages widespread	Government provides food; local traders exchange grain
1922	**	Crop failure and food shortages widespread	Government supply of food on loan; traders sell grain for cattle; local cattle-for-grain exchanges
1926-27	** then *	Patchy impacts; small grains survived	Local livestock-for-grain exchanges; more traders from outside the district involved in the late 1930s
1933, 1935, 1937, 1939	*	Localised crop failure compounded by locust attacks	
1947	**	Widespread crop failure and livestock mortalities	Migration and government food relief; maize imported from Kenya
1949	**	Patchy crop failure; lack of grazing	Grain purchases from stores; livestock movement
1960	*	Crop failure	Grain purchased from stores; food-for-work
1967	*	Crop failure followed by 1968 cold spell killing many cattle	Local attempts to keep cattle alive
1972	**	Some cattle mortality; crop yields down	Cattle movement locally
1982-83	** then *	Major crop failure and cattle mortality	Major food relief effort by government and NGOs; large-scale cattle migration
1986	**	Some livestock mortality; crop yields down	Local cattle movements; food-for-work programme
1991-92	* then **	Total crop failure in second year; major cattle mortalities	Government and NGO food relief; supplementary feeding and movement of cattle

Sources: Archival records; local interviews. ** = Very severe (DI=<-1.3); * = Severe (DI=< -0.8). Seasons are based on July–June rainfall figures starting in the year indicated. nd = no data

people had both cattle and money sufficient to buy grain, it was unavailable in the district. This exchange failure was due to the poor transport infrastructure and the inability of traders to reach the remote parts (NC Chibi, 1912). By mid-1912 Fort Victoria province (now Masvingo) had to import food. This was distributed as part of a food-for-work programme, with limited amounts distributed free to the old and infirm. A government post was also opened in Chivi where grain could be purchased or exchanged for stock (Iliffe, 1990: 46). This pattern was repeated in 1916. Again, this drought hit the marginal, peripheral areas of the country the hardest (Iliffe, 1990). Chivi was not spared. Cattle were exchanged for grain in large numbers, with private traders again supplying much of the grain, although this was supplemented by government relief.

The next major drought period was in 1922. This was made worse by the collapse in the cattle price, prompted by international changes in the beef market (Phimister, 1978). This combined with an outbreak of East Coast Fever, with quarantines preventing animal movement and trading. In many parts of the country an adult ox could be exchanged for only a single bag of grain. This contrasted dramatically with the much more favourable terms of trade in 1912 and 1916, when a beast would realise between two and five bags (Mosley, 1983). Local responses included purchasing grain or exchanging livestock with the successful local agricultural entrepreneurs (*hurudza*). Young girls were sometimes married off in exchange for bride-wealth payments. Wild resources were particularly important in providing alternative foods when crops failed. Drought response strategies in this period were recalled during discussions in the area:

> After the influenza [1918] there were many droughts. People were given maize or they sold cattle. But the droughts were mild by comparison to these days ... those who did well had farms on the *dambo*s [low-lying, wetter areas], the others in the plains suffered. The *hurudza* [agricultural entrepreneurs] succeeded because of good rainfall in the years between. [Discussion, Zihove, Chivi]

> In 1922 grain was brought, but it was for sale, unlike in 1916. In those days people used to organise hunting parties in times of drought and round up wild animals for slaughter. Also you had to rely on the *hurudza* or relatives in distant places where there had been rain and food was plentiful. [Discussion, Maringire, Chivi]

Archival records also record the impact on livestock of the early droughts and government's facilitation of stock movement.

> The effect of the drought on native stock threatened to be very serious if not disastrous, by reason of lack of water and pasturage. Early in the year ... arrangements were made to move cattle to better grazing and water before they should grow too weak to travel and large numbers were moved and saved in this way. [CNC, 1922]

In many years, drought impacts were patchy and no large-scale response was required by the state. Reports note that local exchange of livestock for grain between surplus and deficit areas was sufficient to sustain people's food supplies in most years. For instance, the Native Commissioner for Chivi commented in 1942 that 'local bartering of cattle and cash for grain amongst themselves was sufficient to supply those in need of food' (NC Chibi, 1942).

The recurring theme of commentaries, from the 1920s through to the 1940s, is the importance of cattle as exchange entitlement during drought. This was to change over time, with shifts in the terms of trade, especially during the recession of the 1930s, with the reduction in the number of cattle people owned through government destocking between 1945 and 1961 and through gradual human population increase and the decreasing number of livestock owned per person (Chapter 2). By the mid-1980s, the importance of cattle as an exchange commodity and a source of drought security had been seriously reduced (Figure 10.1).

Terms of trade during drought were also seriously affected by changes in the maize marketing system in the early 1930s. The control of maize marketing from 1931 (Chapter 2) resulted in low prices for African-produced maize as it was produced far from the railheads and Control Board buying points (Palmer, 1977; Mosley, 1983). In addition, the reduction in competition amongst European traders with the advent of maize control again reduced sales prices. However, purchase prices in times of food shortage increased as a consequence of monopolistic control of sellers and the price stabilisation imposed by the Control Board.

Figure 10.1 Terms of trade between cattle and grain, 1923–93

Improved infrastructure, particularly the expansion of the road network and the arrival of motor vehicles, from the mid-1920s certainly increased the ability of people in remote areas such as Chivi to survive during drought. The encouragement of private traders during the drought periods of the 1930s meant that government intervention was kept to a minimum. By contrast to the major drought relief operations of 1916 and 1922, the government was able to rely on an increasingly effective infrastructure and private enterprise (CNC, 1933; 1935; NC Chibi, 1933).

One of the most important factors that has changed the nature of drought responses over time has been the changing links with the urban economy. In the early part of the century, people had an ambivalent attitude to wage labour. The local sources of employment were largely underground mining jobs, which were both poorly paid and dangerous. The Native Commissioners regularly complained about the lack of labour supply to the urban and mining sector, especially during the cropping season and following good harvests when plentiful food and beer was available in the rural areas. As the NC for Belingwe (now Mberengwa) commented in 1927, 'The labour demand is far in excess of the supply. The asbestos mines are not popular and experience great difficulty in recruiting' (NC Belingwe, 1927).

By the 1940s, however, an increasing number of younger men were being forced to work in town in order to support their families in the 'reserves' (Chapter 2). They became an important source of support both in normal times and in drought. Incentives to migrate for seasonal employment fluctuated over the period, with changes in real wage rates and variation in returns to agricultural production, but the general trend has been towards a greater level of participation in the formal labour economy. By the mid-1940s the migrant labour pattern had been firmly established in the reserves, as highlighted by the Assistant NC of Shabani (now Zvishavane): 'The reserve native is being forced to maintain a dual existence working away from home and leaving his family behind; particularly when the economy of an overpopulated reserve such as Lundi [now Runde] is productive of few marketable surpluses' (ANC Shabani, 1947).

The 1947 drought was perhaps the worst drought since the beginning of the colonial period. A series of crop failures precipitated widespread food shortages which had to be filled by the importing of yellow maize. Transport delays from South Africa, and later from Argentina and Kenya, resulted in some serious problems. These are reported vividly in the NC reports from Gutu and Gwanda for that year:

> Had it not been that natives in neighbouring districts had food to spare at a time when supplies of imported grain were arriving here at irregular intervals and in amounts far short of what was estimated to be necessary, a very serious position may have arisen. ... Because of the uncertainty many men who would otherwise have gone to work stood by to go foraging. [NC Gutu, 1947]

> There has been an acute shortage of food this year and at one stage the position became critical and many natives were very close to starvation. Crops were a complete failure everywhere and natives were compelled to buy all food from traders. There was little in the granaries after two consecutive years of failure. There is a severe lack of seed for the next season. [NC Gwanda, 1947]

During 1947 some 202,815 African cattle were sold and most were exchanged for grain. About 500,000 bags of grain were supplied by the government but strictly on a sale basis, with limited concessions to the seriously needy (Illife, 1990: 100). The Chief Native Commissioner commented: 'This is the first time in the colony's history that we have had a major drought and famine which has cost the government practically nothing by way of famine relief to the native population' (CNC, 1947). This was achieved because of the availability of livestock for exchange. This was noted by the Assistant NC for Zvishavane: 'Were such a drought as this to strike the local reserve [Lundi] with its present economy at a time when it had no bank in the form of excess livestock, the results would have been more than calamitous' (ANC Shabani, 1947). The 1947 drought was thus in many respects typical of more recent droughts, with local coping mechanisms being important for a period, but with government intervention and food relief being required later. However, it contrasts starkly with later drought events in one important respect: the availability of exchange assets, notably cattle, meant that government intervention was largely paid for.

From the 1950s to the present, a different pattern has emerged, with local stores and assets being inadequate. This erosion of the asset base, and an increased reliance on external claims, can be attributed to a number of factors. The impact of destocking meant that the average number of cattle per household in Chivi declined. Studies in other areas show that ownership by the 1960s was highly skewed, with as many as 30% of households not owning cattle (Johnson, 1968; Weinrich, 1975). Land availability in Chivi was also adversely affected by the implementation of government policies during this period. The eviction of African settlers from European-designated land following the Second World War resulted in major influxes of people into reserves such as Chivi. This was combined with the implementation of land reorganisation policies with centralisation and the Native Land Husbandry Act (Chapter 2). These interventions often disrupted production by moving arable plots to new, often more marginal, sites. The banning of riverine gardening also undermined food security. With these changes, people were increasingly reliant on off-farm sources of income. Remittances had been important since the 1920s, and rises in real wages during the post-war boom encouraged more and more people to join the labour market. Between 1948 and 1960 real wages rose by around 35% and the number of indigenous Africans employed increased from 387,000 to 647,000 (Chapter 3).

Fortunately the 1950s were a wet decade, with good harvests resulting in large stores. This pattern was upset in 1960 with a drought year which necessitated some food relief in Chivi. This was organised around a food-for-work programme, involving the construction of small dams. However, most droughts in this period are remembered as ones affecting cattle rather than people. Local people particularly recall the movement of cattle between areas. For instance, a group in Masinire, Chivi, recalled that 'in 1950 cattle were driven here from other parts of Chivi. In 1960 a lot of cattle were loaned here again and some people came and built camps in the forest. Plenty also came around 1965 to find grass.' An informant from Mazvihwa remembered that 'in 1965 drought seriously affected the cattle. They were taken to Shabani [Zvishavane] area and further to Mapanzure. This happened again in 1982 and 1983. In 1973 cattle moved locally, just across the river to Masinire in Chivi.'

Following the good harvests that immediately followed Independence in 1980, drought struck hard in 1982–84. This required a major drought relief effort – with around two million people receiving food handouts during the period. Local coping strategies were inadequate and particularly vulnerable groups, such as single women with families, were most at risk (Cheater and Bourdillon, 1982; Leys, 1986).

Drought relief has been almost continuous in Chivi since this period. The lack of an effective local asset base has undermined the ability of local populations to cope. The collapse of cattle populations during the 1970s (due to disease) and during the 1980s (due to drought) has meant that fewer and fewer people have access to cattle. Prior to the 1982 drought around 25% of households area owned no cattle. Following the drought this percentage rose to over 50%. By the end of the 1992 drought, nearly 70% of households in the Chivi household sample owned no cattle at all (Chapter 11). Increased human populations have also meant that pressure on land resources has increased, with arable plots decreasing due to subdivision, and sources of wild produce declining due to arable expansion. The pace of resettlement has also been slow, providing limited relief to resource constraints in the communal areas. Drought responses in the 1980s and 1990s have thus been characterised by an increasing reliance on external claims on the state, in the form of drought relief, and on relatives sending remittances.

Drought in 1991–92: official responses

The drought that struck Southern Africa during 1991–92 was of unparalleled proportions, requiring major region-wide responses to the emergency. The way government, NGOs and donors responded in Zimbabwe during this period is described below. This sets the scene for a more detailed look at what happened in Chivi, where external responses combined with local responses to the crisis.

Over the past decade, much effort has been invested in Zimbabwe in improving the capacity of administrators (and the politicians they serve) to anticipate the onset of drought. Various early warning systems have been initiated, working at both the national and regional level. The national crop forecasting committee derives information from district-level assessment by field-level agricultural extension workers at various points during the season. This provides information on expected harvests on the basis of rainfall levels and crop performance in the field. This data is combined with information provided by the Meteorological Office and the Central Statistics Office. The national committee compiles the information into national-level maps which give indications early in the season on expected harvest shortfalls. This in turn relates to the national process of food security planning which assesses expected harvests from different sectors (communal, resettlement, small-scale and large-scale commercial) in relation to stocks of grain held in storage by the Grain Marketing Board. The national early warning system is complemented by a regional food security and early warning unit under the auspices of the Southern African Development Community (SADC). Information from national reports, plus some limited additional data collection, is compiled in a regional bulletin published each quarter with monthly updates.

Each of these early warning mechanisms provides information, at varying scales and with varying degrees of accuracy. Information is provided to administrators and politicians on the likelihood of drought and its potential impacts and consequences. Information is provided in a digestible form, with data aggregated, standardised and simplified. The limitations of the science of anticipation, imposed by uncertainty and indeterminacy, go unacknowleged, at least in public. Where caveats are applied it is argued that more prediction and more assessment will fill the knowledge gap and provide better, more reliable information. Early warning systems thus rely on the ability to reduce uncertainties to probabilities, to remove the fear of ignorance and the unknown and to provide some basis for action. The science of anticipation thus provides a comforting assurance of control over an uncertain, unpredictable and potentially threatening natural world. For politicians and administrators, who must make decisions about what to do, this can provide a reassuring rationale for intervention.

But do administrators and politicians take any notice of early warning systems? The evidence is mixed. The gap between early warning prediction and on-the-ground action is highly variable. In most cases there appears to be a 'missing link' between early warning and response (Buchanan-Smith and Davies, 1995). There are many reasons for this. In many cases it is unclear what the early warning system is trying to measure. Most are geared to identifying famine, or major food deficits, but are not well attuned to highlighting other forms of risk, stress or vulnerability. Crisis responses of national governments or international donors may be too late and the benefits of anticipatory information are lost. Early warnings tend to be linked to a single response of food delivery, rather than triggering support to vulnerable populations in other ways. Different messages are responded to in different ways; different information sources have different levels of credibility, even if the information's origin is the same. An understanding of responses, therefore, must be situated within an understanding of the social and political context of risk perceptions. If governments or donors are unwilling to respond for whatever reason, excuses for inaction can always be found. Inadequate details, suspected inaccuracies or untimely data delivery can be used to discredit early warning information or to delay response. The link between information delivery and response is also plagued by the practical, logistical difficulties of transport, finance, administrative capacity and so on. Whilst the ability of early warning systems to increase their predictive power with ever more sophisticated indicators and systems of measurement has undoubtedly improved over the past decade, the ability to respond to and mitigate drought impact in Africa has not (Buchanan-Smith and Davies, 1995).

The story of drought response among adminstrators and politicians in Zimbabwe during 1991–92 has many similarities with the wider African story.[1] The national Early Warning Unit first sounded the alarm about impending food shortages in July 1991. At that time they alerted the government that food stocks would run out in early 1992. This proved to be ominously accurate. The national bulletin noted: 'If the present trend of intake, local commercial sales and export of maize continues, the stock of maize in the GMB will be at a record low level by December 1991' (National Early Warning Unit, Vol 5(7)). The SADC report echoed this concern, pointing to the problem posed by the GMB's export obligations and the need to import grain to maintain strategic reserves. These warnings were basically ignored. Indeed, no one appeared to trust them. Even when the situation was obviously critical, the government insisted on commissioning its own monitoring exercise to investigate the food situation in the country. Similarly both the United Nations World Food Programme and the Food and Agricultural Organisation sent their own missions to confirm the results emerging from the early warning system, before committing themselves to food relief activities.

It was only when the failure of the 1991–92 rains became very clear and the national press started to highlight the issue, that government started to act. In April 1992, the *Herald* reported the concerns of Syndey Malunga MP: 'The government must ensure that its promises to the nation to make food available during the drought are met, otherwise the rift between the Government and the people will cause the failure of the economic reform programme' (*Herald*, 8 April 1992). Stories of how people were driven to extreme lengths by the failures of the relief effort were common. For instance, the *Herald* reported how Mberengwa villagers forced a train driver to stop and stole over 300 bags of maize and how Masvingo residents were scavenging for food in dustbins (*Herald*, 5 October 1992).

In February 1992 the government announced significant increases in producer prices for white maize, raising the price from Z$270 to Z$550 per tonne, with added incentives for early delivery. However, such incentives were too late to provide the necessary maize for the year. By February the GMB only expected 250,000 tonnes of maize to be delivered from Zimbabwean producers, but demand was likely to rise during the year to around 150,000 tonnes per month because of the near-complete failure of the communal area crop. The chairman of the GMB suggested at a seminar held in February that Zimbabwe would have to import up to two million tonnes of maize to meet local demand, at a cost of up to Z$1,500 per tonne (*Herald*, 21 February 1992). A columnist in the *Financial Gazette* commented thus:

> This predicament need never have arisen. The primary cause of the problem has been the totally impractical maize price. Droughts do come but the nation has had three reasonable seasons. ... Stockpiles are a necessity. It is now evident that at least one year's supply should always be retained rather than selling maize for foreign currency. [*Financial Gazette*, 13 February 1992]

The food import programme started during December 1991. The arrival of food aid in the country was plagued by logistical problems, made worse by the widespread nature of the drought in the region. Road and rail transport was commandeered in order to bring American grain from South Africa and Mozambique (SADC, 1993). By March 1992 the country had effectively run out of reserves and people waited expectantly for supplies. The first American maize arrived at the ports at the end of March, but by the first week of April there was still none inside the country, although six trains a day, supplemented by road transport, were expected (*Herald*, 7 April 1992). The government committed itself to the feeding of some 4–5 million people during the drought, requiring the eventual importing of around 1.7 million tonnes. The initial monthly ration allocation of 10kg per person was later reduced to 5kg as supplies became uncertain and costs escalated (Thompson, 1993).

Politicians therefore trusted neither the information emanating from their own civil servants nor that from international sources. Despite the claims of scientific certitude of the early warning bulletins, the government failed to act early on. It was only a wider political process of lobbying and petitioning, by government officials in the districts, by the press and by churches, NGOs and others, that forced action. By mid-1992, public and political pressure mounted sufficiently and by most accounts a highly effective and efficient drought relief and food distribution campaign was launched. By this time, the cost of relief was around Z$30 million per month, much of which was paid for by government. During 1992 in Masvingo Province, around 250,000 children were being given regular supplementary feeding rations and around one million people (practically the whole communal area population) were receiving food relief. Churches and NGOs played an important role in providing distribution facilities (Thompson, 1993). The total costs of the drought relief operation were estimated to be around 2.7% of GDP in 1991–92 and 4.5% of GDP in 1992–93, requiring a significant increase in government borrowing (Benson and Clay, 1994).

For a time during 1992 the government had lost control; its food security policy was completely discredited, its maize pricing policy was suddenly drastically revised, the Minister for Agriculture was hurriedly shifted, and the highly unpopular economic structural adjustment policy looked to be going off course. The rumblings of discontent had reached even the remotest rural areas, usually the stalwarts of support for the ZANU–PF party and government (Chapter 9). Uncertainty over what to do about the drought had resulted in a certain helplessness and a loss of political control and power. Not until the launch of the food aid programme and the countrywide tours by President Mugabe was some confidence restored. Only then was it realised by rural people that Mugabe and the ZANU–PF government had not broken their post-Independence bargain and would not let the people of Zimbabwe starve.

Thus the perceptions of drought on the part of scientists, administrators and politicians were different, resulting in very different types of action. Scientist confidently predicted disaster using scientific indicators, neatly packaged in early warning bulletins. Faith was placed in the statistics, the aggregated inferences, and the composite conclusions. The scientists' view was based on what they claimed as a scientifically 'rational' response to impending disaster. Administrators responded in mixed ways. Some lobbied politicians on the basis of the early warning predictions and their own experience in the districts; others, especially those surrounded by the well-watered lawns and golf courses of Harare, maintained a more cautious stance. The politicians did not know what to do. They refused to believe the science of prediction and would not listen, at least initially, to their constituents. The uncertainty surrounding drought resulted in a perilous loss of control and an unnerving loss of power. Power and control were only regained by firm action later on, when political and social process, and not rational scientific argument, provided the impetus for action.

Drought coping strategies: local responses

Across rural Zimbabwe the drought forced people to employ a variety of coping strategies; some involved assistance from outside, others made use of local resources. The press was full of comment. According to a report from Mberengwa communal land (*Bulawayo Chronicle*, 13 January 1992): 'Each morning women could be seen carrying buckets on their heads heading for the forests to collect wild fruits'. In other areas, people were reported as going back to the 'old ways', hunting animals for food and abandoning new settlements (*Herald*, 10 April 1992). In many areas gold panning became a way of life. The *Herald* records the views of a 'self-confessed' gold panner from Mupfure: 'Maize handouts from food-for-work took a long time to come for distribution. With gold panning the cash is instant. ... The Government says it is illegal. We are only trying to survive.' (*Herald*, 20 February 1992).

A wide variety of drought coping strategies were followed by members of the 146 households in the Chivi sample. Different individuals and households, with different levels of assets or different access to various types of claim, were able to respond in different ways. The analysis below examines this differentiated response, exploring the factors influencing the nature of coping strategies.[2] The various drought coping activities that were employed in order of their frequency of occurrence among the sample as a whole (Table 10.3) are taken in turn and information is presented on how survival strategies differed by area, time and socio-economic group during two periods of the drought.

Government aid

Chivi has been receiving food handouts almost continuously since Independence. Although peaks coincided with the 1982–83 and the 1991–92 drought periods, there has been only one year (1985–86) when no food was distributed. By 1993 practically the whole communal area population (over one million people) was being fed regularly in Masvingo Province at enormous cost to the government and aid donors (Tobaiwa, 1993). Nearly 80% of people in the Chivi sample benefited from claims on the government food aid programme at some stage during 1992, despite the restrictions imposed on joining the programme. In a number of instances councillors allowed families to join even if they had husbands working in full-time employment. This was the result either of political patronage or pity for those families suffering because no remittances were being sent home.

The organisation of the food relief programme changed through the year from food handouts to a food-for-work programme organised by local *kraal* heads and village development committee leaders. People were

Table 10.3 Activities carried out by Chivi households during the two periods of monitoring during 1992, ranked by frequency of occurrence by household

	Period 1: Feb to May 1992	Period 2: July to Nov 1992	Overall
Government aid and food-for-work	71.2	72.6	79.5
Remittance income (cash or kind)	67.8	69.2	76.0
Vegetable vending	22.6	32.8	43.8
Gold panning	28.0	19.8	35.6
Goat sales	26.0	9.6	28.8
Beer brewing and sale	22.6	2.7	22.6
Trading	14.4	4.1	16.4
Poultry sales	15.0	2.7	15.1
Off-farm work (general)	10.9	6.8	13.0
Sewing, crocheting	10.3	2.7	13.0
Cattle sales	5.5	3.4	7.5
Building	6.8	3.4	6.8
Prostitution	2.7	2.7	4.8
Clay pot making	3.4	1.4	3.4
Church aid	2.0	2.7	3.4
Collection and sale of tree pods	0.7	2.0	2.1

Note: all activities where three or more households were involved are noted

involved in a variety of projects largely determined by local officials. These ranged from blocking of erosion gullies to the repairing of roads to the destumping of fields. Most work involved a few hours in the day, allowing people other time to engage in activities such as gold panning, trading etc. Rations were calculated according to the claimed family size (again open to some abuse) and people worked initially for 10kg per person per month. The number of days a person from any family was allowed to work was determined by the family size. Government rations arrived intermittently and in variable amounts. Later in the season the ration was cut to only 5kg per person per month, equivalent to around one quarter of total food requirements. This cut in the ration resulted in all sorts of accusations about inefficiency, stealing and corruption. The *Herald* commented: 'Family rations have been cut down to a paltry 5kg of mealie-meal a month. ... Supplementary feeding programmes have not taken off in many areas and in others officials are still bogged down in the paperwork' (*Herald*, 18 September 1992). MPs warned: 'people could die of hunger if the government does not ensure that enough drought relief food reaches the people' (*Herald*, 20 September 1992).

Despite this, government aid provided food for a wide section of the population. Although it was not a very reliable source and made up only a small proportion of consumption needs, it was unquestionably important in people's food provisioning strategies, especially towards the end of 1992. There was no significant difference in participation in government food programmes between the three study sites. In addition, there were no significant differences in participation between households of above and below average size and average age of household head or between those of different wealth status. Those in receipt of remittance income were significantly less involved in food-for-work activities in line with the regulations, although the numbers of those dodging these increased in the latter part of the drought. By contrast, female-headed households were significantly more involved in both periods. Although there was some level of targeting, it was not thorough. However, the benefits of a strictly means-tested approach to support during such a widespread drought are doubtful (Thompson, 1993).

Remittances

Remittances in cash or direct provision of food were probably the single most important contribution to people's livelihoods during the drought. Although this study did not attempt to quantify the remittance levels received, many people indicated how important these claims were. Remittance levels vary significantly: some people receive substantial and regular income from husbands or close relatives working in full-time employment, whilst others receive lower and occasional, but none the less important, amounts (Chapter 3). The proportion of households receiving some form of remittance did not differ significantly between the two periods studied. A significantly higher percentage of the wealthier household group received remittances in both drought periods. In the first period, a significantly higher proportion of households with heads older than the average received remittances, reflecting their stage in the demographic cycle, with greater numbers of adult children sending money home. This distinction disappeared in the second period, when most people in all age groups gained at least some source of remittance. Proportions of households receiving remittances were not distinguished by household size.

The Takavarasha area had the highest percentage of households receiving remittances in both drought periods (75% and 79%) and the Ngundu area had the lowest in both periods (64% and 53%). These patterns reflect the migration history of the area (Chapter 2): the Takavarasha area has a long history of rural–urban migration, particularly to the mining town of Zvishavane. The Ngundu area has had less out-migration over time with a greater attachment to a farming existence in the relatively better agricultural environment found there. Nevertheless, migration to the Chiredzi sugar estates and to South Africa has been important, although a number of people were made redundant as a result of water shortages in Chiredzi and Hippo Valley during 1991–92.

Vegetable sales

In the early part of 1992 women in Ngundu area were heavily engaged in vegetable trading. Most of these vegetables were bought from traders in Masvingo and were sold for marginal profits at Ngundu Halt business centre and at various small townships along the main Masvingo–Beitbridge road. There were significantly more households involved in this activity in the Ngundu area, although this trade declined dramatically between the two periods, reducing from 40% of households to 25%. In the latter period, women took up dry season riverbank and *dambo* gardening and marketed a proportion of their produce. This dry season activity was particularly important in the Takavarasha area, where the number of households involved in vegetable selling increased from 18% to 68% in the latter part of the drought. Vegetable vending was associated with the relatively better-off, as they still had extra cash with which to purchase vegetables for resale. The poor were engaged in a battle for survival, and were not indulging in the relative luxury of business life. However, in relation to all other categories of difference (remittance access, household size, age/gender of household head), there were no significant differences in involvement.

Gold panning

Gold panning was initiated by a few households during 1991, usually with one or two people joining forces to pan as a team in one of the nearby rivers. In the early periods it was particularly women and younger people who engaged in gold panning; this resulted in income flows to those who, in previous years, did not have access to any significant income source. Reported tensions between husbands and wives and parents and children resulted from this shifting access. In this early period a number of women and younger people were able to purchase assets (goats, radio-cassettes, watches and clothes were all reported). However, soon the imperative of food provisioning took over and gold panning incomes were diverted to the buying of maize meal. By early 1992 whole families became involved in gold panning. In some cases they migrated *en masse* to live by the rivers and jealously guard their panning site.

Over the whole period, 35% of households were involved in panning gold at some time. In both periods of the drought, those without access to remittance income sources were significantly more involved. Panning was thus an important alternative form of security, especially in the latter part of the drought. Panning decreased in the second period (from 28% to 20%) as a consequence of the reduced amounts of gold being gained per unit of labour input, the lower prices offered for gold, the reduced marketing opportunities (the result of the arrest of a number of key dealers) and the difficulties of investing such a huge amount of effort when food intakes had been reduced. The demands of land preparation by hand (as most of the cattle had died) also drew people away from panning. As a result, more people switched to the less demanding government food-for-work programme. Gold panning attracted a diversity of households and it was not differentiated significantly by wealth status, age of household head, gender of household head or household size.

Degrees of gold panning differed between research sites. A trend of decreasing activity over time was shown for the Takavarasha and Chivi sites, while the opposite was the case for Ngundu. This reflects different market conditions and the reduced number of alternative activities available for Ngundu people in the latter part of the drought, with the drying up of the vegetable buying-and-selling trade and the lack of building contracts in the area. Overall, the Takavarasha and Ngundu sites had the highest percentage of households involved in panning, reflecting their proximity to major rivers (the Runde and Tugwi or Tokwe respectively).

Goat sales

The sale of goats was significantly higher in the early part of the drought, dropping from 26% to 9.6% of households in the latter part of 1992. Most goat sales occurred in the Takavarasha area (50% and 20% of households selling in the two periods). This was significantly higher than the other sites throughout the drought. The dry environment of Takavarasha is good goat-rearing country and the level of goat ownership is higher here than in the other study areas (Chapter 1). Takavarasha goat sales boomed because of the panners' market along the Runde river; goat prices shot up at the height of panning as demand increased. The drop in goat sales over the period was a result of the severe depletion of flocks and decreasing demand, as people became increasingly frugal with available cash. This hit the Takavarasha households particularly hard, as it came alongside the dramatic drop in the gold market and price in the area. People were consequently forced to diversify into other activities, notably vegetable gardening. Goat sales were not differentiated by household wealth status, size or age of household head. However, fewer female-headed households sold goats during the drought, a reflection of the resource-poor status of this group.

Beer brewing

The brewing and sale of beer at commercial beer parties was significantly higher in the early periods of the drought. Many people at this point still had grain stores and were able to add value to grain through brewing. Others purchased grain from other areas, especially the agriculturally more successful areas around Madamombe to the north, and brewed it at home, making sufficient profit to buy more grain for brewing and provide food for the family. However, beer brewing practically ceased by late 1992, as grain stores across the whole district ran out. The proportion of households brewing beer did not differ significantly between the three research sites, or between households of different wealth status, size or gender of household head. However, significantly more older people brewed beer, reflecting the fact that older people opt for small grain production.

Trading

A variety of trading activities was initiated by members of 16.4% of households during the drought period. Trading activities were dominated by women who concentrated on the purchase and resale of second-hand clothes and the marketing of goods imported from South Africa and Botswana. Men were occasionally involved in the selling of hides and skins or the illegal sale of cannabis. Trading activities were significantly higher in the earlier period of the drought, and their occurrence was higher in female-headed households and in those households without access to remittance incomes. Trading was highest in Ngundu (with easy access to South Africa and Masvingo), with 21% of households involved, next highest in Takavarasha (with closer links through working husbands to Zvishavane and Bulawayo), and lowest in Chivi central.

Poultry sales

The sale of poultry was important in the first period of the drought, when 15% of households were involved. The price of a chicken rose from around Z$10 to Z$18 during the period as the supply of chickens reduced. Three households in the sample had broiler chickens that continued to be fed through the drought with grain or chicken meal bought by working husbands. Another source of broiler feed was maize received from the food-for-work programme. Sales to teachers and other civil servants at Chivi Office, Ngundu Halt and at outlying schools continued to provide an occasional income throughout the drought. However, for most, poultry sales were sporadic and served as a supplement rather than as a main income source. Incomes derived were small and were spent on such items as soap, tea and sugar. Those with poultry in sufficient numbers to sell tended to be the relatively better-off. There were no significant differences in poultry sales between households of different size, age of household head and gender of household head, and the pattern of sales was similar across all three areas throughout the drought.

Off-farm work

Various off-farm work options were taken up by 13% of households. These included casual labour (herding, working for teachers, piecework for the District Development Fund etc.), hiring out of scotch carts or other assets, the setting up of small businesses (shops, hair salon) in the villages, and the continued practice of particular professions such as traditional healing (*n'anga*s and herbalists). These activities persisted through the drought and among all household categories. A greater proportion of households were engaged in the first part of the drought, when the local money supply was greater. The number of households involved in off-farm work activities was significantly lower in the Chivi area, with under 2% involved. This compared with 15% and 10% in the other areas. This lack of activity does not relate to lack of opportunity, as Chivi Office is very close; the lack of enterprise shown may be related to the absence of historical association with locally based off-farm work (Chapter 3).

Sewing, crocheting

Over 10% of households were engaged in the making of clothes, doilies, bed covers and other items for sale. This was the exclusive activity of women. The proportion of households with members selling sewn or crocheted craft items dropped during the drought, but the distribution of activity was not significantly different between different household types. Such activities were concentrated in Takavarasha and Ngundu, again making use of connections with urban centres and export opportunities. No such commercial craft activity was occurring in any of the Chivi households.

Cattle sales

In contrast to previous droughts, relatively few households managed to sell or exchange cattle during the drought (7.5%). This was the result of small herd sizes, poor condition of the cattle and poor marketing opportunities. Cattle sales were held on occasions by the Cold Storage Commission (CSC) in the area, supposedly as a means to allow farmers to destock animals prior to major drought mortality. Early in the drought, farmers were understandably reluctant to destock, thinking that the rains might come and cattle would survive. As this became increasingly unlikely the market supply rose as many farmers realised the urgency of the situation. At this point the market was saturated, prices dropped drastically, and the CSC refused stock on the grounds of their poor condition. The organisation of the sales caused frustration among farmers and local officials alike as dates would be announced, cattle would be penned and

CSC sales officials would not arrive. The consequence was a significant number of deaths from starvation or water shortage in the sales pens themselves. Later in the drought, farmers tried to sell to local butchers, but again this was at a very low price. In most cases cattle died on the hoof or were slaughtered just before they collapsed and died (Chapter 11). Meat was then shared locally, with small amounts sold. Larger households were significantly more likely to sell cattle in the first period of drought. As such households have greater cash needs for food and school fees this is not surprising. Cattle sales were not differentiated by age or gender of household head or by access to remittance income. Clearly those with higher levels of assets, including cattle, were more likely to sell.

Building

Building is a traditional dry season activity for male specialists, who often have a background in the business, with skills picked up during previous work in town. A total of 7% of households were involved in building during the drought. Building activity was highest in the early period of the drought and was concentrated in Ngundu and among relatively asset-rich households. There are a large number of builders in Ngundu, many of whom have been apprenticed with each other. They service a wide area and will travel across Chivi on contracts. As the drought progressed the availability of local contracts reduced dramatically. People ran out of money and builders had to divert their attention elsewhere. Many Ngundu builders switched to gold panning; the lucky few were able to get temporary contracts on government building schemes, notably the building and refurbishment of schools in the area.

Prostitution

Prostitution was an important source of income for women in 4.8% of sample households. Prostitution is particularly important for younger, unmarried women and older divorcees. Trade is concentrated around the business centres of Chivi Office and Ngundu Halt. Others migrate to the larger towns and remit cash to their rural homes. In addition, there is a certain amount of rural prostitution around beer parties (*dikondo*). However, business was down during the 1992 drought. A combination of a lack of cash and the fear of contracting HIV/AIDS has reduced demand for sexual services. But despite this, the 'month end' pay day for civil servants remains an important cash earning opportunity. Prostitution occurred in all research sites and in both periods of the drought, with no significant differences in occurrence between area and period. Members of female-headed households and those with lower asset levels were more likely to practise prostitution.

Clay pot making

Clay pot making is a specialist activity of a few women. As with other craft activities, the involvement of households dropped during the drought. As with other off-farm activities, clay pot making was concentrated in Ngundu and Takavarasha, with no households involved in Chivi. The pattern of activity did not vary between household groups in any significant way.

Wooden crafts

The making of wooden items (cooking sticks, furniture, drums etc.) occurred in all areas and was done by men. The highest level of activity was in the Ngundu area, where the markets along the Beitbridge road were important sites for sale. As with other craft activities, the making of wooden craft items reduced in the second drought period when markets dried up. Craft activity was not significantly differentiated by household characteristics.

Church aid

A few households were associated with churches that handed out food and clothes. Some members of the Catholic, Apostolic Faith and Methodist churches received aid in this way. This provided additional support that complemented government aid.

Collection and sale of tree pods

Three households from the Takavarasha area engaged in the collection of *Acacia* pods for sale to cattle owners. A bucket of pods sold at Z$1 and provided an occasional source of income for these homes. Children were usually employed in the collection of the pods after their return from school.

Coping with drought: case studies from Chivi

A series of case studies illustrate how the various coping strategies described in the previous section were combined during the 1991–92 drought period. Ten different anonymous cases, a representative selection from the household sample, are presented, illustrating a wide diversity of strategies. The cases are ranked according to wealth levels prior to the drought (using livestock ownership as a proxy). The cases show how strategies changed over time, shifting between different options in order to make ends meet. They show how different individuals within a household were involved in different activities, with men, women and children often all doing different things. They also show how people with different asset levels, whether productive assets or stores, are differentially vulnerable. Finally, they show how households may call on claims on different sources, whether people living locally, relatives living in town, or the state, church or NGOs supplying aid, in order to cope.

Case 1 Mr M. is a widower and lives alone. He has limited means to cope with the drought. When he runs out of food he borrows maize meal from relatives. On occasions relatives living nearby invite him to eat as they know he has little food. Otherwise he relies on government food aid through the food-for-work programme. He received a bucket of maize in April and June from the programme. This can last a long time and from April it was complemented by relish (vegetables and tomatoes) grown in a small garden.

Case 2 Most of Mrs M.'s support comes from government aid. Without this, she says, things would be really bad, as no one in the family has any employment, except one daughter who is a prostitute in Masvingo. She manages to send some money home to her mother, but it is only Z$20 or so and then only once every few months. Prostitution, she explains, no longer pays because of the fear of AIDS. Food-for-work maize is thus the key to survival and Mrs M. works on the programme almost daily. In the early part of the year, the whole family used to go to the river following the completion of food-for-work duties in order to pan for gold. But they found the work hard and sometimes the panning did not yield anything. They abandoned the activity in favour of government programmes in the second part of the drought.

Case 3 During the drought, Mr and Mrs R. found it difficult at times to secure enough food. The most important source of income was through the sale of goats. In the early part of the year they sold one goat each month, each one raising between Z$45 and Z$55. Beer brewing was also an important activity in the early part of the year. For instance, Mrs R. brewed one bag of pearl millet *(mhunga)* in March and realised Z$110. These activities depleted the goat flock and grain store to zero. Mr and Mrs R. live alone and receive an occasional amount from their daughter who is working in Zvishavane, but this is very irregular and only sufficient to buy the odd tin of maize. In the latter part of the year Mrs R. started vegetable production. However, because of late planting there were only very limited sales. No further remittances were received and they became increasingly reliant on government food relief.

Case 4 Mr D. is a not a long-term resident of the area as he came from the Charumbira area in another part of Chivi. He consequently does not have any relatives to assist him during the drought. This presents a major problem, and he found it difficult to feed his family of twelve. In February 1992 he decided to go gold panning at the Runde river. He comments: 'This at least provides some income. If you find a good place to pan, then you can get around Z$50 in two days.' In addition, he and his family were heavily reliant on government food aid. But the intermittent supply of food caused Mr D. some serious problems, as he could not rely on this source. Later in the year he abandoned gold panning as a result of low prices, and resorted to selling his livestock capital. This was a big loss as he was forced to sell three of his five donkeys during April and May in order to get food. Each donkey provided between Z$150 and Z$170, all of which went towards the purchase of maize meal. In addition, he sold one of his remaining goats at Z$40 in June in order to buy food.

Case 5 Mr T. worked at Hippo Valley Estates at Triangle. During early 1992 he was working full-time and earned sufficient money there to support his family. At this time the whole family was staying together at Hippo Valley and the home in Chivi was being looked after by relatives. The job income was supplemented by the sale of goats and by beer brewing at home. However, later in the year, because of the effect of the drought on the estates, Mr T. was only working two weeks in the month and getting only Z$60 per month. Obtaining food was now a problem. The parents failed to pay school fees and the children ceased to attend school. On occasions the family went without maize meal porridge (*sadza*) for days. Mr and Mrs T. decided it would be best to move back to Chivi, as staying away from home was very difficult. In July Mrs T. returned home to sell two of their remaining goats. This money was used to pay for maize meal and to transport the family and their belongings back to Chivi.

Case 6 Mrs M. and her family concentrated on different activities in order to survive the drought. Mrs M. made clay pots, baskets and mats. These were sold to local people, either for cash or in exchange for grain. Their daughter was employed under the government food-for-work scheme for the whole year. One son worked at least four days a week at the river where he panned for gold, selling it at Z$50–60 per gram. On occasions he was assisted by other sisters when they were free from other commitments. These income sources were supplemented by occasional remittances from sons working in Chipinge and Chiredzi. These sons assisted their mother by inviting some of their brothers and sisters to stay, thus relieving her of the burden of finding food for them at home.

Case 7 Mr Z. relied on his own grain stores until April 1992. This meant that he was in a much better position than many of his neighbours who had long run out of food. However, it was necessary to supplement this with cash from other sources. Both Mr and Mrs Z. went gold panning in February for two or three days in the week. This was enough to get 1 gram of gold, which at that time sold for Z$50. Later in the year they abandoned gold panning because of the dropping prices for gold and the incredibly hard work involved. In addition, Mrs Z. organised a vegetable trading business which continued throughout the year. This involved buying vegetables from Masvingo and selling them locally. This was done during the weekends, when the daughters earned around Z$15 per day. Mr Z. had hoped he would get employment through building, but with the exception of receiving Z$80 for the building of a toilet, he was unlucky as no one in the area had any surplus cash to invest in building projects. Instead, he was forced to work at the food-for-work programme for most of the year, carrying stones to fill gullies; this at least provided something.

Case 8 Because of the severity of the drought in Chivi, at the end of 1991 Mr S. took his chidren to Gweru to live with him. From that time Mrs S. remained at home relying on money sent from Gweru and money raised from the sale of crochet work to traders travelling to Botswana and South Africa. From May 1992 Mrs S. also migrated to Gweru, leaving only two boys who are relatives at the home. The boys survive in part off the money sent by Mr S., but also by selling the occasional goat and working on the food-for-work programme.

Case 9 Mr D. is a soldier in the Zimbabwe National Army and most of the support to his family came from his salary. Around Z$300 each month is sent to his wife at home. This money was used to buy maize meal and other household articles. Mrs D. supplemented this money by working hard at home. She kept broilers which she sold at Z$13 each and eggs at 40c. In addition, Mrs D. has a very productive garden at her homestead. Using piped water she grew tomatoes, onions, rape and carrots. She is always getting cash from the sale of vegetables as most people in the vicinity do not have gardens.

Case 10 Income-generating activities at home combined with remittance incomes to make the conditions at Mr H.'s home quite satisfactory, despite the terrible drought. Home activities included poultry production, livestock selling (cattle and goats), beer brewing, vegetable production and the selling of skins and hides. All this was supplemented by food received from the government, as the father attended the food-for-work programme. The activities changed during different phases of the drought. Livestock were sold extensively early in the year, but, as the condition of the animals worsened, the CSC was unwilling to purchase animals presented for sale. Mr H. thought it better to slaughter the animals and eat the meat. Beer brewing, carried out by Mrs H., was equally important early in the drought, but as the grain ran out brewing was no longer possible. These activities were replaced by vegetable production and an increased flow of remittances from Mr H.'s son and daughter, who are teachers in Ngundu and Bulawayo respectively. Poultry keeping was a continuous source of income throughout the drought, providing regular cash for the purchase of maize meal, groceries or stock feed.

The case studies show how increasing the diversity of coping strategies by widening the portfolio of income-earning activities is an important way of offsetting risk and reducing vulnerability. Successful coping is thus often the result of exploiting a range of livelihoods. Most households in the sample had around three sources of income during the drought, although the number ranged from one to seven. The number of activities decreased in the second part of the drought as opportunities became more constrained. Wealthier households had significantly more activities throughout the drought, in part because their larger household sizes meant there was a greater number of people in the home available for a variety of different activities. Larger households generally had significantly higher numbers of activities. The largest portfolio of activities was to be found in the Takavarasha area, this being significantly greater than those in the other two areas in both drought periods. Chivi central had the lowest number of activities in both periods. The age and sex of the household head did not significantly affect the number of activities employed, although the type of activities was certainly influenced.

The mix of different activities changed over time, as different individuals within a household tried out different activities to exploit different options. This dynamic element is a particularly important characteristic of how people compose their livelihoods in a drought setting. Coping may occur in a series of phases, with increasing commitments of domestic resources made (Campbell, 1990; Frankenberger, 1993). Strategies employed later in a drought thus tend to be less reversible, often involving the disposal of productive assets or, at the most extreme, complete abandonment of the area (Maxwell and Frankenburger, 1992).

As the case studies illustrate, different individuals within a household may be involved in different activities at any one time. Women's cash incomes tend to have a different pattern of expenditure to men's. In the case of women, the small amounts of cash raised are usually spent on family grocery items and clothes rather than on the purchase of maize meal. On occasions, women are able to purchase assets such as goats; these are sometimes kept at the marital home, but are often sequestered at the woman's parents' *kraal*. Basic food provisioning is generally the responsibility of the husband. However, these intra-household relations changed in the drought. There was little opportunity for the purchase of 'luxuries' among most households (clothes, shoes etc.) and certainly no opportunity for accumulating assets. Nearly all household income was diverted to food provisioning, although school fees remained an important preoccupation.

How vulnerable are rural livelihooods?

The case studies illustrate the diversity of coping strategies employed, both within and between households. But how vulnerable to drought stresses are the people of Chivi? The 1991–92 drought was perhaps the most severe shock ever experienced by the rural economy, coming at a time when local asset levels were low and the wider economy was depressed. Can livelihoods continue to be sustained in Chivi or can we expect further near-catastrophes as in 1991–92, requiring massive levels of external support from government and NGOs? In order to begin to answer these questions, it is necessary to examine what form coping strategies took in the face of massive production failure in 1991–92, asking whether livelihoods are more vulnerable today than they have been in the past, and if there are measures that can be taken to support locally based coping, in order to reduce the dependence on external aid.

It is important to understand the interactions between the various components of livelihood. A useful conceptual model for understanding the relationships between local production, off-farm income sources and exchange entitlements is provided by Jeremy Swift (1989), which extends the exchange entitlements analysis of Amarthya Sen (Sen, 1981; Drèze and Sen, 1990). This model charts the options open to households in

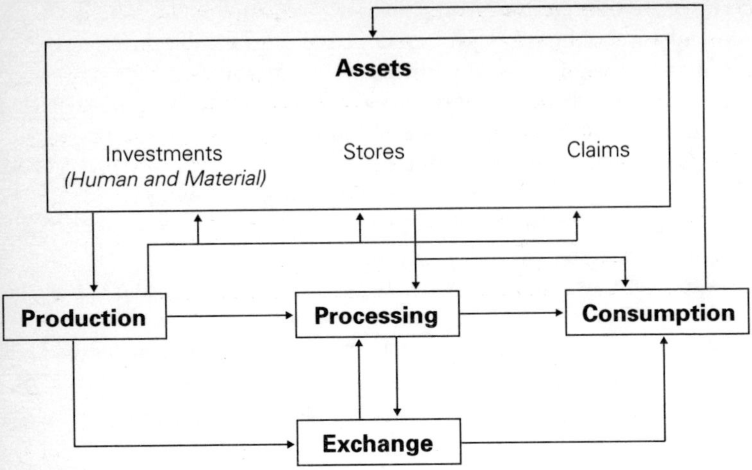

Figure 10.2 Livelihoods and vulnerability: a model adapted from Swift (1989)

providing food in the face of production failure. In the Zimbabwean context it reveals a great diversity of coping strategies for dealing with vulnerability in food supply. The following sections discuss the pattern of drought response during 1991–92 in relation to this model of livelihood vulnerability.

Production, storage and consumption

A single year of drought should not cause calamity if grain storage is sufficient to tide people over. In the past, grains (largely millets and sorghum) were stored for up to ten years, and many people had large amounts in their granaries sufficient for their own needs and for selling on to others. Today storage levels in most parts of Chivi are low. Output levels in the years leading up to the drought were minimal, with an average of only 1,416kg of all grain types being produced per household in the 1988–89 and 1989–90 seasons. Production was highly skewed, with some households producing close to zero and others producing over 8,000kg. Poorer households (non-draught owners) produced on average 861kg while richer households (draught owners) produced 2,301kg. Storage levels were equally varied across households. The average levels per household by crop are shown in Table 10.4 for the years following the 1988, 1989, 1990 and 1993 harvests.

The grain retentions were insufficient to meet consumption demands. A simple food balance calculation gives an indication of the level of food security each year. If grain consumption (estimated at 200kg a year per head) and storage losses (estimated at 10%) are removed from the stored

Table 10.4 Retention (production minus sales) of crops (kg and SE)

Crop	1988		1989		1990		1993	
Maize	955.8	(69.6)	717.4	(64.9)	757.5	(66.1)	1,156.4	(99.1)
Pearl millet	392.9	(57.8)	214.7	(34.2)	221.8	(35.4)	387.04	(56.64)
Sorghum	126.3	(22.4)	63.7	(11.8)	51.9	(15.3)	178.2	(21.2)
Finger millet	101.5	(17.7)	64.9	(15.3)	932.2	(102.6)	251.34	(27.14)
Groundnuts	191.2	(22.4)	139.2	(17.7)	213.6	(17.7)	81.42	(16.5)
Sunflowers	22.4	(8.3)	17.7	(4.7)	24.8	(7.1)	nd	

levels of grain (maize, pearl and finger millet and sorghum), then a food balance level is derived. Average levels are shown in Table 10.5 for each year leading up to and immediately following the drought. In all years nearly half the population is in food deficit. This means that even in non-drought years households must find other sources of income in order to purchase food. In contrast to the past, household stores are insufficient. Although there are always some households with large stores, ranging from two to ten tonnes, these may not be large enough to supply the rest of the population, even if they had the resources to buy the grain. Ngundu area shows a level of food deficit that is significantly higher than the other two areas. This is because of the greater reliance on maize and higher sales levels in Ngundu. Instead of relying on millets and local stores, as is more common in Takavarasha, the area with the highest average storage level, Ngundu farmers prefer to sell maize and rely on the cash received to purchase food. The poor storage properties of maize in comparison to millets and the better access to markets in Ngundu makes this strategy appropriate; however, it does open farmers in Ngundu to different types of risk, including market failure and price changes (Chapter 5).

During the 1991–92 drought, few households had stored grain. There had not been a big harvest in Chivi since 1985 and most households with stored millet had stored grain from the 1988 harvest and a little from the

Table 10.5 Food balance estimates, 1988–93

	1993	1990	1989	1988
Average (SE) kg	305.4 (132.3)	308.2 (149.9)	−502.9 (78.1)	−43.2 (101.2)
Minimum	−4,014	−3,113	−4,961	−3,589
Maximum	+7,320	+10,094	+2,342	+3,685
% of population in deficit	47	55	79	63
Average kg Chivi	349	767	−508	198
Average kg Ngundu	82	−469	−789	−574
Average kg Takavarasha	498	617	−190	249

1989 and 1990 harvests. Thitrteen % of households had some grain stored in the first part of 1992 and they continued to eat from these stores. Only two farmers had any maize; the rest stored only millet and a little sorghum. However, these stores were not, for the most part, large, and by the second half of the drought only three households had any grain stores left, apart from small seed stores. Those with higher asset levels were significantly more likely to have grain stores in the first part of the drought. In the second part of the drought most of these stores were eaten and only 1.2% of richer households had any stores, while the poorer households had maintained theirs. In both periods, female-headed households were more likely to be without grain stores. Those with remittance incomes were significantly more likely to have stores in the first period, presumably because, with alternative income sources, they had not eaten into them significantly. However, by the second period of the drought the percentage of remittance-receiving households with stores had dropped to only 3.5%, while the non-remittance-earners had nothing left at all. The store holders in the first period were older householders with larger household sizes. As other forms of income failed, these stores got quickly consumed, due to the large number of mouths to feed, leaving most people in the same position by the latter period.

Since most households in nearly all years are net food purchasers, food marketing and supply policy is a key issue (Chisvo *et al.*, 1991). Chapter 3 has already highlighted the importance of the rural grain trade and the opportunities opened up with the liberalisation of grain markets. In order for households in food deficit to provision themselves adequately, access to and efficient operation of markets is key. In periods of drought such markets come under particularly acute stress as supply dries up and prices escalate. As we have seen, the role of government food aid, either as drought relief or as food-for-work, may become important, although it is vital that such interventions do not disrupt other forms of provisioning and exchange.

This pattern of food insecurity is typical of most dryland communal areas in Zimbabwe (Stanning, 1989; Christensen and Stack, 1992), where structural food insecurity appears to plague a majority of the population. This is why it is of particular importance in the Zimbabwean context to look beyond the production–storage–consumption component of livelihoods to the role of other assets, investments, markets and claims.

Commodity and labour exchange

Exchange entitlements have been highlighted in many discussions of famine and coping strategies since Sen's classic work (Sen, 1981; Drèze and Sen, 1989; Swift, 1989). Exchanges of either commodities or labour offer important opportunities for raising income when farm production has failed. Commodity exchanges in Chivi included selling beer, vegetable vending, livestock sales, selling gold, collection and sale of tree pods and trading of clothes or craftwork. Labour exchanges included building, piecework and prostitution.

The success of any of these strategies depended on the supply levels of the commodity or labour, the demand for the good or service and the functioning of the market. All these elements are subject to risk and uncertainty. In some cases the supply of commodities to sell was dependent on the asset or storage levels of the household, in other cases it depended on the availability of other forms of capital to set up a trading operation. For instance, it was only those with significant livestock holdings or large stores of grain who were able to sell animals or brew beer for sale. Equally, it was only those with some capital base who were able to establish trading operations, selling second-hand clothes from South Africa or vending vegetables from Masvingo. Labour availability and skill are also critical factors; for instance only adult men were employed for piecework by the District Development Fund, and only people with recognised skills in building would be hired.

The demand for goods and services was highly variable during the drought. Those exchanges that were reliant on income from outside the rural economy fared best. For instance, schoolteachers and civil servants continued to receive salaries throughout the drought and their demand for poultry or goat meat remained steady, if small. Similarly, building contracts from schools or public institutions proved much more reliable than from local people, who were not in a position to pay. Access to such markets was thus a critical aspect of survival. This access was easier for those living near the business centres where government offices are sited and where civil servants live. Proximity to transport routes in order to capture trade from people travelling on buses or tourists driving along the main roads was also key for those selling certain commodities. For this reason, the people in Ngundu were particularly fortunate. In addition, seeking access through contacts and networks was also key. Being trusted as someone who offers a good deal, who provides a regular service and offers good quality for the money paid is often critical in a competitive marketplace. Networks based on friendships, kinship links and past contacts were used to the full in securing exchange entitlements during the drought.

Well-functioning markets offer a reliable source of income if supply and demand conditions are right. Even if competition is intense, traders know what to expect. However, with external interference all sorts of uncertainties are introduced. The illegal nature of certain coping strategies, and government restrictions on trading, through licensing and regulation, affected patterns of exchange. For instance, the government's attempt to stop gold panning and arrest gold dealers introduced major disruptions. Instead of panning during the day, people were forced to pan at night;

rather than dealers coming to the sites directly and exchanging with limited transaction costs, intermediaries arrived in order to protect the main dealers from the police. The consequence was price rises, and uncertainties were introduced into the market. The same applied to the enforcement of traders' licensing requirements for clothes and vegetable selling. Attempts to raise revenues by the local council acted to cut the margins of traders to minimal levels. Although the authorities relaxed the restrictions during the drought, recognising that illegal trading was critical to people's survival, they did not formally abandon restrictions and the threat of being apprehended and being fined remained. This put off some, and added anxieties for others.

The purchasing power of money realised through such exchanges is another critical factor that affects the ability of people to cope. For most of the drought period, except for a few months in early 1993, maize meal was available in the shops in Chivi. However, the price shot up. Inflation during this period was running at over 40%, and the local price of a bag of maize meal almost doubled. Changes in the macro-economy, combined with the impacts of drought, caused massive price hikes, hitting the poorer consumers hardest. As most people in Chivi are net consumers of grain in most years, food prices are as important to rural residents as they are to the urban population. But if prices paid for labour or commodities in local markets do not keep pace with price rises elsewhere in the country, then entitlements are undercut. This certainly happened during the 1991–92 drought, when many were unable to afford the high cost of maize meal being sold commercially.

Claims and assistance

When a household's own immediate means of sustaining livelihoods fail through production failure, asset disposal or lack of savings or stores (Figure 10.1), then people must turn to other sources of support and draw upon claims from outside. Such linkages are key aspects of normal economic life, part of the 'moral economy' of the rural areas (Scott, 1976; Watts, 1989). In periods of drought they become even more significant. State assistance through food relief and food-for-work programmes became increasingly important as the drought progressed. Officially, claims on the state were only available to those without immediate family in full employment and rations were calculated according to family size. However, the rules were inevitably manipulated to some extent and a large proportion of the population enjoyed the benefits of food support. Although supplies were irregular, and rations were reduced, the drought relief operation was vital for many.

Local networks of support were also important, particularly for vulnerable households with limited alternatives. These took a variety of forms.

At the local level, households continued to be connected together in clusters based around labour and draught sharing (Chapter 4). These clusters, usually centred around close kin relationships, are important social structures for mutual aid. Food sharing within clusters increased during the drought; this was particularly important for children, who could get food from a range of homes. With the abandonment of agriculture during the 1991–92 season, co-operative labour and draught sharing ceased and most other activities that emerged were carried out on an individual basis. But sharing of food or borrowing of money became critical for the very poor. Social networks may be drawn on in other ways. For instance, the marriage of a daughter may realise a bridewealth payment. Although daughters were not pawned in order to raise income as happened in the past (*kuzvarira*), drawing on social obligations, affirmed by marriage-related payments, can be an important source of support.

Claims on relatives living in town were perhaps the most important in terms of local livelihoods. In many instances these claims were a key source of food for survival. However, reduced levels of real wages meant that sending remittances home was increasingly difficult. Redundancies also struck hard, especially with the large lay-offs occurring in the sugar estates around Chiredzi. This increased hardship dramatically among some households. Reduced remittance flows lowered the circulation of money in the rural areas. By mid-drought, teachers and a few other government civil servants resident in the rural areas were the only sources of potential cash. Migration to urban workplaces was also a strategy employed by a number of households. In some cases children were sent to relatives in town for periods during the drought. In other cases the whole family left to go and stay in town, usually with the working husband. However, because of the tight economic situation for most low-income wage earners, supporting a family in town proved difficult and some families returned home to continue with other activities.

Drought recovery

Recovery from drought is a slow and painful process. With livestock assets wiped out, debts accumulated and grain stores empty, many people in Chivi were in a bad way as the rainy season of 1992–93 approached. The success of the 1992–93 harvest was thus vital. The prospects of a further year on government food relief was alarming many. The following sections discuss the various elements of drought recovery in the two seasons following the drought, from the period of land preparation through to harvest and the sale of crops.

With the arrival of the rains in 1992, huge efforts were invested in land preparation by hand. Lack of seed meant that people were reliant on government handouts or friends and relatives with seed stores. The lack of draught power during 1992–93 meant that most people had to rely on hand-hoeing to prepare their land (Chapter 4). Despite promises, the tractor services never materialised. District Council tractors operated in some areas, but only those who paid well in advance or had good connections benefited. Otherwise, private operators hired out tractors, but very few could afford the cost. By 1993–94 the situation had improved: cattle populations had begun to recover and 38% of households were able to use their own draught spans and another 22% were able to share or borrow. Those with access to cash, but not draught, hired local ox teams (19%) or tractors (0.75%), while the remainder (22%) continued to prepare their land by hoeing.

During 1992–93 the government, with assistance from European donors, distributed seed and fertiliser packs in Chivi at a total cost of Z$3.8m. The total cost, including distribution, at the province level was Z$43.8m (Agritex Masvingo, 1993). The packs were meant to be sufficient for 0.5ha of fertilised maize and 1ha of unfertilised millet and sorghum. Due to supply and distribution problems, not everyone received the packs on time, nor did they always contain the standard compliment of seed and fertiliser. Despite this, the supply of seed, in particular, proved vital and allowed people without cash resources to plant at least some of their land with maize or sorghum. The high costs of hybrid maize seed following the removal of subsidies (around Z$160 per 50kg at local stores in 1993 and Z$202 in 1994) encouraged many to talk of using open-pollinated varieties for the first time in decades. The free fertiliser was less used, as people are wary of using the prescribed amounts (Chapter 7). Much of the free fertiliser was sold on to those farmers who use fertiliser regularly.

The 1992–93 cropping season thus saw a large influx of new genetic material. Although the hybrid maize varieties were similar to those used prior to the drought, many small grain varieties were new to the area. Some of the government seed handouts were produced from bulked-up Indian varieties or were a mix of varieties from elsewhere in the region. Other varieties were imported from other areas through connections with relatives or friends. The mixing of this new genetic material may have undermined the survival of locally adapted landraces which were severely hit by the drought. According to farmers in Chivi, some varieties of sorghum and millet completely disappeared during the drought.

The lack of draught cattle was a major concern for farmers following drought, and cattle were the first major asset purchase made when sufficient income was raised. During 1993, there was a limited programme of restocking in Chivi sponsored by the Lutheran World Federation: 20 heifers were distributed to five different grazing schemes in the district. By 1994 a government-supported group-based credit scheme for restocking was in place and several sample households were making use of the facility. However, these schemes have had very limited impact and most people relied on purchasing replacement animals themselves. But the lack of available animals meant people were forced to buy from the commercial farms. Owners of commercial farms were able to cash in successfully on the high demand for breeding stock during the post-drought period. They set up regular markets at various sites in Chivi where they would sell heifers or exchange them for old oxen. Alternatively, farmers organised themselves in groups, hiring their own transport, and went direct to commercial farms which were known to have animals for sale. Some local businessmen with transport also profited from this trade, bringing heifers into the area for sale. The heifers were often exotic breeds (Herefords, Sussex) and ill-suited to the harsh environments of Chivi. The introduction of exotic breeds in Chivi is, of course, not new (Chapter 2), but experience tells us that indigenous breeds are far more successful at adapting to drought conditions than exotic breeds, and any undermining of this adaptation through the introduction of new genetic material may have negative impacts on the survival capacity of herds in the longer term.

The rapid recovery of grass cover following the rains of 1992–93 was remarkable. Grass species that had not been seen for years reappeared, germinating from seed that had for years lain dormant in the hardened soil. Tall grass dominated the landscape, as reduced livestock populations ensured that little was consumed. Those livestock that did remain alive prospered. Natural growth of the cattle population was rapid. Nearly every fertile adult cow reconceived and gave birth during 1992–93, an illustration of the impressive physiological responsiveness of indigenous stock. The result was that people were able to benefit from milk (both fresh and soured), a luxury not seen for years. While the grass recovery was spectacular, transforming the environment from a barren wasteland to lush, green pasture, the recovery of other components of the ecosystem was less consistent. In the year following the drought everyone commented on the lack of birds, as most non-migratory species had perished in the drought. During 1994 there was a major explosion of the rodent population, which caused havoc to growing crops, grain stores and anything edible in people's homes. No one knew the reason for this plague, although some speculated that the eradication of snakes during the drought had caused an imbalance in predator and prey populations.

Expenditure and investment following the harvest

The 1993 harvest proved to be, by and large, a bumper one (Chapter 4), with most people reaping sufficient crops to sell. Crop sales during 1993 occurred in a piecemeal fashion, with people selling to private traders in exchange for much-needed goods in the early period, and only later selling for cash at GMB depots or to traders (Chapter 3). This cash was vital for the recovery process. Much of the money realised from the sale of crops

Table 10.6 Patterns of expenditure in 6 months following the 1993 harvest

Item of expenditure	% of households
School fees	45.3
Groceries	34.9
Blankets and clothing	29.0
Agricultural inputs (seed etc.)	18.6
Cooking utensils/household items	18.6
School uniforms	11.6
Chickens	15.1
Goats	9.3
Loan repayment	5.8
Labour hire	5.8
Banked (POSB)	5.8
Plough/agricultural implements	4.6
Beer party	3.5
Oxen	3.5
Building	3.5
Bridewealth	3.5
Scotch cart	2.3
Donkey	1.2
Funeral	1.2
Transport hire	1.2
Grinding mill	1.2

was spent on immediate consumption needs, including food, clothes, school uniforms and vital groceries. Other money was spent on paying off debts with friends and relatives, schools and storekeepers. Only when these obligations had been met did people contemplate spending money on new investments. Material investments included the rebuilding of cattle herds, and the purchase of furniture, building materials or agricultural equipment. Longer-term investments included ensuring that children could return to school and take their exams. Other expenditures included investments in social relationships through the payment of bridewealth costs.

Access to crop incomes and control over expenditure within households are extremely varied. In most cases where the husband is resident, he will take formal control of the money raised, especially when crop incomes are received in large lumps through the marketing board or from bulk sales to traders. However, if the husband is absent, women have a greater degree of financial autonomy. This is also the case when small transactions are made. Since women dominate the grain barter and exchange markets which have expanded over the past few years (Chapter 3), they have greater control over crop incomes than in the recent past.

Because of the levels of indebtedness that many people had reached following the drought, few could contemplate major productive investments. Most people faced major difficulties in raising sufficient cash to purchase cattle, which were now priced at exorbitant levels. During 1994 only 3.5% of households in the Chivi sample purchased cattle. Each oxen purchased averaged Z$1,500, equivalent to around ten bags of maize on the local market. It was only those households who could supplement the income received from their harvest with other sources, notably remittances, that were able to purchase animals.

Adding value to the crop harvest and ensuring that money raised is saved effectively are critical elements of people's drought recovery strategy. One of the surest ways of adding value to harvested crops was the brewing of beer. Although religious prohibitions prevented some people from getting involved, 37% of households brewed regularly during 1993 and 50% during 1994. Sometimes beer brewing is combined with a savings mechanism (Chapter 3), allowing people to raise relatively large cash sums. Otherwise, simple rotating savings systems are used for the same end. Following the harvest in 1993, many savings clubs were established as mechanisms for recycling the benefits of harvest sales and beer brewing. During 1994 around 25% of households were involved in savings clubs – involving beer parties (*baroni*) and rotating savings (*kukandirana*). These allowed people to make expenditures involving lump sums.

Social networks and changing vulnerability

During the drought, social networks came under high levels of strain as increasingly urgent claims were made. Sometimes this resulted in the fracturing of such relationships with accusations and insults flying. As tensions rose during the cropping season of 1992–93, with the uncertainties over the harvest dominating people's minds, the number of accusations of witchcraft rose as people blamed misfortune in their cropping enterprise on others who were jealous, malicious or evil. During 1994, taking advantage of this discontent and growing rifts in the community, a number of prophets arrived in the area claiming to be able to resolve conflicts. The prophet Elisha of the *Matenga Azarurwa* sect offered a mix of Christian and traditional solutions to the people of the Takavarasha area, including all-night prayer services, herbal treatments for the afflicted, and traditional medicines and appeasements to ancestral spirits.

In spite of these tensions, more often than not social networks remained intact and once again became important during the cropping seasons of 1992–93 and 1993–94 (Chapter 4). However, with the limited availability of draught power in 1992–93, the extended draught sharing and cattle loaning networks of the past could not reform. Instead, much tighter relationships emerged around those who still had draught animals. As in the past, such networks were usually based around lineage clusters, but involved much more individual negotiation than in previous years. This increasing individualisation of production – or at least retraction of the clusters to smaller groups – meant that those outside such networks became even more vulnerable. By the 1993–94 and 1994–95 seasons there was a return to more group-based work and sharing. Newly purchased livestock were widely shared through networks; co-operative work parties (*humwe*) were very noticeable during land preparation and weeding periods. The drought had not permanently undermined the cluster-based system of production; instead a flexible and responsive series of networks expand or contract depending on the situation.

In contrast to droughts in the past, most people suffered during the 1991–92 period; some lost more than others, but no one gained in the way the *hurudza* (agricultural entrepreneurs) had once done. Droughts today produce, it seems, only losers. However, the impacts are felt differentially, making recovery more difficult for some than others. Under the harsh economic conditions of the 1990s, it is particularly hard for those who must regularly purchase increasingly expensive foodstuffs without support from off-farm income sources. Independent, younger men and unmarried women who are unable to get work, and so unable to establish themselves as farmers, are particularly hard hit, as are older people who do not produce and store enough food for themselves and whose asset base has been depleted by the sequence of droughts of the past decade and who do not have sons or daughters who regularly send remittances home.

Conclusion

The drought of 1991–92 could easily have resulted in calamity in the communal areas. The implications have provoked discussions in the highest of policy circles. So what was so different about the 1991–92 drought? What patterns of coping have changed over time that have affected people's ability to survive? In many respects the drought of 1991–92 was very similar to previous droughts: people had to rely on grain stores and exchange (of livestock and other goods) to provision themselves with food; remittance income from relatives in town were key to survival; movement of people and animals was an important response to local deficit; wild foods were extensively eaten as a supplement; and people relied on external aid. But there were significant differences in the details of these responses. These relate to the scale and severity of the drought and to significant changes in the wider economy and its impact on the rural areas.

As production has become more constrained, due to declining field areas and reduced land quality, and local storage levels have become more limited, due to shifts in cropping patterns and greater crop sales, farmers in Chivi have become increasingly reliant on off-farm income sources, particularly during drought. In examining drought response policies, the role of local markets, the importance of removing burdening restrictions and the significance of trade and exchange should not be underestimated. Policies that ensure that exchange entitlements can be realised are vital.

Contrary to Michael Bratton's claim (1987: 239) that 'the family is in decline as an institution of social insurance against hardship in Zimbabwe', it appears that social networks, especially those based on the extended family, remain central to coping strategies in Chivi. Access to remittances, opportunities for food sharing and other linkages are key to survival strategies. Although sharing relationships centred on agricultural production are abandoned during drought and in the period of recovery when draught power is scarce, other forms of relationship and new types of network arise. With the stresses of drought and food scarcity, relationships may be strained, but they are nevertheless important. As Michael Watts notes (1989: 262) such patterns of 'moral economy and subsistence security are embedded in the wider system of economic and political relations'. Thus the pressures of macro-economic reform were being felt particularly acutely during the 1991–92 drought, with high inflation resulting in reduced buying power of the money received from trading, piecework or remittances.

External support – from the state, local networks or rural–urban connections – will almost certainly remain key in sustaining livelihoods in Chivi. The range of local coping mechanisms is clearly inadequate during major calamities such as the 1991–92 drought. The reduction in people's asset levels over time has increased vulnerability and added to poverty. Nevertheless, experience in Chivi during this period demonstrates the importance of coping strategies: how the range of activities may be focused or diverse; how they change over time in response to evolving circumstances; how divisions of labour and responsibilities within households are key to survival; and how coping strategies shift during different phases of a drought. A more complete understanding of local responses to risk in drought conditions is clearly essential if more effective drought relief, mitigation and proofing strategies are to be designed. Appropriate policies for coping with drought must therefore take the dynamics of local response into account.

Notes

1. This section is based on information from national and regional food security bulletins, newspaper articles and interviews with officials of the national and regional early warning units, the Department of Social Welfare, and the Economics and Marketing branch of the Ministry of Agriculture.

2. Sample households were grouped by various criteria and statistical comparisons were made (full details are contained in FSRU/IIED, 1994). The groupings include: draught access as a broader wealth proxy; remittance access; household

size differences compare households above and below mean household size (7); age differences compare households above and below the mean age of household head (aged 49), and examine very young and very old households (aged 23–30 and 70–83); gender differences compare those households with male and female household heads (female household heads include widows, divorcees and households where the husband is employed full-time outside the area); area differences compare the different strategies employed by households in the three research areas – Chivi central, Takavarasha and Ngundu; time differences compare the strategies seen among sample households in the first part of 1992 (approximately February to May) and the second part of the year (approximately July to November).

CHAPTER ELEVEN

Cattle and drought: impact, response and recovery

This chapter contrasts three droughts that have affected cattle populations in southern Zimbabwe in the past decade. The chapter focuses on the impacts of prolonged below-average rainfall on cattle populations, exploring the impacts on herds in terms of mortality levels and the differential responses of herders in terms of supplementary feeding, herd movement and destocking sales. The three drought periods under scrutiny (1982–84, 1987 and 1991–92) have both similarities and differences. In each case, the peak impact on livestock populations followed a year or two of rainfall significantly below the average (Chapter 10). Although some rain fell in each year, the amounts were insufficient to allow grass growth. The major droughts of the period since Independence are characterised by two or more years when rainfall was 25% of more below the mean. For Chivi and surrounding areas, this coincided with the periods between 1982 and 1984 and 1991 and 1992. The only other season where significant rainfall deficits were felt was in 1986–87. This represented a single season's deficit and so differs in important respects from the other two drought periods.

Population trajectories: collapse and recovery

The population trajectory of cattle populations in the communal areas shows a pattern of 'boom and bust'. The non-equilibrium nature of dryland environments means that during periods of good rainfall cattle populations build up, with birth rates increasing and death rates decreasing as a result of high levels of available fodder. During drought periods, the populations collapse as fodder availability drops off (Behnke *et al.*, 1993). This pattern of population dynamics means that cattle populations in the dry communal areas only rarely reach a stable ecological carrying capacity level where births and immigration equal deaths and emigration. During the past 60 years, cattle populations in Chivi and surrounding areas have only reached such levels for brief periods, such as during the mid-1970s, when an extended period of good rainfall meant that populations increased significantly before crashing again (Chapter 2). However, in most periods, due to a combination of drought, disease and government interventions, cattle population densities have been lower than ecological carrying capacity

(Scoones, 1993). Cattle population levels are shown for two dip tank populations in nearby Mazvihwa communal area between 1981 and 1994. Figure 11.1 shows both populations collapsing during the 1982–84 drought. This was followed by a period of recovery until 1987 when another drought period cut back populations again. From 1989 populations again recovered, almost back to pre-1982 levels, until 1991 when drought hit again. A slow period of recovery began in 1993.

Differences in patterns of collapse and recovery between sites are dependent on a range of factors. These include ecological conditions, with sandy soil savanna areas showing more resilience to drought shocks, but slower recovery, than clay soil savanna areas (Scoones, 1990). This is due to the growth patterns of the grass species and the availability of browse in the different savanna types. Access to particular types of grazing resource is also key. Certain grazing resources, notably lower-lying patches such as riverine strips or *dambo*s are often 'key resources' in dryland grazing systems (Scoones, 1992c; 1995b). Movement to such areas is often critical to the survival of herds. These ecological factors combine with social and economic factors, such as availability of herding labour, distance from markets and the existence of sharing and loaning networks.

Population dynamics

The overall population trajectory described above is made up of the interaction of births, deaths, slaughters and sales, as well as of movements

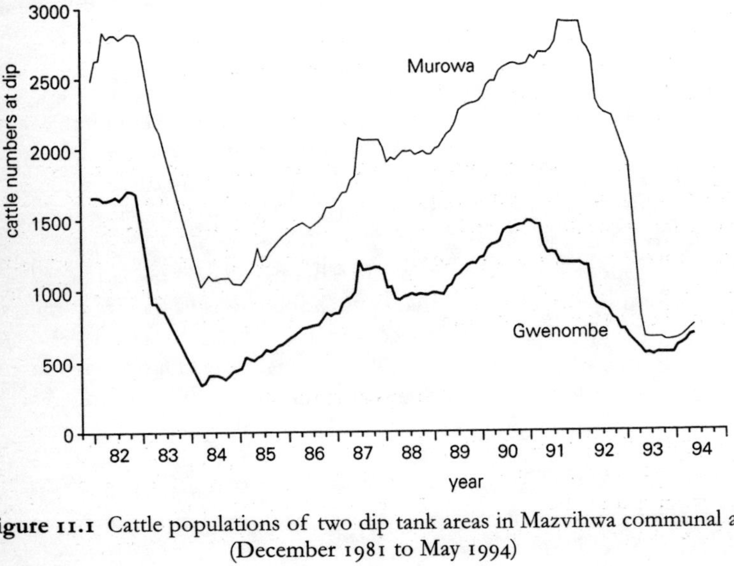

Figure 11.1 Cattle populations of two dip tank areas in Mazvihwa communal area (December 1981 to May 1994)

and exchanges in and out of the area. These are recorded on a weekly basis in dip registers and compiled in monthly statistics by the Veterinary department.[1] Table 11.1 shows how these population parameters changed over the period from 1983–84 to 1993–94 on an annual basis (October–September). The data show the high variability in population parameters over time, with death rates rising during the drought periods and birth rates increasing during recovery phases. Sales and slaughters are generally at a low level, as the economic returns from cattle are higher when they are alive (Scoones, 1992b). However, sales and slaughters do rise during drought when animals cannot be kept alive or immediate household income needs cannot be met.

Table 11.1 Births, deaths, slaughters and sales in all dips, Mazvihwa communal area (as percentages of total cattle census in October)

Years	Deaths	Births	Sales	Slaughters
1983–84	39.20	0.97	13.15	8.24
1984–85	0.28	18.11	0.75	2.64
1985–86	0.64	22.87	1.13	2.09
1986–87	0.54	16.56	3.16	2.42
1987–88	11.83	6.71	0.92	1.30
1988–89	0.48	23.51	2.26	2.56
1989–90	0.43	16.82	1.70	2.29
1990–91	0.83	12.74	5.45	3.65
1991–92	21.91	1.55	2.01	0.73
1992–93	19.83	0.08	1.39	0.94
1993–94	0.05	12.80	1.26	1.28

Note: Years relate to the period between October–September, except for 1993–94, which is between October 1993 and May 1994

In all three droughts broadly similar seasonal patterns are observed. Birth rates drop off dramatically to practically zero prior to the onset of significant mortality. Mortalities start slowly but then rapidly accelerate. Peak mortality periods are during the onset of the 'rains' (November to December), late 'rainy' season following mid-season drought (February) and in the middle to late dry season (June–September).

Survival rates

The aggregate data described above give no indication of how mortality affects different age and sex categories of cattle. This has, of course, important implications for the dynamics of recovery of the population as a whole. Table 11.2 looks at survival rates (% of animals alive at the end

Table 11.2 Survival of cattle by age and sex category in three droughts

Cattle type	Survival (%) 1982–84	Survival (%) 1987	Survival (%) 1991–92
Bulls	20.0	90.6	34.0
Oxen	30.9	96.0	33.6
Cows	15.7	71.3	26.9
Heifers	32.7	76.3	76.9
Male Calf	24.6	81.4	37.5
Female Calf	24.5	58.3	41.2

Note: Calves were defined as animals up to weaning age and heifers as female animals aged between weaning and reproduction

Table 11.3 Herd composition in the Chivi sample, before and after the 1991–92 drought (%)

Cattle type	Pre-drought (N = 583)	Post-drought (N = 247)
Bulls	8.1	6.5
Oxen	22.5	17.8
Cows	34.5	21.9
Steers	5.7	8.1
Heifers	20.8	37.7
Male Calves	2.7	2.4
Female Calves	5.8	5.7

of drought) for the three main drought periods over the last decade. For 1982–84 and 1987, data are derived from Mazvihwa (Scoons, 1990) and for 1991–92, data are derived from the Chivi sample.

In each case, cows had lower survival rates than any other category, with the exception of female calves in 1987. Mortalities were especially high among pregnant cows or cows with calves. With their resources drained, many could not feed sufficiently to maintain body weights. This was despite selective supplementary feeding strategies carried out by a number of farmers. Heifers seemed to fare relatively well; their smaller body mass required less food intake for maintenance and their greater agility meant they were able to forage in more inaccessible sites. Oxen and bulls (with the exception of 1982–84) also survived reasonably well. They were usually left unkraaled and were allowed to forage freely for much of the drought period. As long as they were not used for ploughing or transport, they also had larger body reserves to draw on than other animals. Calf mortality was very varied. In some cases, calves were kept alive by supplementary feeding. But many died, especially younger ones still exclusively reliant on milk. In most cases the cow's milk completely dried up, and in many instances the cow died soon afterwards.

The differential mortality of different age and sex groups of cattle clearly has an impact on herd composition. Again, this has important implications for the recovery dynamics of the cattle population.

Causes of mortality

During 1991–92, the largest cause of mortality was death due to starvation or extreme water shortage (47.7%). A significant number of animals were slaughtered just prior to death in order to salvage some meat for local consumption or sale (30.3%). Low nutritional status is linked with disease susceptibility, and a number of animals died either directly from illness or were slaughtered because of disease (4.5%). Extensive searching for food required animals to wander far. This meant that a number were permanently lost; either they died while out foraging or they were stolen (5.7%). Foraging also had to take place in dangerous places (road edges, mountains, riverbanks) and a number of cattle died due to accidents (7.2%). Only very few animals (4.5%) were purposefully slaughtered.

The Takavarasha populations were the first to suffer appreciable mortalities. There, 13.5% of cattle died during 1991, mostly in November and December. The annual mortality rate in Takavarasha was significantly higher than in either Chivi or Ngundu, where 1991 death rates were 4.1% and 1.8% respectively. By 1992 the impacts had shifted south to Ngundu, where 51% of the cattle population died during the year. This was significantly higher than in Takavarasha, where the remaining population was reduced by a further 15%. High mortality rates were also felt during 1992 in Chivi area, where 36% of the cattle perished by December.

Cattle slaughter rates (including the killing of nearly dead animals) were at levels above the long-term averages in Takavarasha (9%) and Ngundu (7%) during 1991. These levels were significantly higher than the 1.4% rate shown in Chivi area. In 1992 these rates rose further with all areas showing high slaughter offtake, ranging from 27% in Takavarasha to 24% in Ngundu and 20% in Chivi.

Ownership patterns

Nearly 75% of households had one or no cattle following the 1991–92 drought (Table 11.4). Many who had previously owned between five and ten cattle ended up with only one or two. The consequences for draught access were dramatic. There were different impacts in different parts of

Table 11.4 Changes in household cattle ownership (not including loaning arrangements) as a result of drought (% of total households (N) with cattle holdings of different sizes)

Household cattle ownership	Before 1982–84 N = 73	After 1982–84 N = 73	Before 1987 N = 68	After 1987 N = 68	Before 1991–92 N = 146	After 1991–92 N = 146
0	23.3	50.7	33.8	32.4	54.8	67.8
1	6.8	10.9	5.9	8.8	1.4	5.5
2	2.7	8.2	1.5	5.9	4.1	11.6
3–4	4.1	13.7	8.8	5.9	6.8	9.6
5–6	6.8	4.1	16.2	27.9	12.3	2.7
7–10	16.4	5.5	19.1	11.4	10.3	1.4
11–15	16.4	1.4	10.3	4.4	7.5	0.7
16–20	9.6	2.7	1.5	2.9	0.7	0.0
21–25	1.4	1.4	1.5	0.0	0.0	0.0
26–30	4.1	1.4	1.5	0.0	1.4	0.0
31–50	4.1	0.0	0.0	0.0	0.0	0.0
50+	4.1	0.0	0.0	0.0	0.7	0.7

Note: 1991–92 data are derived from the full Chivi sample. Other data are from nearby Mazvihwa (Scoons, 1990; 1992c).

the study area, with Ngundu seeing an additional 19% of households with no cattle at all following the drought. In Takavarasha and Chivi an additional 12.5% and 8% of households were stockless post-drought. During 1991–92 overall cattle survival was 41%. This was the case for both large and small herd owners, with no significant relationships being shown between pre-drought herd sizes and survival rates.

Co-operative draught sharing relationships

The 1991–92 drought's impact on the livestock population saw a number of significant changes in the sharing relationships between households. The lack of draught power resulted in the breaking up of long-standing co-operative draught sharing arrangements amongst kin and friends. These were replaced by an increasing individualisation of production, some degree of commercialisation (although there are very few spans for hire) and the formation of new relationships for ploughing during the 1992–93 season. However, by the 1993–94 and 1994–95 seasons, with the partial recovery of cattle populations, previous sharing networks were beginning to be re-established (Chapter 10). Box 11.1 highlights three cases, typical of many others, that illustrate the consequences of stock loss on draught-sharing relationships.

Box 11.1 Draught-sharing relationships

1. Prior to the drought, Junica and Shanduka both owned a pair of donkeys each. They would join them together to form a single span. With the death of both of Junica's donkeys and one of Shanduka's, this arrangement was no longer operable in the 1992–93 season. During this season, Junica had to work alone, cultivating the whole field by hand, while Shanduka managed to arrange a loan of donkeys from a relative in Mapuvire.

2. Before the 1992–93 drought, Matye used to provide draught power (cattle and donkeys) for a number of relatives. These included Ebson, Tariro and Stefan (Chapter 4). At first, the animals were used in rotation between different fields with the men working together to work two days on each field. Later, as the herd size increased, individual spans were loaned out. Over recent years Tariro acquired cattle and so no longer worked with his father, and only occasionally hired them out to others. Meanwhile Ebson and Stefan still relied on donkeys from Matye. But the conditions of the remaining draught animals in the 1992–93 season was so bad that Matye concentrated on his own field, with some help given to Stefan's wife who is resident in the father's compound. Ebson had to seek alternative support and found another relative from Takavarasha who loaned him a span for ploughing.

3. In 1990–91 Tariro owned a span of cattle. These were used to plough both his own and his mother's field. Unfortunately all the animals died during the drought, so at the beginning of the 1992–93 season Tariro and his mother, Zinofa Chineka, had to resort to hand hoeing. This they did together, sharing labour between their respective fields. Later on, during early February, when the surviving cattle had fully recovered and were fit, some relatives offered to plough the remaining fields for a nominal cash payment. This ploughing was used to plant two plots with sunflowers.

Economic impacts

The economic costs of drought are high. The loss of animals on the scale witnessed in 1982–84 and 1991–92 is a huge burden to be carried by an already weak rural economy. A rough calculation of economic losses resulting from drought mortalities can be made using data on the economic value of cattle in the communal areas. The value of different animals can be calculated according to their functions. Cattle provide a variety of functions in the communal areas, ranging from draught for ploughing and transport, to milk and manure production, to capital growth or sale. A number of researchers have made calculations of the value of these functions (e.g., Dankwerts, 1974; Barrett, 1992; Scoones, 1992b). Although the figures in the different calculations do not exactly coincide, the studies broadly agree that the value of cattle in the communal lands is high – much higher than conventionally acknowledged in policy analyses. This is

Table 11.5 Economic impacts of drought on a cattle herd of 100 animals

Year	Survival (%)	Economic loss from herd (Z$)	Loss of economic value (%)
1982–84	25	24,556	79
1987	80	5,875	19
1991–92	41	21,720	70

because of the multifunctional nature of cattle and because high stocking rates give high per hectare returns.

Barrett (1992) reviews a number of these studies suggesting a series of values for different functions.[2] Using the 1991 pre-drought herd composition (Table 11.3) for the Chivi herd as the starting point, the gross value of a herd of 100 animals with this herd composition comes to Z$31,174 (1991 prices). If the age- and sex-specific mortality levels found in 1982–84, 1987 and 1991–92 are imposed on this herd of 100 animals the impact on potential annual herd value is dramatic (Table 11.5). If we assume similar losses were felt across the whole of Chivi district, then the economic loss from the district herd in 1991–92 would amount to some Z$21m.[3] At a province-wide level the economic loss would amount to Z$145m. Although a certain amount would be recouped through salvage slaughters, this represents a huge loss of value from the drought.

These losses are felt over a number of years. The response time for a 50% mortality impact on a cattle population is estimated to be 5–7 years in different parts of Africa (Toulmin, 1986). Longer periods are also found, especially if the drought affects female animals in a disproportionate manner and if there is a limited potential for bringing in new breeding stock. The pattern of recovery of cattle populations in Mazvihwa communal area following the 1982–84 drought is shown in Figure 11.1. This shows a six-year recovery period, interrupted by a one-year drought. The impacts of the 1991–92 drought are likely to be felt over a period of at least six years. During this time the economic impact will decrease each year as herds grow to their former size. From a 41% survival rate a six-year recovery period represents two years of 25% growth (high reconception rates and buying-in following drought) followed by four years of 12% growth.

The point of presenting these calculations is to demonstrate that the magnitude of loss is very high. It is not the exact figures that are of interest, simply the orders of magnitude. Even if the calculations were ten times too high, the losses experienced would still be significant in terms of the impact on the local economy. These figures provide a strong argument for investment in mitigation measures in order to offset the scale of impact of drought.

However, some commentators argue that the high costs of drought loss are the price paid for high stocking rates. According to this argument, if animals were stocked at a lower, conservative stocking rate, then per animal productivity would be higher and drought losses lower. Lower stocking rates will inevitably result in higher per animal productivity (Jones and Sandland, 1974), but are less likely to result in higher productivity per unit area. The relationship between stocking density and drought mortality is complex, and evidence suggests that much drought mortality is not density-dependent (Scoones, 1993), thus weakening the argument for destocking. So, despite the costs of opportunistic stocking at high levels, the returns per unit area remains high.

If we assume an opportunistically managed population (high stocking rates, high drought losses) to follow a pattern of stable output over five years followed by a drought collapse as seen in 1991–92 (41% survival) and then a recovery of 25% over two years and 12% over the following four, then the total output value from a starting herd of 100 animals over ten years comes to Z$210,342 (assuming no inflationary component and the same value functions as used above). By contrast, a conservatively managed population might yield (generously) 20% more per animal (due to greater milk, meat, draught outputs) and might suffer no drought mortality (unlikely, see above). The output of such a population stocked at one third of the level (approximately the differential between peak communal area stocking rates and recommended commercial levels) over ten years would be Z$124,700 from 33.33 animals; about 40% less than the output of the opportunistically stocked population. In other words, according to these, admittedly rough, calculations, opportunistic stocking is a better bet over a ten-year period.

Local responses

During the droughts over the past decade, three different types of drought response have been observed. These are movement responses at different spatial scales, supplementary feeding of both locally available fodder and imported foodstuffs, and drought-induced sales and slaughters. The contrasting nature of the three drought periods under study resulted in different patterns of response and different effects on cattle survival rates. The pattern of response among Chivi herds during 1991–92 is shown in Table 11.6. This differentiates between two phases of the drought: the early period during 1991 and the late period during 1992.

Movement responses

Movement of animals from food deficit areas to food surplus areas can happen at different spatial scales. In 'normal' dry seasons or low-intensity

Table 11.6 Percentage of herd owners following particular drought mitigation practices in two periods of the 1991–92 drought (Period 1: 1991; Period 2: 1992)

Response	Period 1 (%) (N = 64)	Period 2 (%) (N = 48)
Illegal grazing	9.7	25.0
Movement out	29.0	35.4
Leasing	14.1	10.4
Commercial feed	16.1	14.6
Pods and hay	3.2	4.2
Cut-and-carry grass	12.5	4.3
Tree products	100.0	100.0
Crop residues	34.4	2.1

droughts, such as in 1987, local movement at a landscape level may help to offset drought mortality. Movement to key resource habitat patches within the landscape, such as riverbanks, drainage lines or *dambo* grazing areas, allows animals to maintain fodder intake when grass availability is poor in the topland areas (Scoones, 1995b). Such movement may involve the transfer of animals between different ecological zones. Typically this involves the movement of animals from clay soil grazing areas, where grass production collapses early in a drought, to sandy soil areas, where, under low-rainfall conditions, grass production is higher. A greater diversity of graze and browse resources is found in the sandy soil *miombo* environments of southern Zimbabwe. Movement to such areas affords the opportunities of grazing in *dambo* patches or from hillsides and of browsing from the early shoots of *miombo* trees. In all three droughts, patterns of movement of this type were recorded for cattle populations. During 1991–92 in Chivi, most early movement occurred from the largely clay soil Takavarasha plains area to the hilly zone to the east.

Local movements are facilitated by loaning arrangements between kin and through friendship networks (*kuronzera*). In all droughts, loaning increased during the drought period as herd owners tried to spread the risk of mortality by splitting herds and moving them to lower-risk areas. During 1991–92, 14% of herd owners loaned or leased animals during the early part of the drought; this number decreased later as some herds were recalled as a consequence of high mortalities being experienced at the loaning site. Indeed, the survival rates of herds that were loaned out were higher than others where no loaning took place, although not significantly so.

Larger-scale movements may also occur. These happened on a major scale during the 1982–84 drought. Once grazing resources had been depleted in the area, in both clay and sandy soil areas, Mazvihwa communal area cattle were moved to Zvishavane town and on to Runde communal area. Other animals were moved further north and southeast to vacant

Table 11.7 Movement strategies during the 1982–84 drought and the impact on cattle survival

Strategy	Nature of movement	% survival	N (herds)
A	Out of area (c. November 1982)	40.1	287 (17)
B	Out of the area in the dry season (Aug.–Oct. 1983)	22.9	402 (18)
C	No movement outside area	3.3	181 (21)

Note: Survival relates to the percentage of the starting population (N) alive at the end of the drought. The number of herds following each strategy is shown in brackets

Source: Scoones, 1992c

commercial ranches in the Shurugwi and Chiredzi areas. Grass availability in Runde communal area, Shurugwi farms and Chiredzi farms was higher than in the Mazvihwa area and such movements, especially if carried out early in the drought, increased the chances of survival (Table 11.7).

During 1991–92 such large-scale movements were not so much in evidence. This was because of the widespread nature of the drought and the increasingly policed restrictions on cattle movement imposed by government authorities. Cattle were moved from Chivi to a variety of sites during late 1991. In the first part of the drought, 29% of herds were moved out of their home area to another site within the communal lands. By the second part of the drought this percentage had risen to over 35%. Illegal grazing outside the communal area (in resettlement areas or commercial farms) represented another type of movement. Nearly 10% of herds had been moved to such sites in the first period of drought and by the second period one quarter of all herds were using illegal grazing. From the Ngundu area, animals were transferred to the resettlement areas across the Tokwe river, as well as further south to commercial farms in the Mwenezi area. Cattle from Takavarasha were moved within Chivi communal area to the hills to the east and some were moved to graze illegally in commercial farms along the Zvishavane road. Movement from the Chivi central area was more constrained, as the area does not border resettlement or commercial farm land. However, some animals were moved to commercial farms to the west and to communal land grazing, farms and resettlement areas to the north of Chivi. Because of the widespread impact of the drought, such regional movement strategies were ineffective in increasing the survival chances of cattle. There was no significant difference in the survival rates over the whole drought between those herds that were moved out of the area and those that stayed behind or between those that were sent out of the area to illegal grazing areas (commercial farms, resettlement areas) in both 1991 and 1992. Indeed, herds that were moved out of the area to illegal grazing sites had lower survival rates than those that were kept at home, especially over the 1992 period. This was particularly so for Ngundu herds that were sent to resettlement grazing nearby. This area was deluged by cattle from Chivi, Mwenezi and Mazvihwa communal areas during early 1992, which resulted in the decimation of the grazing resource. Animals became too weak to travel on to other areas or back home, and perished in large numbers.

The contrast between the 1982–84 drought and 1991–92 is stark. In the earlier drought, movement proved a successful strategy as herd owners were able to exploit the variable availability of fodder resources within 100km or so of their homes. Restrictions on movement, although officially in place, were not upheld strongly, and night-time movement around police and veterinary roadblocks meant that officialdom could be bypassed to some degree. The 1991–92 drought presented a different situation. Although there were patches of available fodder during 1991, largely in the under-used ranches and resettlement areas, this was quickly used up. The drought's impact was so extensive and so dramatic that movement within a large radius was pointless. Animals that had been moved earlier got stranded, unable to benefit from the micro-management afforded to cattle resident at home *kraals*. Movement restrictions were more effectively enforced during 1991–92, with EC regulations (a condition of Lomé Agreement beef export deals) requiring strict adherence to prevent foot-and-mouth disease outbreaks. Although the Veterinary Department awarded movement orders to a number of communal area farmers, blanket lifting of movement restrictions was resisted despite extensive petitioning to District Administration officials. Another difference between the two periods was the higher occupancy of both resettlement and commercial farm areas. In 1982–84 the resettlement areas were only just beginning to be settled and commercial farms were run down following the long liberation war. By 1991–92, communal area farmers had less room for manoeuvre; resettlement areas had been settled, commercial farmers had returned and were increasingly defending their land against intruders, and the state regulatory machinery (notably Veterinary Department movement restrictions) was operating more effectively.

Supplementary feeding

A variety of strategies for increasing drought survival chances can be employed without resort to movement over long distances. Very often, localised herding movement to key resource patches is combined with supplementary feeding at the home *kraal*. Supplementary feeding may involve the collection of tree pods (notably *Acacia* spp.), the preparation of hay, the cutting and carrying of fresh grass, the lopping of trees (branches, leaves, fruits), the feeding of crop residues and the supply of commercial feed supplements (Table 11.6).

Each of these responses occurred to varying extents during the three droughts. During 1982–84 crop residues were fed to animals during the early periods. However, these soon ran out and herd owners resorted to the lopping of trees as the primary feed supplementation strategy. In 1987 a similar pattern was observed. In this period, 83% of Mazvihwa sample farmers fed animals stover (mostly maize and pearl millet) and this lasted for most of the drought. Fewer farmers thus resorted to the lopping of trees. During both the 1982–84 and 1987 droughts, only one herd owner fed his animals with commercial feeds (Scoones, 1990).

In 1991–92 the practice of purchasing commercial feeds (direct feed, supplement or appetite lick) had increased. In the Chivi sample 16% of herd owners made use of purchased feed in the first period and 14.6% in the second period. This increased reliance on imported feeds reflected the widespread nature of the drought and the difficulty of finding local feed supplements. However, in 1991–92, commercial feed supplementation was combined with a variety of strategies. These included feeding of tree products,[4] feeding of crop residues and the collection of grass and pods (Table 11.6). Tree product feeding remained high throughout the drought, with all herd owners actively lopping trees in both periods. The feeding of crop residues dropped from 34% to only 2% as sources ran out. Cutting and carrying of grass to animals was important for 12.5% of herd owners during the first period of drought. People travelled to mountains and other inaccessible places to harvest grass in order to feed it to their weak animals at home. However, even this resource was exhausted by 1992 and only 4% of herd owners were involved in cutting and carrying during this period. The purchase of collected tree pods or grass hay was recorded for 3–4% of herd owners during the drought. A number of children and women made small amounts of money through the sale of buckets of *Acacia* pods or bundles of collected grass hay (Chapter 10). These were collected either from the communal area woodlands or from neighbouring commercial farms. Although each of the supplementary feeding strategies enabled animals to survive longer during 1991–92, the differences in overall survival between those herds with a particular type of supplementary feeding and those without were not statistically significant in any case.

Sales and slaughters

Sales rates increase during drought periods; this is only significant, however, in very severe droughts. According to the dip data (Table 11.1), sales rates were 13% between October 1983 and September 1984, 3% during 1986–87 and 2% during 1991–92. High sales rates in 1982–84 were encouraged by the larger pre-drought herd sizes of many owners, who could risk sales while still retaining animals within their home *kraal*. Low sales levels were recorded of cattle during 1987, with most sales occurring in the post-ploughing and dry seasons. Drought stress sales accounted for only 13% of all sales and most sales were the result of regular income needs, such as school fees (Scoones, 1990).

During 1991–92 only 34 of the Chivi sample cattle were sold live, representing a 3% offtake. Most herders avoided sale early in the drought, preferring to try to keep animals on the hoof. As the severity of the drought became more apparent, increasing numbers of farmers tried to sell their animals. However, by this stage the condition of their animals was so poor that the Cold Storage Commission buyers refused to take them. Attempts to sell locally were also made. Some butchers and neighbouring commercial ranchers bought up live animals at very low prices. Sales were thus sporadic with no particular seasonal pattern. The total number of animals sold was higher in 1991 than in 1992; many of the 1991 sales occurred in the Ngundu area, where a significantly higher offtake (9%) was recorded. The other areas did not show such a pattern of early drought destocking, and sales levels remained low at around 1–2%, rising to 4% in 1992.

The pattern observed during 1991–92 parallels that in previous droughts. Because cattle are considerably more valuable live (for draught power, manure, milk etc.) than dead (sale value), there are very strong incentives to try and maintain livestock. Destocking is a risky option as the terms of sale during drought and repurchase following drought are not favourable to the herd owner. The costs of not having animals available to plough in the rainy season (assuming rains come) is so high that most farmers retain their stock as long as possible. In the case of both the 1982–84 and the 1991–92 droughts this was too late. Buyers refused to purchase them and many died.

Slaughter rates (Table 11.1) do not increase in droughts largely because major events, such as marriages, occur with decreased frequency during such periods. However, the dip register does not record slaughters that occur immediately prior to death from starvation, illness or accident. This is a major source of meat during drought, but is recorded as mortality rather than slaughter in the data. In 1991–92 this was a major type of slaughter in the Chivi sample, representing 77% of all recorded slaughters and 30% of all mortality during the period under study. During 1991, slaughters of all types (purposeful and due to imminent death from other causes) were as high as 9% in Takavarasha and 7.3% in Ngundu; both rates were significantly higher than the 1.4% recorded in the Chivi area. By 1992 slaughter offtake had risen in all areas to above 20%, with no significant differences between areas.

During 1991 the sales rate was significantly higher and the slaughter rate significantly lower among households with access to remittance income. Higher slaughter rates among non-remittance-income-earning households reflect the greater need for local food subsidy, either through local consumption of meat or sales of meat. Those with remittances may risk sales knowing that they are in a better position to repurchase animals following the drought. By 1992 such differences had disappeared as sales reduced to practically zero and slaughters increased dramatically across all household types.

Contrasting responses

The 1982–84 drought was patchy, so movement to other areas where fodder was still available proved a successful strategy. In contrast the 1991–92 drought was very widespread and movement proved an inadequate response; local feed supplementation was the only option. The single-year 1987 drought was short-lived and localised, so local-level movement, combined with feed supplementation, proved an effective response.

Micro-management of feed supply, with human beings actively foraging on behalf of weak animals, was the most effective way of increasing survival among animals during 1991–92. By contrast, movement strategies appear to have been more effective in the previous two drought periods, in combination with a certain amount of supplementary feeding. Low-impact, single-year droughts (marginally more severe than 'normal' dry seasons) and severe, extended (two–three-year) droughts, whether patchy or widespread, require different types of local-level response.

Policies for drought response and mitigation

Experience over the past decade has shown how different droughts can be. There therefore can be no single policy response to drought. If the objective of government policy is to reduce the impact of drought on the rural economy, lowering the potentially very high costs of livestock loss (Table 11.5), then it will be necessary to support existing drought mitigation strategies employed by farmers. Planning must take into account the range of alternative drought scenarios described above and be based on a flexible response to an uncertain set of contingencies.

It is difficult to gauge what existing policy with respect to drought response and mitigation is. The national livestock policy (Zimbabwe, 1992) is not very specific. It argues for sustaining communal livestock populations through drought, as well as advocating more aggressive destocking through sales during drought periods. However, the details of policy and the justification for the existing statements remain vague.

A range of policies can be examined in relation to three different drought scenarios. These are: a single-year rainfall deficit resulting in temporary dry season feed shortages (as in 1987); a two-or-more year rainfall deficit resulting in local feed shortages (e.g. over a whole district) over several seasons (as in 1982–84); and a two-or-more year rainfall deficit resulting in widespread feed shortages (over a whole province or country) over several seasons (as in 1991–92). The frequency of occurrence of each of these type of events varies. Single-year rainfall deficits (rainfall below 25% of the 1914–92 mean) occurred in Chivi in 26% of years since 1914, and two consecutive year deficits occurred five times. In most instances the scale of impact has been relatively local, with surplus fodder being found within 100km. Only on two occasions (1947 and 1992) have impacts been felt over very large areas, where virtually no surplus fodder areas could be found (Chapter 10).

Low-intensity droughts and other dry seasons

Government (and other development aid) policies should concentrate on supporting and enabling existing dry season grazing management strategies. In particular, this involves the selective use of key resource grazing areas and the extensive use of browse as fodder. Management of key resources, such as *dambo*s, riverbanks and drainage lines, through deferred grazing rotations can ensure late dry season fodder reserves. Reseeding with high biomass production grass species and rehabilitation of degraded key sites, through protection and selective use, should also be central to drought mitigation strategies. Complementary management of the browse resource through selective thinning and pruning of woodland areas to encourage high-value browse species and the establishment of natural woodland or planted fodder banks is also critical. These measures will help livestock production in 'normal' as well as drought years. They should be central to all grazing management interventions, such as grazing schemes, and managed at a local level, planned and organised by local institutions (Cousins, 1992). Investment requirements for such activities would be minimal, simply meaning redirecting extension efforts to areas currently not well covered.

Longer drought with patchy impact

When a single-year drought extends into a multi-year drought and the response mechanisms previously applied are failing to work, it is necessary to assess whether the impacts are patchy or uniform. If areas of feed surplus can be identified within trekking distance of herds in feed deficit, then movement options need to be facilitated. Policy responses should include the lifting of movement restrictions (providing this does not jeopardise animal health) and the provision of information to herders as to where surplus feed is available. This may mean movement within communal areas or outside them. Government officials may play an important role in negotiating access between areas. In cases where surplus feed is available on government or private land, such areas can play a critical role in providing grazing either free or according to a grazing charge system. The opportunity costs of not doing anything are so large that a subsidised grazing system is warranted under such conditions. This might include the issuing of exchangeable grazing rights to state or commercial land that would allow each household the right to graze a limited number of animals.

Longer drought with widespread impact

Movement options become limited when drought impacts are widespread. In such situations support for *in situ* feeding is necessary. This would involve the subsidisation of feeding pens for selected cattle (e.g. limited numbers of breeding stock per village). Government support could come through the financing of stock feed delivery (purchased commercial feeds or hay collected elsewhere) to village feed lots. The costs of selective feeding would be less than the transport of animals over long distances (Agritex, 1984)[5] and returns in reduced mortality losses would exceed the costs of feed investment. Limited attempts were made at survival feeding during 1991–92. The Veterinary Department set up a series of feed pens as an attempt to save breeding stock. However, they were set up late, as funds for fencing and feed supply were delayed. Feed supplies were intermittent and the survival rate of animals was disappointing.

What is clear from the 1991–92 experience is that advance contingency planning is needed in case of widespread and prolonged drought. In order for local-level feed supplementation to work, support mechanisms must be in place early on and supplies must be guaranteed. This requires planning for implementation, including securing the funds, when a single-year drought is experienced. When drought is widespread and prolonged, there are good arguments for destocking animals for later restocking. However, the difficulties of effecting this are well known (Oxby, 1994). If there is a chance of keeping animals alive, herders will try to do so for good economic reasons. But by the time the chances have receded, the market is depressed and the animals are in very poor, often unmarketable, condition. Providing added incentives for sale, linked with some form of guarantee of post-drought restocking, seems to make sense under such conditions (Toulmin, 1994). Various options are open including: a guaranteed sale channel, even if animals are in poor condition, with a minimum price; sale to the state marketing authority or other land owner who keep animals alive for a fee, with repurchase at sale price minus fee; and sale to the marketing authority, which retains the money and organises re-purchase of animals at the value of the sale price, plus interest earned.

The distinctions between drought types is obviously not clear-cut. Single-year droughts lead into longer-term droughts with different spatial impacts. The probability of this will always remain uncertain. Impacts are not solely related to rainfall deficits. As the discussions above have shown, wider changes clearly have an influence. For instance, the ability to purchase feed sources will be affected by the wage levels derived from off-farm employment or the value of agricultural produce sales. These in turn are affected by economic policies (Chapter 3). In the current context of declining wage levels with high inflation, the ability of farmers to purchase commercial feeds is severely constrained. Changes in land pressure equally affect the ability of farmers to respond through flexible movement. As the pressure on land becomes greater, both within and outside the communal areas, the availability of surplus land to move cattle onto in times of drought diminishes.

Few of the policy options outlined above are cost free. Most involve some kind of temporary subsidy in order to offset drought losses. Is this justified under current economic conditions? We believe the answer is yes. If the very high potential costs of drought mortality are to be offset – with long-term impacts on agricultural productivity, food security and rural livelihoods – then focused investment in drought mitigation must be justified. Government needs to invest, together with others, in longer-term strategies for drought contingency response. This will entail investing in the rural development support for livestock that this key sector deserves (e.g. grazing and browse management, water supplies, dipping services), as well as setting up flexible drought response strategies, able to respond early and effectively to the onset drought.

Notes

1. Veterinary dip data are collected on a weekly or fortnightly basis, depending on the time of year. All cattle are dipped and all births, deaths, sales and purchases are recorded in the dip register. There are currently no incentives to avoid registration, as dipping is free and there are no imposed stocking restrictions. The data are therefore reliable and accurate.

2. Using Barrett's estimates of gross value (excluding costs) for different functions (milk, manure, sales, draught etc.) in 1991 Z$ prices, the gross value of different animals' outputs per year is equivalent to: bull = 355.1; ox = 358.7; cow = 516.2; heifer = 18.0; calves = 0. Steers are assumed to have the same value as oxen.

3. The Chivi cattle population in 1990–91 was estimated at 99,859 in the communal areas. The provincial total was 667,668, according to Veterinary Department statistics.

4. The most important lopped trees were: *Lonchocarpus capassa, Combretum apiculatum, Kirkia acuminata, Kigelia africana, Afzelia quanzensis, Julbernadia globiflora, Colophospermum mopane, Combretum hereroense, Grewia monticola, Sclerocarya birrea, Euphorbia sp., Brachystegia glaucescens, Peltophorum africanum.*

5. Following the 1982–84 drought, Agritex calculated the relative costs and returns of *in situ* drought feeding and large-scale movement using trucks and train transport. The results showed that movement was economic if the animals were

moved out and then were sold later. Return movements were not found to be cost-effective. However, commercial ranchers during 1991–92 did transport their breeding animals from low-veld ranches to high-veld farms, suggesting that economic conditions have changed.

PART FOUR

Policies

CHAPTER TWELVE

Policies for an uncertain world: lessons from Zimbabwe

Risk and uncertainty are all-pervasive in dryland farming systems. During any 'normal' agricultural season in a dryland area, a variety of events impinge on farming practice. Rainfall patterns are unpredictable, with occasional downpours interspersed with mid-season droughts. Pest infestations may suddenly arise, requiring immediate attention to avoid crop failure. Similarly, labour or draught power availability are often uncertain, with negotiations within and between households being required to ensure an effective response. The realisation of income from crop or livestock sales may be affected by variability in price levels or market conditions. The risks faced are not only affected by conditions in the agricultural sector, as off-farm work is often vital to people's livelihoods. Changes in the broader economy affect remittance flows and so influence the ability of farmers to supply inputs for agriculture. Wider social obligations also carry with them uncertainties. Funerals, marriages, meetings or other social gatherings may mean that farming priorities must change. Droughts add to the degree of risk and uncertainty. With the failure of agricultural production, alternative income sources must be found and claims on others must be made.

A consideration of risk and uncertainty during the formulation of policy seems inescapable. Yet most policies assume a certain world, one guided by predictable relationships and assumptions about standard responses and equilibrium patterns. Whether we are talking of economic policy, land and natural resource policy, agricultural research and extension policy or even drought management and relief approaches, policies tend to come in blueprint format. A standard response is offered for what is assumed to be a standard situation.

Policy-makers recognise that this is problematic, and it is always easy to see, with hindsight, why certain policies failed. The usual response is to urge researchers to collect more data, so that a more accurate picture of reality can be built up and better policies can be designed. But this response fails to deal with the indeterminacies of the real world. More and more data may offer increasingly impressive models of decision-making, but if uncertainty prevails, then to invest large amounts of research time in trying to reduce what is ultimately uncertain into a probability distribution amenable to conventional risk analysis may not be worth the effort. This approach may be both expensive and self-deceiving, although it does offer the security of a clear and definitive answer.

Recognising uncertainty: adaptive management and policy

If uncertainty is taken seriously, a very different type of policy-making is needed, one that relies on incremental learning from experience and adaptive responses. This is known as the adaptive management and policy approach (Walters, 1986; Holling, 1993). The adaptive policy-maker never pretends to know everything, but must make decisions on the basis of current knowledge. As Mary Douglas notes (1985: 43), 'we should learn to suspend judgement and not pretend to precision we lack'. Responses to policy are then monitored and interventions are changed accordingly. Adaptive policy-making and management have a number of key features which can be contrasted with more conventional modes of policy-making and management.

Levels of decision-making: the subsidiarity principle.

In complex situations, where full knowledge of every permutation is an impossibility, allowing solutions to emerge from the local level is essential. There is no point in imposing a blanket policy solution, whether this is a fertiliser recommendation or a drought response strategy, when local conditions will inevitably mean that the policy is inappropriate for most people most of the time. The principle of subsidiarity suggests that administrative and management tasks should be carried out as near to the level of actual users as is compatible with efficiency and accountability. Zimbabwe, as with many other countries in Africa, has experienced a history of intense, centrally directed and top-down intervention, whether from government research and extension services, environmental legislation or development projects (Chapter 2). The subsidiarity principle suggests different roles for local groups, district-level service providers and national government. National policies need to be enabling, setting the ground rules and providing a broad framework for consistent action, rather than being interventionist, attempting to regulate and plan every last detail. This offers a greater role for local organisations, who need to be supported in order to be able to respond to the hazards and opportunities of the local level. For Zimbabwe, as elsewhere, taking the principle of subsidiarity seriously will necessitate some major shifts in the direction and style of policy (see below).

Openness, transparency and accountability

If policies are to be acted upon, they must be credible. People must believe in them and policy-makers must be accountable for them. This requires a level of openness and transparency in policy-making that is very rare. An admission that the exact solution is not known, that there is some degree of uncertainty, is often seen as an admission of inadequacy. Embracing error and accepting adaptive, incremental change also imply letting go of a degree of power and control, which is usually guarded jealously (Korten, 1980; Chambers, 1993). This makes adaptive policy-making a high-risk strategy for the cautious and conservative professional and requires some fundamental rethinking of the way organisations and the people within them behave (Agyris and Schön, 1978). But, as we have seen with many examples from Zimbabwe, ranging from policies on plant breeding to food security, opening up the process to a wider constituency, and so increasing the range of options, is the only way of addressing the fundamental problems of risk and uncertainty.

Participatory approaches to encourage learning

Planning and policy-making in an uncertain world require a continuous process of learning, in order to adapt and change. Different experiences offer different insights to different people. For this reason it is vital that planning and policy-making is seen as a co-learning process (Russell and Ison, 1993), whereby different worldviews are acknowledged and different voices are heard. Participatory approaches, ranging from participatory rural appraisal to participatory action research, training-for-transformation or theatre-for-development, offer useful opportunities for exchanges of ideas and learning (Cornwall *et al.*, 1994). The expanding range of methods that encourage the sharing of perspectives between different stakeholders increases the possibilities for successful participation in planning and policy-making (e.g. Mascarenhas *et al.*, 1991; Webber and Ison, 1995). But it should not be forgotten that participation is a political process whereby different actors engage, debate and contest alternatives in forums where issues of power are crucial (Fals-Borda and Rahman, 1991). The opportunities for successful participation are thus dependent on the attitudes and behaviours of the participants, as well as on the instititional and political contexts of the encounter (Long and Long, 1992).

Most government departments responsible for agricultural policy have few of the qualities mentioned above. The need for organisational change, combined with shifts in methodological approach and individual behaviour, is enormous, but unlikely to happen quickly. There are many obstacles to transformation, including simple bureaucratic inertia, the power of vested interests in the status quo, and the need for wholesale retraining and reskilling of agricultural professionals (Chambers, 1993; Pretty and Chambers, 1994).

As previous chapters have shown, the agricultural policy, research and extension system in Zimbabwe, as in many other countries, is poorly equipped to deal with challenges of dryland development and the management of risk and uncertainty. What new challenges for policy-makers are suggested? What steps might be taken to encourage a more effective response? What are the elements of government (and indeed non-government) policy and practice that need urgent reform?

Policies for risk and uncertainty: lessons from Zimbabwe

Previous chapters have touched upon the implications of a variety of policies, either in historical context or in the contemporary setting. These have included economic policies affecting urban wage employment, agricultural commodity marketing and informal sector activity (Chapters 2–3); land and natural resource policies affecting land distribution and settlement, the regulation of resource use and tenurial and institutional arrangements (Chapters 2 and 6); agricultural research and extension policies affecting the approaches and methods of on-farm work (Chapters 4–8); and food security and drought policies affecting local drought coping strategies, drought early warning response mechanisms and drought proofing (Chapters 9–11). The following sections pick up these themes and explore the implications for policy change in Zimbabwe, drawing lessons for elsewhere in dryland Africa.

Economic policy and rural livelihoods

As we have seen, many areas of policy impinge on rural livelihoods. It is not just agricultural, or even rural, policy that is important, but a whole range of cross-sectoral policies that provide the framework within which rural people's livelihoods are embedded. In Zimbabwe today, as elsewhere, these policies are often contradictory and potentially disenabling. For instance, little thought seems to have been invested in exploring the rural–urban dimensions of economic policy reform. While certain aspects of reform in recent years have enhanced the ability of small-scale producers to deal with risk, other areas, such as the induced contraction of the economy and reduction in real wage rates, clearly have not. If economic policies do not work in concert, recognising that people's livelihoods traverse sectoral barriers, then problems inevitably arise.

Agricultural liberalisation in Zimbabwe since 1990 has transformed agricultural pricing and marketing policy (Chapter 3). In particular, the new policy allows for much greater flexibility in marketing. Although product prices are allowed to vary seasonally, this should not increase consumers' exposure to risk if local storage and trade are options. The removal of movement restrictions and price controls and the abandonment of a central marketing system should also allow greater competition and efficiency. With deregulation there has been an expansion of small-scale milling at a local level which has increased the local availability of food and reduced costs. However, increased flexibility and the ability to respond to risk will only come about if the starting conditions are right. For instance, the current lack of transport limits the opportunities for new entrants into crop marketing, resulting in market imperfections and profit-seeking. Policies to support flexible marketing must therefore also take account of the conditions required and this may mean more than simple deregulation and liberalisation: it may require investment in such areas as transport infrastructure and active support for new market entrants, millers and traders. Flexible marketing and price arrangements may be all right when harvests are good and farmers are able to take advantage of the new opportunities, but when drought strikes and most households are grain consumers rather than producers, policies that create safety nets to avoid destitution are also necessary (see below).

Non-farm sources of income are of major importance to people's livelihoods in dryland Zimbabwe. The significance of remittance income to patterns of investment in the rural areas should not be underestimated. In Southern Africa, rural and urban areas are intimately linked through migrant work, kinship networks and flows of people, money and resources back and forth. Policies that affect off-farm employment, in the towns, in the mines, or on the commercial large-scale farms, also affect livelihoods in the communal areas. As Chapter 3 has shown, historical changes in real wage levels have influenced the incentives and opportunities to invest in agriculture in the dry zones. For people with a limited asset base in terms of land and livestock, securing a living from farming alone in dry areas is a major struggle. Recent declines in real wage levels, and increasing levels of unemployment, have hit rural households hard. The long-term effects of this are unknown, but some trends are apparent. These include declines in investment in rural assets (livestock, farm implements, housing), declines in input levels (hybrid seeds, fertilisers, pesticides), reductions in school and health care attendance (especially when cost-recovery schemes are introduced), and shifts in social formations (increased individualisation, reduced effectiveness of support networks, changes in marriage arrangements). Rural policies, whether farm support services or social welfare policies, will have to shift to accommodate these changes.

As farming livelihoods become increasingly constrained and off-farm formal employment options become more and more limited, policies that support the diversification of the rural income base become vitally important. Support for income diversification through the encouragement of rural manufacturing, industry and trade is thus a vital component of rural development policy (Moyo, 1991). A combination of appropriate deregulation and targeted credit, subsidy and training is needed to realise this. But many options remain constrained by over-regulation and needless quality controls – an inheritance of the colonial era when regulations restricting the growth of small-scale (African) business proliferated.

Land and natural resources policy

Land and natural resources are basic requirements for rural people's livelihoods, yet policies in the past have limited people's access to and control over them. Highly inequitable land distribution, inadequate tenure security, weak rural institutions and draconian natural resources legislation have combined to make land and natural resources policy a troubled area to this day. On the post-Independence record, Mandivamba Rukuni comments that 'land policy has been Zimbabwe's biggest failure' (Rukuni, 1994: 35). The failure of the resettlement policy to provide for substantial shifts in land ownership is well documented, as are the inadequacies of the settlement models adopted (Chapter 2). The rigidities of the Zimbabwe approach, with the insistence on a farm model, following particular farm management and agricultural extension recommendations, has been found wanting. The limited capacity of government to support such settlement schemes, in terms of extension, credit and infrastructure, has added to the slow pace of purchase of suitable land.

If the viability of the communal areas is to be sustained, urgent solutions to the problems of land scarcity will have to be sought in the coming decades. It may now be time to explore a wider range of land redistribution opportunities, abandoning the strict adherence to a standardised, packaged settlement model and testing other options. If they are to address the fundamental problems of the communal areas, such options must offer new land of adequate potential and in sufficient quantities to begin to satisfy land needs. Such areas must be supported, perhaps through innovative credit schemes, but not constrained by excessive planning and intervention from outside. Settlement areas must also have tenure arrangements secure enough to encourage investment. If these conditions are satisfied, evidence suggests that a vibrant small-scale sector can offer Zimbabwe a bright future, both satisfying food needs and entering cash crop production for export (Christiansen, 1993). However, if the challenges of land redistribution are not met, then the exposure of communal area people to risks will increase and livelihoods will continue to be undermined with the associated costs of food aid, social disquiet and spontaneous migration.

A revival of agriculture and resource management *within* the communal areas is a parallel policy challenge to the land redistribution issue. There has been much public debate about the importance of tenure and institutions, which led to the establishment of a Land Tenure Commission in 1993. Much of the debate has been focused on the merits and demerits of land privatisation and titling in the communal areas, with supporters of land titling arguing that this is the only way of securing rights to land and credit collateral that will allow long-term investment. Others argue that there is *de facto* tenure security in most communal areas and that there are other ways of securing collateral and releasing credit. In many respects the concentration on land tenure is a diversion from basic questions about the range of appropriate institutions for agricultural and resource management. As various sections in this book have illustrated, tenure arrangements in the communal areas are complex, with overlapping and diffuse claims to particular sites which are always shifting and being renegotiated. For instance, one portion of a grazing area may have strong claims on it by a small lineage cluster during the dry season, with outsiders being excluded. But the same area may be more widely used in the wet season by a larger group. Such arrangements make it very difficult to envisage the strict allocation of rights of use according to a particular tenure regime. Instead, a much more sophisticated system of negotiated rights to land use at a local level is needed. In the past, this process of negotiation was mediated by lineage leaders and family heads. Today, the multiplication of institutional authority, with the arrival of the village and ward committees, has made the process more difficult, and in many instances unworkable. The failure of the committees to serve as legitimate local authorities is now widely recognised, yet the process of institutional revitalisation has failed to happen. The vacuum of authority at the local level presents many problems and requires some major policy initiatives to fill it.

One of the central roles for local leadership in the past was the implementation of rules and regulations over resource use. During the colonial era this function was increasingly removed and taken up by the state. The barrage of environmental legislation that emerged from the 1940s was framed in a way that removed the opportunities for local-level negotiation of rules and regulations. Instead, rules were formulated centrally with blanket regulations governing the whole country. Among the most celebrated of these were the 30m rule preventing stream bank cultivation and *dambo* use (Chapter 6), but there are many more scattered across a range of Acts of Parliament (Scoones and Matose, 1993). A policing approach to environmental management has proved invidious. Many of the laws are deeply resented and, with limited policing capacity, many are flouted. With so much effort being invested in regulation and enforcement, little attention has been paid to supporting local institutions for environmental management. The consequence is that local-level natural resource protection suffers and, in the long term, people are exposed to more risks. It is widely recognised that much land and natural resources legislation is outdated and based on premisses that are inappropriate to today's circumstances. Rather than attempting to meddle with the margins, what is needed is wholesale redrafting. This is a major challenge requiring a rethink in approach on the part of key departments in government. New environmental and natural resources legislation would be enabling in character, devolving responsibilities to the lowest level appropriate to the task. It would thus encourage local responses to local specificity, while at the same time providing guidelines on the process and indications as to appropriate limits and standards for different circumstances. Such a decentralised approach to land and natural resource management must necessarily work in tandem with a process of revitalising a variety of local institutions to ensure legitimacy and accountability.

Agricultural research and extension policy

This book has shown how responses to risk and uncertainty are varied in space and time and among different people. Farming is thus not an ordered and predictable affair, but one highly influenced by contingency and uncertainty, embedded in social relations and patterns of economic differentiation. This makes the design of agricultural research and extension policy particularly challenging. Yet research and extension approaches often appear to ignore this fundamental finding. In the design of trials or the production of packages the vagaries of the real world are often screened out and an assumption of stasis and uniformity is adopted. This is, of course, grossly misleading.

Why has the research and extension establishment in Zimbabwe largely failed to address the complexities of the small-scale farming sector? A number of reasons can be sought. First, the undoubted successes in serving the large-scale commercial sector prior to Independence were regarded by many as a model for the post-Independence era, with adjustments in scale and target group rather than basic content. Second, the dominant models of research and extension have emphasised a top-down approach to technology design. This applies as much to the Green Revolution model for scientific breakthroughs in plant breeding as it does to the diffusion models for extension. The result has been organisational approaches that reduce flexibility and responsiveness. For example, commodity-focused trial programmes on particular crops often limit attention to wider issues such as processing or marketing, while the Training and Visit extension system (or the variety of group-based approaches common in Zimbabwe) limits extension to a process of calendar-timed and message-based contacts. Third, professional norms, reinforced by funding patterns, have supported adherence to the dominant models, limiting innovation and experimentation. Agronomists, for instance, are loath to embark on on-farm experimentation for fear of 'uncontrolled variables' and 'non-statistical results', preferring the sanctity of the research station where outputs are amenable to standard tests and, as a result, more likely to find their way into reviewed journals. With career rewards reinforcing this pattern of professional behaviour, it is only the brave few who venture out and try to address complex issues confounded by risk and uncertainty. Fourth, funding and staffing constraints have severely limited the ability of the key government departments to seek out alternatives and innovate. High staff turnover, due to a young and mobile staff cadre always on the lookout for greener pastures, has combined with a continued squeeze on funding. Non-salary, recurrent budgets have dropped to levels that mean that extension staff are now unable to travel for significant portions of the year and on-farm research support has been cut back. In addition, increasing reliance on external donor funds means that government departments must increasingly play the donor's tune and are unable to look beyond a short-term project time frame.

International experience suggests that there are alternatives to the conventional model of research and extension, that do allow risk, uncertainty and local complexity to be taken seriously in the process of agricultural technology development (cf. Chambers *et al.*, 1989; Amanor, 1990; Reijntes *et al.*, 1992; Scoones and Thompson, 1994). These alternatives do not mean jettisoning the unquestioned merits of high-quality on-station research for which the Zimbabwe research system has became renowned. They merely mean recognising that there are a variety of ways of carrying out agricultural research involving different actors and appropriate to different circumstances. Modes of research include farmers' own experimentation, on-farm trials involving both farmers and researchers, and on-station or laboratory research involving mainly research scientists (cf. Merrill-Sands *et al.*, 1991; Worman *et al.*, 1991; Heinrich, 1993). All result in learning of different types and all are legitimate ways of exploring the world and seeking solutions to problems.

In Zimbabwe there is a growing experience of farmer participatory research (Scoones and Cousins, 1988; Clarke, 1991; Hagmann and Chuma, 1994) which demonstrates the effectiveness of the approach in diverse areas such as agroforestry, soil and water conservation, agronomic management and crop variety testing. As Chapter 8 has shown, farmers are continuously engaged in experimentation of their own; the challenge for researchers is to explore ways in which this process can productively articulate with the more formal research process. How can crop breeding or agronomy be made more relevant to communal area users? How can farmers' research priorities feed into on-station research agendas? How can farmers become more involved in evaluating the outputs of formal research?

These basic issues were one of the many things that prompted the initiation of the Farming Systems Research (FSR) approach in the 1970s. As Chapter 8 has shown, much FSR failed to meet these challenges as it fell into the trap of becoming wedded to a tightly defined and linear model of implementation. Instead of continuously engaging with farmers in a process of problem redefinition, diagnostic studies were often seen as one-off events, largely run by outsiders with limited participation. Equally, on-farm trials became associated with on-farm testing of station-derived technologies, using methodologies defined by researchers, rather than being an opportunity to test out a variety of options with farmers taking the lead. Today, FSR in Zimbabwe is in a process of transformation. The range of methods offered by Participatory Rural Appraisal (PRA) means that diagnostic studies, trial monitoring and evaluation are all much more participative. Equally, the introduction of farmer-designed and -managed trials as a major function of village research groups offers a cost-effective opportunity to link farmers' own processes of innovation and experimentation with the formal research process.

The adoption of a more participatory on-farm research process suggests some major shifts in our conception of research and extension. Conventionally, in Zimbabwe as elsewhere, research was seen as the site of innovation and the process of extension was seen simply as one of transferring the technology to a wider audience. But if multiple sources of innovation (cf. Biggs, 1989b) are recognised (from the research station to the farmer's field), together with multiple ways of assessing the validity and appropriateness of the results (from statistical tests to farmers' assessments) and multiple ways of spreading information (from formal sessions to informal networks), then the distinction between research and extension becomes increasingly blurred. This is particularly so for the farming system researcher who, as broker of information, facilitator of the experimental process and convenor of research groups, must bridge the gap between the conventional roles of research and extension (Chapter 8).

Participatory approaches to extension also suggest many new challenges. If extension is no longer to be seen as simply the process of information or technology diffusion from expert to farmer, but instead involves networking amongst many sources of innovation, offering a range of choices to farmers, encouraging a process of farmer-to-farmer extension and supporting the on-going process of local innovation and experimentation, then new skills and priorities are required. In Zimbabwe, innovatory approaches are being tried out by Agritex, the government agricultural extension agency, together with NGOs in a number of provinces. In order to consolidate such innovation, support for organisational reform in agricultural support services will be necessary. This will involve retraining of staff, redefining professional incentives and restructuring departments. Under conditions of continuing budgetary cutbacks, such investment may seem unlikely. But ultimately a leaner, more effective government support service may evolve that draws on the complementarities in private and non-government sectors (Farrington, 1994). But a demand-led agricultural research and extension service requires mechanisms by which demand from a wide range of stakeholders is expressed through effective lobbying and political influence. Weak farmer's organisations, with poor representation of marginalised groups, remain a major constraint in Zimbabwe (Eicher and Rukuni, 1994).

Policies for livelihood security

The reduction of levels of risk exposure has been a neglected area of public policy. Food security policies have tended to focus on grain reserve targets, early warning systems and emergency relief plans, rather than taking a wider view that encompasses the various dimensions of vulnerability. Robert Chambers (1989: 1) defines vulnerability, a concept distinct from the conventional income-based definitions of poverty, as 'defencelessness, insecurity and exposure to risk, shocks and stress'. Large sections of the communal area population are highly vulnerable to the risks, shocks and stresses of uncertain environmental and economic conditions. Whilst much of this population may not be defined as poor (certainly not by comparison with other rural populations in the Southern African region), people are certainly exposed to a variety of income and food insecurities. What has been termed the 'paradox of food insecurity' in Zimbabwe (Jayne and Chisvo, 1991; Rukuni and Eicher, 1994), means that in the midst of apparent plenty (maize exports, national food silos brimming and food in the shops), significant levels of food insecurity are faced by large portions of the rural population on a regular basis. A disaggregated analysis of risk and vulnerability is essential, in which differential entitlements to food through direct production, market exchange or a variety of claims are assessed. Only with such an approach can the hidden consequences of risk exposure be uncovered. The historical analysis of entitlements attempted in Chapters 9–11 suggests that vulnerability is on the increase. Long-term changes are occurring that increase the stresses on rural livelihoods, resulting in increased exposure of rural populations to sudden shocks, such as drought or rapid economic change.

Long-term increases in levels of vulnerability are the product of a combination of factors resulting in regular household food deficits for at least half the rural population (Chapter 10). The inability to grow enough food is caused by the erosion of farmers' asset base. Plot sizes are shrinking as population increase results in greater pressure on limited land areas; livestock holdings are decreasing as recurrent droughts hit cattle populations; and savings levels are vanishingly small as the real value of remittance incomes declines and the amount of money circulating in the rural economy is cut back. This means that coping strategies that previously worked well enough to tide people over are no longer as effective. Without livestock or cash, regional trading for grains collapses; without extensive forest areas, hunting and foraging are no longer options; and without access to new lands, local migration is impossible. In order to secure food, rural people must increasingly rely on other options. The demands on a variety of claims – from relatives, from churches, from development organisations or from the state – appear to be on the increase as the risks to rural livelihoods escalate. The consequence is that, as social networks of support get stretched to breaking point, there is an increasing reliance on food aid on the part of a significant minority of the rural population in poor harvest years.

There is no better way to reduce rural vulnerability and ensure the viability of people's livelihoods than to increase the productive base. Proofing the system against drought (and other risks) means strategic investments in key areas. First, addressing land redistribution with more flexible and imaginative approaches than in the past is a major priority (see above). Second, investment in technologies that increase outputs while reducing risk is essential. For the dry areas the obvious investment is in water management, whether in the form of water harvesting or residual moisture *dambo* cultivation (Chapter 6), or small-scale pump-assisted irrigation schemes. Third, longer-term investment means commitment to strategic research that is focused on tackling the key problems of dry areas. This requires a new approach to research which is driven by the demands of farmers (Chapter 8). Finally, diversification of income-earning options is also vital, so that people are less reliant on farm-based cash and can generate income from sources less dependent on the vagaries of rainfall.

Policies to protect entitlements are vital to ensure that productivity improvements are sustained and act to reduce vulnerability (Frankenberger, 1993). The erosion of the asset base is undermining people's abilities to cope with risk. Policies that protect livestock assets during drought periods are essential, lest the ratchet effect of sequential droughts continues to undermine rural production. As Chapter 11 has shown, the economic loss due to cattle mortalities during the droughts of the last decade has been enormous, and public investment to protect such key assets should be regarded as money well spent. Enhancing people's exchange entitlements is another important area for policy attention. Market liberalisation, particularly for the whole and milled grain trade, has opened up a wider range of opportunities for exchange. In periods when there is grain to sell and buy, this has positive effects. However, in times of widespread drought and food shortage there remains a role for the state in offering guaranteed opportunities to purchase or sell grain. Increasing the efficiency of markets, whether for food products or other tradable items, is an important challenge which must combine a reduction of restrictive practices, imposed by legislation, licensing or other regulations, with increasing market entry and competition. The process of rationalising the regulatory structure of marketing and small enterprise development is proving long and arduous. The inevitable trade-offs between liberalisation for market efficiency and regulation for the social good present many dilemmas. However, even once the regulations and restrictions have been pared down to the minimum necessary, this does not mean that markets will work. Again, strategic investment in transport, road infrastructure, market facilities and so on will be necessary.

The provision of safety nets for the most vulnerable is another policy area that requires attention. Zimbabwe's record in public support during times of crisis has been impressive. Despite major food shortfalls in the last 15 years, the government, together with aid donors and NGOs, has managed to feed people in times of crisis. However, the cost has been enormous and is growing. An alternative to the permanent supply of food aid to the communal areas must be sought. The experience of the most recent drought has shown that both national and regional early warning systems are effective in recognising food deficits at the aggregate level (Chapter 10), but such systems are inadequate in two respects. Even if a food deficit is predicted accurately this does not mean that politicians will act in a timely manner. The disastrous experience of 1991–92 suggests that a tighter linkage between early warning and decision-making is required (Buchanan-Smith and Davies, 1995). But, perhaps more important, a much more disaggregated view of the range of local coping mechanisms is needed in order to be able to target support more effectively and move beyond blanket access to either food aid or food-for-work schemes.

Conclusion

Through the discussions of farming practice and drought responses, this book has addressed two types of risk: the first relating to the regular adaptive responses to 'normal' variation, and the second relating to responses to major shocks, such as drought. Despite these contrasts, people's responses to such risks can be placed along a continuum, ranging from marginal adaptations of farming practice to major shifts in livelihood strategy (Frankenberger, 1993; Davies, 1993). With low-impact risks which are, by and large, expected in the normal course of events, responses require limited investment. This may involve shifting a planting strategy, reallocating labour to new tasks, or making use of a new area in the agricultural landscape. By contrast, during a serious drought period drastically different coping strategies must be employed. This may involve redeploying labour to new tasks outside agriculture, disposing of farm assets such as livestock, or, at the most extreme, abandoning the area completely.

The ability to cope with risks and uncertainties of all types along this continuum of response will depend on the entitlements of individuals, households and resource-sharing networks or clusters. Availability of assets, in the form of capital, labour and land, as well as access to claims from elsewhere, notably through access to remittances from close kin, is critical.

Equally important is access to markets, for, without the ability to exchange agricultural produce or labour, the flexibility of livelihood strategies decreases. With limited access to such entitlements, options are constrained. For instance, those without draught power, and particularly those outside sharing networks, find it difficult to farm effectively. Consistently, such individuals produce less, market less and have lower income levels overall. It is the same people who find it most difficult to cope in drought. With fewer resources and with less opportunity for drawing on claims from others, such people must rely on the government to supply food in times of crisis.

Policies to reduce vulnerability must respond to the whole range of risks faced, increasing the ability to respond flexibly through the diversification of livelihood opportunities. As this book has shown, policies to increase the viability of the asset base by making land available for agriculture and livestock through land reform must be combined with research and extension support that allows local-level innovation and adaptation to diverse and changing circumstances. Diversification requires policies that traverse the rural–urban divide and encourage non-agricultural income earning opportunities. Such policies to ameliorate the effects of 'normal' variation, will inevitably increase the ability of people to survive extreme shocks and stresses, such as drought. But additional support may be required. Drought policies need to be attuned to local coping strategies, as well as providing safety nets for those in extreme need.

Risk and uncertainty will always be part of dryland farming livelihoods. If an alternative to continuous food subsidy to dry areas is to be found and sustainable livelihoods are to be created, an adaptive policy process should help avoid the temptations of universal solutions. Instead, it should recognise the complexities of living with the hazards of dry areas and create the opportunities for local-level innovation, adaptation and change.

APPENDIX ONE
Methodology

Study sites

The research focused on three contrasting study sites in Chivi communal area (natural regions IV and V). Chivi is broadly representative of the conditions found in the drier parts of southern Zimbabwe, especially Masvingo Province and the southern Midlands. The Chivi study sites are representative of the range of ecological conditions found within Chivi. All sites were previous trial areas for the FSRU and so the team was known well at each site. Each site has a variety of topographical settings, vegetation associations and soil types; all have some sandy soil areas (typically associated with *miombo* woodland) and some clay soil areas (typically *mopane* and/or *Acacia* woodland). The three sites are: Chivi central (around Chivi Office), with a clay-soil-dominated area to the north (Shanduka) and a sandy soil area to the south (Mapuvire); the dry Takavarasha area, with two largely clay soil sites (Gwarega/Havurovi Mazhambe); and the wetter Ngundu area, represented by the sandy soil Tandare village and the clay soil Zivhu village.

Between 45 and 50 households were chosen at each site (total sample, N = 146). Households were defined by local informants as spatially distinct residence units. Following the construction of a full village list with the assistance of local village leaders, a stratified random sample was drawn up with the help of local informants. Stratification by draught ownership was chosen on the basis of previous socio-economic research in the area. Meetings were held to introduce the research and invite people to participate in the sample study. Very few drop-outs were recorded. Involvement of others in the area increased during the research, during rapid rural appraisal exercises and following the formation of farmer research groups.

Data sources

Unless otherwise specified, the graphs contained in this book are based on the following data sources:

1. Livestock numbers are derived from Native Commissioners' annual reports (1923–46) and subsequently from Chief Native Commissioner and Secretary for Native Affairs reports (1946–61). From the 1960s data are derived from Veterinary Department files. Cattle numbers were estimated from dip returns, whilst donkey and smallstock numbers are based on occasional censuses. Dip records from 1981 to 1994 from Mazvihwa communal area are also used.

2. Crop price series are derived from Mosley (1983) for 1930–60, Muir-Leresche (1985) for 1954–81, Stanning (1985) for 1970–85 and MLAWD (1994) for 1980–94. Livestock price series are derived from Native Commissioners' reports up to 1961. Subsequently prices are derived from Cold Storage Commission and Economics and Markets branch market records where the average sales price per animal is calculated.
3. Crop production from the communal areas is derived from MLAWD (1994) for the period since 1970, based on CSO data to 1985–86 and National Early Warning Unit data from 1986–87.
4. Crop marketing data are derived from MLAWD (1994) and based on annual Grain Marketing Board reports and accounts.
5. Fertiliser use and price data are derived from MLAWD (1994) and World Bank (1991) and based on data from fertiliser companies and Agritex surveys of use.
6. Human population estimates are based on census figures for 1969, 1982 and 1992 (CSO, 1985; 1992). Earlier estimates are derived from Native Commissioners' annual reports. Total populations prior to 1950 are based on taxation estimates for Africans only (Mosley, 1983); subsequently census data are used.
7. Employee levels and wage rates are derived from Mosley (1983) for 1906–63, Muir-Leresche (1985) for 1954–81 and CSO records subsequently. Data relate to Africans specifically up to 1977 when the racial categorisation was abandoned.
8. In the absence of a rural consumer price index, the low-income urban African CPI is used to deflate prices and wage levels. The basket used for calculating the CPI changed at various times, with additions to a basic basket of food, fuel and lighting made in 1941, 1964, 1970 and 1981. The indices have been combined for the purposes of comparison of trends over long periods. Sources for CPI include Mosley (1983) for 1914–39, and subsequently the Southern Rhodesia yearbook series and Central Statistics Office records. Base dates used in the price-and-wage data presented here are either 1914 or 1960 depending on the data series.
9. Rainfall data are based on daily records from Chivi Office supplied by the Meteorological Department.
10. Cash sums are presented in Zimbabwe dollars. Over the period since 1975, the currency has changed in the following way in relation to the US dollar:

Year end	**US$**
1975	0.62
1980	0.63
1985	1.64
1990	2.63
1991	5.05
1992	5.48
1993	6.93
1994	8.12

Source: Reserve Bank of Zimbabwe

Unpublished sources

A variety of archival material is used in the historical sections of the text, drawing from the following sources.

Archival sources (National Archives of Zimbabwe)

Annual reports of Native Commissioners, 1923–48 (S235/501-546).
Annual reports of Matabeleland Native Commissioners, 1901–12 (NB 6/1-12).
Annual reports of Native Commissioners, 1898–1922 (N9/4-25).
Oral evidence: Native Affairs. Natural Resources Board Native enquiry, 1947 (S988).

Unpublished series

Annual reports of the Secretary for Native Affairs and Chief Native Commissioner, various to 1961 (S1051/SRG3/INT4).
Annual reports of the Secretary for Internal Affairs and Chief Native Commissioner, 1962–72 (SRG/INT4).
Annual yearbooks of the Colony of Southern Rhodesia. Government Printer, Salisbury.

Methods

Various quantitative and qualitative methods were used during the research. The following list outlines, in approximate chronological order between 1990 and early 1994, the phasing of different research elements.

1. Agenda-setting workshops, attended by researchers, development workers and policy-makers, to establish priority areas for the study.
2. Establishment of field study sites and choice of sample. Village meetings at all sites to introduce and review the research objectives. Five members of the research team were permanently resident in the study area and continued to monitor changes throughout the study.
3. Field activity monitoring: regular discussions with farmers throughout the season (October–April) with weekly monitoring of all agricultural activities by field plot (N = 1,008 in 1990–91 season) was carried out in two seasons: 1990–91 and 1992–93 with all sample households.
4. Crop choice, output and sales patterns: retrospective data were collected on crops planted on all plots, as well as total output and sales by crop type for the period from 1988.
5. Drought coping strategies: regular discussions with farmers during the drought (1991–92), focusing on how people and animals coped during the drought.
6. Household surveys to investigate in more depth particular issues (e.g. household asset ownership; household demography; remittance incomes; off-farm work; stover and fodder management). Quantitative data analysis allowed variables to be related to other factors (e.g. agronomic practice or drought coping).
7. Thematic studies: rapid rural appraisal exercises were carried out to investigate key themes identified by other research activities. These included: the impacts

of structural adjustment, soil fertility management and indigenous chicken management.

8. Time-series data analysis: existing data sets from Chivi derived from on-farm crop trials (1984–90) and livestock monitoring (mostly 1985–88) were analysed to explore trends over time. These were combined with government data on human and livestock populations (Central Statistics Office and Veterinary Department), wage levels and employment statistics (Central Statistics Office), commodity prices, marketing levels and outputs (Economics and Markets Branch, Ministry of Agriculture).
9. Historical change: archival material, including secondary literature and district records, held by the Zimbabwe National Archives were examined in order to reconstruct changes over time.
10. Formation of farmer research groups: research groups were formed initially by participants in the research, and later more widely, to tackle key issues identified through on-farm trials supported by the FSRU.
11. Policy workshop: a workshop was held for government and NGO researchers, extensionists and policy-makers to review the findings of the research. Farmer representatives from all study sites attended. Feedback to the farmer research groups was provided by the representatives.
12. Local feedback and evaluation meetings: findings from the research were discussed with farmer groups in all study sites. Research participants reviewed the findings and suggested new areas for study.
13. A technical report and summary policy paper was produced and widely circulated for review and comment in Zimbabwe.
14. Review of FSRU strategy: the project provided the opportunity to reflect on the FSRU's strategy towards on-farm research. The previous concentration only on researcher-managed on-farm trials with highly controlled conditions (through researcher choice of site, treatments and inputs) was found to be inadequate. A more interactive, participatory approach to on-farm work, directed and managed by farmer groups, has been initiated. This will complement more formal on-station and on-farm work.

APPENDIX TWO

Extension recommendations and farmers' practices

The material on extension recommendations is based on a series of interviews with Masvingo Province and Chivi District Agritex staff, as well as on consultation of official extension handbooks. Information on farmers' practices is derived from the Chivi field study (1990–91 season). Aggregate data are presented for the full sample. However, farmers' practices are highly differentiated, by gender, by wealth group, by soil type etc. (Chapters 4–7). This differentiation is not reflected in extension recommendations, which are standard for particular natural regions.

Table A2.1 Cropping extension recommendations and farmer's practices

Cropping activity	Extension recommendation	Farmer's practices
Crop varieties	Maize: R201, R200, R215; sorghum: SV2; pearl millet: PMV1; finger millet: 25C; sunflower: peredovik, musasa; groundnuts: plover, Natal common, GMB Spanish; cotton: G501, K602.	As recommendations, mixed in with local varieties for sorghum and millets.
Land preparation	Winter plough (June–July) to 20–25cm; early manuring (August–September).	5% of area winter ploughed, to c. 10–15cm depth; 6% of area manured.
Planting	Early planting dates from first effective rains in November until late December.	Staggered, from dry planting of millets in October to late planting of replacement crops (e.g. sunflower) in February/March.
Planting	Seeding rates (25kg/ha for maize, 15kg/ha for sorghum, 10kg/ha for millets, 8kg/ha for sunflower) and 90 x 45cm for maize spacing. Plant with hand hoe or ox-drawn planter in straight rows.	Variable seed rates and spacing according to seed availability and field conditions. Row planting with hoes for maize, cotton; otherwise broadcast.

Table A2.1 (*cont.*)

Cropping activity	Extension recommendation	Farmer practice
Fertility management	For grain crops: inorganic fertiliser (basal at 100–200kg D/ha and top at 100kg AN/ha). Blanket D and split top dressing application. Oil seeds – sunflower: 150kg L/ha and 100kg AN/ha; groundnuts: 200kg SSP/ha and 200kg gypsum/ha.	6% of area with basal fertiliser applied; >1% with top dressing. Low concentration, spot applications for certain crops (maize, cotton); otherwise none.
Weeding and cultivation	Intensive weeding for first 8 weeks. 2–4 weedings recommended. Use hoe, mouldboard plough or cultivator.	80% of area with 1 weeding; 20% no weeding; 20% weeded twice; >1% weeded 3–4 times. Weeding depends on crop. Hoe weeding dominates. >5% of farmers with cultivator.
Pest and disease control	Various pesticides: e.g. for maize Diptrex or Thiodan 4–6 weeks to control stalk border.	No pesticides used, except on cotton.
Intercropping, relay cropping, late planting, in-filling	No recommendations, disapproved of	Common practice. 75% of maize area intercropped. Relays following crop failure important. In-filling widely practised.
Rotations	Alvord rotation: maize (with manure 37t/ha), then sorghum/maize, then legume crop, then millet crop.	Various, but most common is maize–maize–maize.
Agroforestry	Previously all trees supposed to be removed from fields. Now agroforestry encouraged. Boundary and home garden planting with exotics recommended.	Indigenous trees (especially fruit trees) retained in fields. Growing trees protected and nurtured if valued highly. Some limited planting around homes.
Field water management	Deep winter ploughing; ridges, tied ridges and furrows; early planting; weeding.	Use of microenvironments; water harvesting using bunds; ridging on heavy soils; soil pits; winter ploughing if possible; organic matter management (leaf litter, stover etc.); manipulation of plant populations.

Table A2.1 (*cont.*)

Cropping activity	Extension recommendation	Farmer practice
Soil conservation	Standard contours; construction of waterways and storm drains; planting on contour; manure application; green manure and cover crops.	Contour bunds; planting along contour; soil harvesting in microenvironments or pits; applications of organic matter (manure, leaf litter etc. if available); high plant populations.

Table A2.2 Livestock extension recommendations and farmer practice

Livestock activity	Extension recommendation	Farmer practice
Cattle		
Breeds	Exotic 'improved' breeds.	Indigenous breeds.
Objectives	Beef production.	Multi-purpose use, especially draught power.
Stocking rates	10ha per livestock unit.	2ha per livestock unit.
Grazing management	Rotational grazing in fenced paddocks – grazing schemes.	Key resource grazing, use of high-potential sites (e.g, *dambo*s, drainage lines etc.).
Fodder management	Legume-reinforced pastures in grazing areas.	Browse management.
	Supplementary feeding, salt licks etc.	None, except in extreme drought.
	Stover collection and preparation with urea.	Stover collection and storage only.
	Agroforestry including planting of *Leucena* etc.	Some agroforestry planting; browse management.
Drought management	Destocking – early sales; movement discouraged and highly regulated.	Movement to other areas; supplementary feeding; distress sales.
Disease control	Weekly (wet season) and fornightly (dry season) dipping; dosing; antibiotics; movement controls.	Dipping regime followed except in drought; traditional herbs used to treat disease.
Smallstock	Few recommendations with respect to management, disease control etc.	Indigenous practices.
Chickens	Improved breeds; improved chicken huts; mash feed etc.	Indigenous breeds, free-ranging, little management.

Bibliography

Abel, N. and Blaikie, P. (1989). 'Land degradation, stocking rates and conservation policies in the communal rangelands of Botswana and Zimbabwe'. *Land Degradation and Rehabilitation* 1, 101–23.

Adams, J. (1991). 'The rural labour market in Zimbabwe'. *Development and Change* 22, 297–320.

Agritex (1984). *Report on the Feasibility of Establishing a Fodder Bank for Drought Relief.* Farm Management and Work Study Section, Agritex, Harare.

Agritex Masvingo (1993). *Report on Drought Recovery Programme.* Agritex, Masvingo.

Agyris, C. and Schön, D. (1978). *Organizational Learning.* Jossey Bass Publisher, San Francisco.

Alvord, E.D. (1930). *Agricultural Demonstration Work in Native Reserves.* Department of Native Affairs Occasional Paper 3. National Archives, Harare.

Amanor, K. (1990). *Analytical Abstracts on Farmer Participatory Research.* Agricultural Administration Research and Extension Network Occasional Paper 10. Overseas Development Institute (ODI), London.

Anderson, J. and Dillon, J. (1992). *Risk Analysis in Dryland Farming Systems.* Farm Systems Management Series 2. Food and Agriculture Organisation (FAO), Rome.

Anderson, J., Dillon, J. and Hardaker, J. (1977). *Agricultural Decision Analysis.* Iowa State University Press, Ames.

Anon (1959). Editorial. *Rhodesia Agricultural Journal* 56, 16.

Arrighi, G. (1970). 'Labour supplies in historical perspective: a study of the proletarianisation of the African peasantry in Rhodesia'. *Journal of Development Studies* 6, 197–234.

Ashworth, V. (1990). *Agricultural Technology and the Communal Farm Sector.* Background paper prepared for Zimbabwe Agricultural Sector Memorandum. Agriculture Division, Southern Africa Department, World Bank, Washington.

Avila, M., Whingwiri, E. and Mombeshara, B. (1989). *Zimbabwe: Organization and Management of On-farm Research in the Department of Research and Specialist Services.* On-farm client-oriented research (OFCOR) Case Study 5. ISNAR, The Hague.

Aylen, D. (1942). 'Conserving soil in the native reserves'. *Rhodesia Agriculture Journal* 39, 152–60.

Baker, D. (1992). *The Inability of Farming Systems Research to Deal with Policy.* Agricultural Administration (Research and Extension) Network Paper 35. ODI, London.

Barrett, J. (1992). *The Economic Role of Cattle in Communal Farming Systems in Zimbabwe.* Pastoral Development Network Paper 32b. ODI, London.

Batterbury, S. (1993). *Planners or Performers? Indigenous dryland farmers in northern Burkina Faso.* ODI Agricultural Administration (Research and Extension) Network 42b, 18–31. ODI, London.

Bawden, R. (1992). 'Of systemics and farming systems research: a critique'. In: Raman, K. and Balaguru, T. (eds). *Farming Systems Research in India: Strategies for Implementation.* National Academy of Agricultural Reasearch Management (NAARM), Hyderabad.

Beach, D.N. (1980). *The Shona and Zimbabwe, 900–1850*. Mambo Press, Gweru.

Bebbington, A. (1994). 'Composing rural livelihoods: from farming systems to food systems'. In: Scoones, I. and Thompson, J. (eds), pp. 88–96. *Beyond Farmer First: Rural People's Knowledge, Agricultural Research and Extension Practice*, Intermediate Technology Publications, London.

Behnke, R. (1994). 'Natural resource management in pastoral Africa'. *Development Policy Review* 12, 5–27.

Behnke, R., Scoones, I. and Kerven, C. (eds) (1993). *Range Ecology at Disequilibrium: New Models of Natural Variability and Pastoral Adaptation in African Savannas*. ODI, London.

Beinart, W. (1984). 'Soil erosion, conservationism and ideas about development: a southern African exploration'. *Journal of Southern African Studies* 11, 52–83.

Bell, M., Faulkner, R., Hotchkiss, P., Lambert, R., Roberts, N. and Windram, A. (1987). *The Use of Dambos in Rural Development, with Reference to Zimbabwe*. Final report of Overseas Development Administration (ODA) project R3869. Dambo Research Unit, University of Loughborough, Loughborough.

Bennell, P. and Ncube, M. (1994). 'Jobs for the boys? The employment experiences of secondary school leavers in Zimbabwe'. *Journal of Southern African Studies* 20, 301–15.

Bennett, J. (1985). *A Field Guide to Soil and Site Description in Zimbabwe*. Zimbabwe Agricultural Journal Technical Handbook 6. Harare.

Benson, C. and Clay, E. (1994). *The Impact of Drought on Sub-Saharan Africa Economies: A Preliminary Examination*. ODI Working Paper 77. ODI, London.

Biggs, S. (1989a). *Resource Poor Farmer Participation in Research: A Synthesis of Experiences from Nine National Agricultural Research Systems*. OFCOR Comparative Study Paper 3. International Service for National Agricultural Research (ISNAR), The Hague.

Biggs, S. (1989b). *A Multiple Source of Innovation Model of Agricultural Research and Technology Promotion*. Agricultural Research and Extension Network Paper 6. ODI, London.

Binswanger, H. (1980). 'Attitudes toward risk: experimental measurement in rural India'. *American Journal of Agricultural Economics* 62, 395–407.

Binswanger, H. (1981). 'Attitudes towards risk: theoretical implications of an experiment in rural India'. *Economic Journal* 91, 867–90.

Blackshaw, G. (1915). 'Fertilisers and the relation between cost of production and prices of farm produce'. *Rhodesia Agriculture Journal* 12, 331–3.

Bratton, M. (1986). 'Financing smallholder production: a comparison of individual and group credit schemes in Zimbabwe'. *Public Administration and Development* 6, 115–32.

Bratton, M. (1987). 'Drought, food and the social organization of small farmers in Zimbabwe'. In: Glantz, M. (ed.). *Drought and Hunger in Africa: Denying Famine a Future*, pp. 213–44. Cambridge University Press, Cambridge.

Bratton, M. and Truscott, K. (1985). 'Fertilizer packages, maize yield and economic returns'. *Zimbabwe Agriculture Journal* 82, 1–8.

Brown, W. (1899). *On the South African Frontier*. Sampson Low, London.

Buchanan-Smith, M. and Davies, S. (1995). *Famine Early Warning and Response: The Missing Link*. Intermediate Technology Publications, London.

Burke, E. (ed.) (1969). *The Journals of Carl Mauch, 1869–1872*. National Archives of Rhodesia, Salisbury.

Byerlee, D., Collinson, M., Perrin, R., Winkelmann, D., Biggs, S., Moscardi, E., Martinez, L., Harrington, L. and Benharamin, A. (1980). *Planning Technologies Appropriate to Farmers: Concepts and Procedures.* International Maize and Wheat Improvement Centre (CIMMYT), Mexico.

Campbell, B. (1987). 'The use of wild fruits in Zimbabwe'. *Economic Botany* 41, 375–85.

Campbell, B., Frost, P., Kirchmann, H. and Swift, M. (1993a). 'Nitrogen cycling and management of soil fertility in small-scale farming systems in northeastern Zimbabwe'. Paper presented to the conference on *Livestock and Sustainable Nutrient Cycling in Mixed Farming Systems of Sub-Saharan Africa.* International Livestock Centre for Africa (ILCA), Addis Ababa.

Campbell, B., Grundy, I. and Matose, F. (1993b). 'Tree and woodland resources: the technical practices of small-scale farmers'. In: Bradley, P. and McNamara, K. (eds). *Living with Trees: Policies for Forestry Management in Zimbabwe*, pp. 29–62. World Bank Technical Paper 210. World Bank, Washington.

Campbell, D. (1990). 'Strategies for coping with severe food deficits in rural Africa: a review of the literature'. *Food and Foodways* 4, 143–62.

Cancian, F. (1972). *Change and Uncertainty in a Peasant Economy: The Maya Corn Farmers of Zinacantan.* Stanford University Press, California.

Cane, M., Eshel, G. and Buckland, R. (1994). 'Forecasting Zimbabwean maize yield using eastern equatorial Pacific sea temperature'. *Nature* 370, 204–5.

Carter, S., Bradley, P., Franzel, S. and Lynam, J. (1994). *Spatial Variation as a Factor in Natural Resource Management Research.* Stockholm Environment Institute, Stockholm.

Cavendish, W. (1993). 'The economics of natural habitat utilisation by communal area farmers'. Unpublished mimeo, Centre for the Study of African Economies, Oxford.

Chambers, R. (1989). 'Editorial introduction: vulnerability, coping and policy'. *IDS Bulletin* 20(2).

Chambers, R. (1992). *Rural Appraisal: Rapid, Relaxed and Participatory.* IDS Discussion Paper 311. Institute of Development Studies, Sussex.

Chambers, R. (1993). *Challenging the Professions: Frontiers for Rural Development.* Intermediate Technology Publications, London.

Chambers, R., Longhurst, R. and Pacey, A. (eds) (1981). *Seasonal Dimensions to Rural Poverty.* Frances Pinter, London.

Chambers, R., Pacey, A. and Thrupp, L. A. (eds) (1989). *Farmer First: Farmer Innovation and Agricultural Research.* Intermediate Technology Publications, London.

Cheater, A. and Bourdillon, M. (1982). 'Drought in southern Zimbabwe: 1982'. Paper presented at the the workshop on *Resource Degradation and Development Planning in Semi-Arid Environments.* Hlekweni, Bulawayo.

Chisvo, M. (1993). *Government Spending on Social Services and the Impact of Structural Adjustment.* UNICEF, Harare.

Chisvo, M. and Jayne, T. (1992). 'Is grain availability an important determinant of variation in nutritional status among children?' In: Wyckoff, J. and Rukuni, M. (eds). *Food Security Research in Southern Africa: Policy Implications*, pp. 250–66. University of Zimbabwe/Michigan State University Food Security Research in Southern Africa Project, Department of Agricultural Economics and Extension, University of Zimbabwe, Harare.

Chisvo, M., Jayne, T., Tefft, J., Weber, M. and Shaffer, M. (1991). 'Traders' perceptions of constraints on informal grain marketing in Zimbabwe: implications for household food security and needed research'. In: Rukuni, M. and Wyckoff, J. (eds). *Market Reforms, Research Policies and SADCC Food Security*, pp. 120–40. University of Zimbabwe/Michigan State University Food Security Research in Southern Africa Project, Department of Agricultural Economics and Extension, University of Zimbabwe, Harare.

Christensen, G. and Stack, J. (1992). *The Dimensions of Household Food Insecurity in Zimbabwe, 1980–1991*. Food Studies Group Working Paper 5. Food Studies Group (FSG), Oxford.

Christiansen, R. (1993). 'Implementing strategies for the rural economy: lessons from Zimbabwe, options for South Africa'. *World Development* 21, 1549–66.

Chung, F. (1988). 'Education: revolution or reform'. In: Stoneman, C. (ed.). *Zimbabwe's Prospects: Issues of Race, Class, State and Capital in Southern Africa*, pp. 118–32. Macmillan, London.

CIMMYT (1988). *From Agronomic Data to Farmer Recommendations: An Economics Training Manual.* CIMMYT, Mexico.

Clarke, J. (1991). 'Forestry as a component of participatory rural development: lessons and challenges drawn from the Zimbabwean experience'. Paper presented to the conference on *African Agroforestry*, 19–22 August 1991, Nelspruit, South Africa.

Cleghorn, W. B. (1966). 'Report on the condition of grazing in Tribal Trust Land'. *Rhodesia Agricultural Journal* 63, 57–67.

Cobbing, J. (1976). 'The Ndebele under the Khumalos, 1820–1896'. PhD thesis, University of Lancaster.

Collinson, M. (1982). *A Diagnostic Survey of the South of Chivi District, Zimbabwe for Adaptive Research Planning.* CIMMYT Eastern Africa Economics Programme Occasional Papers Report 5. CIMMYT, Nairobi.

Corbett, J. (1994). *Livelihoods, Food Security and Nutrition in a Drought Prone part of Zimbabwe.* Final report to Economic and Social Research Grants Programme (ESCOR). Centre for the Study of African Economies, Oxford and Centre for Social and Economic Research on the Global Environment (CSERGE), London.

Cornwall, A., Guijt, I. and Welbourn, A. (1994). 'Acknowledging process: challenges for agricultural research and extension'. In: Scoones, I. and Thompson, J. (eds). *Beyond Farmer First: Rural People's Knowledge, Agricultural Research and Extension Practice*, pp. 98–117. Intermediate Technology Publications, London.

Cousins, B. (1992). *Managing Communal Rangeland in Zimbabwe: Experiences and Lessons.* Commonwealth Secretariat, London.

CSO (1985). *1982 Population Census: Main Demographic Features of the Population of Zimbabwe.* Central Statistics Office, Harare.

CSO (1992). *Census Zimbabwe: Preliminary Report.* Central Statistics Office, Harare.

CSO (1993). *Census 1992: Provincial Profile, Masvingo.* Central Statistics Office, Harare.

CSO (1994). *Quarterly Statistical Bulletins.* CSO, Harare.

Dankwerts, J.P. (1974). *A Socioeconomic Study of Veld Management in the Tribal Areas of Victoria Province.* Tribal Areas of Rhodesia Research Foundation, Salisbury.

Davies, S. (1993). 'Are coping strategies a cop out?' *IDS Bulletin* 24, 60–72

de Schlippe, P. (1956). *Shifting Cultivation in Africa: The Zande System of Agriculture.* Routledge, Kegan and Paul, London.

Douglas, M. (1985). *Risk Acceptability According to the Social Sciences.* Russell Sage Foundation, New York.

Douglas, M. and Wildavsky, A. (1982). *Risk and Culture: An Essay on the Selection of Technical and Environmental Dangers.* University of California Press, Berkeley.

Downing, T. (1992). *Climate Change and Vulnerable Places: Global Food Security and Country Studies in Zimbabwe, Kenya, Senegal and Chile.* ECU Research Report 1. Environmental Change Unit, Oxford.

Drèze, J. and Sen, A. (1989). *Hunger and Public Action.* Oxford University Press, Oxford.

Drèze, J. and Sen, A. (eds) (1990). *The Political Economy of Hunger.* Oxford University Press, Oxford.

Drinkwater, M. (1989). 'Technical development and peasant impoverishment: land use policy in Zimbabwe's Midlands Province'. *Journal of Southern African Studies* 15, 287–305.

Drinkwater, M. (1991). *The State and Agrarian Change in Zimbabwe's Communal Areas.* Macmillan, London.

Drinkwater, M. and McEwan, M.A. (1994). 'Household food security and environmental sustainability in farming systems research: developing sustainable livelihoods'. *Journal of Farming Systems Research and Extension* 4, 111–26.

Eicher, C. and Rukuni, M. (1994). 'Zimbabwe's agricultural revolution: lessons for Southern Africa'. In: Rukuni, M. and Eicher, C. (eds). *Zimbabwe's Agricultural Revolution*, pp. 393–411. University of Zimbabwe Press, Zimbabwe

Einstein, A. (1971). *The Born–Einstein Letters.* Macmillan, London.

Elliot, J. (1989). 'Soil erosion and conservation in Zimbabwe: political economy and the environment'. PhD thesis, Loughborough University.

Ellis, F. (1988). *Peasant Economics: Farm Households and Agrarian Development.* Cambridge University Press, Cambridge.

Elwell, H.A. (1983). 'The degrading soil and water resources of the communal areas'. *Zimbabwe Science News* 17, 145–7.

Elwell, H.A. (1985). 'An assessment of soil erosion in Zimbabwe'. *Zimbabwe Science News* 19, 27–33.

Fabian, J. (1990). *Power and Performance: Ethnographic Explorations Through Proverbial Wisdom and Theatre in Shaba, Zaire.* University of Wisconsin, Madison.

Fairhead, J. (1993). 'Representing knowledge: the "new farmer" in research fashions'. In: Pottier, J. (ed.). *Practising Development: Social Science Perspectives*, pp. 187–204. Routledge, London.

Fals-Borda, O. and Rahman, A. (eds) (1991). *Action and Knowledge: Breaking the Monopoly with Participatory Action Research.* Apex, New York.

Farrington, J. (1994). *Public Sector Agricultural Extension: Is there life after structural adjustment?* Natural Resource Perspectives 2. ODI, London.

Farrington, J., Bebbington, A., Wellard, K. and Lewis, D. (eds) (1993). *Reluctant Partners? Non-Governmental Organizations, the State and Sustainable Agricultural Development.* Routledge, London.

Fischoff, B., Lichtenstein, S., Slovic, P., Derby, S. and Keeney, R. (1981). *Acceptable Risk.* Cambridge University Press, Cambridge.

Floyd, B.N. (1959). 'Changing patterns of African land-use in Southern Rhodesia', Vols 1–3. PhD thesis, Syracuse University, USA.

Frankenberger, T. (1993). *Promoting Livelihood Security in Areas Prone to Recurrent*

Droughts and Desertification: Proactive Response Planning for Enhancing Household Drought Resilience. International Fund for Agricultural Development (IFAD), Rome.

Friis-Hansen, E. (1990). *The Zimbabwe Seed Industry.* Background paper prepared for Zimbabwe Agricultural Sector Memorandum. Agriculture Division, Southern Africa Department, World Bank, Washington.

Frost, P., Menaut, J., Walker, B., Medina, E., Solbrig, O. and Swift, M. (eds) (1986). *Response of Savannas to Stress and Disturbance: A Proposal for a Collaborative Programme of Research.* Biology International Special Issue, International Union for the Biological Sciences, Paris.

FSRU (1993). *Soil Fertility Management by Small Holder Farmers. A Participatory Rapid Appraisal in Chivi and Mangwende Communal Areas.* FSRU/DRSS, Harare.

FSRU/IIED (1991). *Structural Adjustment and Communal Area Agriculture: Case Studies from Mangwende and Chivi Communal Areas.* FSRU/DRSS, Harare.

FSRU/IIED (1994). *Coping with Risk and Uncertainty in Africa's Drylands.* Final Technical Report. IIED, London and FSRU, Harare.

Funtowicz, S. and Ravetz, J. (1992). 'Three types of risk assessment and the emergence of post-normal science'. In: Krimsky, S. and Sheldon, D (eds). *Social Theories of Risk*, pp. 251–74. Praeger, London.

Garbett, K. (1963). 'The Land Husbandry Act of Southern Rhodesia'. In: Biebuyk, D. (ed.). *African Agrarian Systems*, pp. 185–202. Oxford University Press, Oxford.

GFA (1987). *Study on the Economic and Social Determinants of Livestock Production in the Communal Areas, Zimbabwe.* Department of Veterinary Services, Harare.

Gilbert, E., Norman, D. and Winch, F. (1980). *Farming Systems Research: A Critical Appraisal.* MSU Rural Development Paper 6. Department of Agricultural Economics, Michigan State University (MSU), East Lansing.

Gill, G. (1991). *Seasonality and Agriculture in the Developing World: A Problem of the Poor and Powerless.* Cambridge University Press, Cambridge.

Gladwin, C. (1983). 'Contributions of decision tree methodology to a farming systems program'. *Human Organization* 42, 146–57.

Grant, P. (1981). 'The fertilization of sandy soils in peasant agriculture'. *Zimbabwe Agricultural Journal* 78, 169–75.

Gumbo, D., Mukamuri, B., Muzondo, M. and Scoones, I. (1990). 'Indigenous and exotic fruit trees: why do people want to grow them?' In: Prinsley, R. (ed.). *Agroforestry for Sustainable Production*, pp. 185–214. Commonwealth Science Council, London.

Guyer, J. and Peters, P. (1987). 'Introduction: conceptualising the household: issues of theory and policy in Africa'. Special issue, *Development and Change* 18(2), 197–214.

Hacking, I. (1975). *The Emergence of Probability.* Cambridge University Press, Cambridge.

Hacking, I. (1983). *Representing and Intervening: Introductory Topics in the Philosophy of Natural Science.* Cambridge University Press, Cambridge.

Hacking, I. (1990). *The Taming of Chance.* Cambridge University Press, Cambridge.

Hagmann, J. and Chuma, E. (1994). *Transformation of Agricultural Extension and Research in Zimbabwe Towards Farmer Participation: Approach and Strategy Based on Experiences in Masvingo Province.* Agritex/Deutsche Gesellschaft für Technische Zusammenarbeit (GTZ), Conservation Tillage Project, Masvingo.

Hagmann, J. and Murwirwa, K. (1994). 'Indigenous soil and water conservation in southern Zimbabwe: a study on techniques, historical changes and recent developments under participatory research and extension'. Unpublished report, IIED/Centre for Development Cooperation Services (CDCS), London and Amsterdam.

Haugerud, A. and Collinson, M. (1991). *Plants, Genes and People: Improving the Relevance of Plant Breeding*. Sustainable Agriculture Gatekeeper Series SA30. IIED, London.

Heinrich, G. (1993). *Strengthening Farmer Participation Through Groups: Experiences and Lessons from Botswana*. OFCOR Discussion Paper 3. ISNAR, The Hague.

Helmsing, A. (1987). *Non-agricultural Enterprises in the Communal Lands of Zimbabwe: Preliminary Results of a Survey*. Occasional Paper 10. Department of Rural and Urban Planning, University of Zimbabwe, Harare.

Herbst, J. (1990). *State Politics in Zimbabwe*. University of Zimbabwe Press, Harare.

Hesse, M. (1980). *Revolutions and Reconstructions in the Philosophy of Science*. Harvester Press, Hassocks.

Holborrow, A. (1915). 'Manuring of maize on Government Experimental Farm, Gwebi'. *Rhodesia Agricultural Journal* 12, 498-501.

Holleman, J. (1969). *Chief, Council and Commissioner: Some Problems of Government in Rhodesia*. Koninkelijke van Gorcum and Co, Netherlands.

Holling, C. (1993). 'Investing in research for sustainability'. *Ecological Applications* 3, 552–5.

Huijsman, A. (1986). *Choice and Uncertainty in a Semi-subsistence Economy: A Study of Decision-making in a Philippine Village*. Koninklijk Institut voor de Tropen (KIT), Amsterdam.

Hussein, J. (1987). 'Agroclimatological analysis of growing season in Natural Regions III, IV and V of Zimbabwe'. In: *Cropping in the Semi-Arid Areas of Zimbabwe*. Agritex, Harare and GTZ, Masvingo.

ICRA (1987). 'Farm systems dynamics and risk in a low potential area: Chivi South, Masvingo Province, Zimbabwe'. *ICRA Bulletin* 27. International Centre for Development Oriented Research in Agriculture (ICRA), Wageningen.

Iliffe, J. (1990). *Famine in Zimbabwe, 1890–1960*. Mambo Press, Gweru.

ILO (1993). 'Zimbabwe: falling wages and rising unemployment: the negative side of structural adjustment'. *International Labour Review* 132, 567–71.

Jackson, C. (1994). 'Changing conjugal contracts in rural Zimbabwean households'. Paper presented at the African Studies Association (UK) conference, September 1994, Lancaster University, Lancaster.

Jackson, J. and Collier, P. (1988). *Incomes, Poverty and Food Security in the Communal Lands of Zimbabwe*. Occasional Paper, Department of Rural and Urban Planning, University of Zimbabwe, Harare.

Jackson, M. (1989). *Paths Toward a Clearing: Radical Empiricism and Ethnographic Inquiry*. Indiana University Press, Bloomington.

Jansen, D. and Muir, K. (1994). 'Trade, exchange rate policy and agriculture in the 1980s'. In: Rukuni, M. and Eicher, C. (eds). *Zimbabwe's Agricultural Revolution*, pp. 175–90. University of Zimbabwe Publications, Harare.

Jayne, T. (1994). 'Do high food marketing costs constrain cash crop production? Evidence from Zimbabwe'. *Economic Development and Cultural Change* 42, 387–402.

Jayne, T. and Chisvo, M. (1991). 'Unravelling Zimbabwe's food insecurity paradox: implications for grain market reform in Southern Africa'. *Food Policy* 16, 319–29.

Jayne, T. and Lawrence, R. (1993). 'Maize milling, market reform and food security: the case of Zimbabwe'. *World Development* 21, 975–88.

Jayne, T. and Nuppenau, E. (1993). 'Maize market reform in Zimbabwe'. *Food Policy* 18, 308–15.

Jayne, T. and Rukuni, M. (1993). 'Distributional effects of maize self-sufficiency in Zimbabwe: implications for pricing and trade policy'. *Food Policy* 18, 334–41.

Johnson, A. (1972). 'Individuality and experimentation in traditional agriculture'. *Human Ecology* 1, 149–60.

Johnson, E.J. and Tversky, A. (1983). 'Affect, generalisation and the perception of risk'. *Journal of Personality and Social Psychology* 45, 21–31.

Johnson, R. (1968). 'The economics of African agriculture in Southern Rhodesia'. PhD thesis, University of London.

Jones, R. and Sandland, R. (1974). 'The relation between animal gain and stocking rate: derivation of the relation from the results of grazing trials'. *Journal of Agricultural Science* 83, 335–41.

Kabeer, N. and Joekes, S. (eds) (1991). 'Researching the household: methodological and empirical issues'. *IDS Bulletin* 22.

Kahneman, D., Slovic, P. and Tversky, A. (eds) (1982). *Judgement under Uncertainty: Heuristics and Biases.* Cambridge University Press, Cambridge.

Korten, D. (1980). 'Community organisation and rural development: a learning process approach'. *Public Administration Review* 40, 480–511.

Krimsky, S. and Golding, D. (eds) (1992). *Social Theories of Risk.* Praeger, London.

Kuhn, T. (1962). *The Structure of Scientific Revolutions.* Chicago University Press, Chicago.

Latour, B. (1987). *Science in Action.* Open University Press, Milton Keynes.

Leys, R. (1986). 'Drought and drought relief in southern Zimbabwe'. In: Lawrence, P. (ed.). *World Recession and the Food Crisis in Africa*, pp. 258–74. James Currey, London.

Lichtenstein, S., Slovic, P., Fishchoff, B., Layman, M. and Combs, B. (1978). 'Judged frequency of lethal events'. *Journal of Experimental Psychology: Human Learning and Memory* 4, 551–78.

Loewenson, R. and Sanders, D. (1988). 'The political economy of health and nutrition'. In: Stoneman, C. (ed.). *Zimbabwe's Prospects: Issues of Race, Class, State and Capital in Southern Africa*, pp. 133–52. Macmillan, London.

Long, N. and Long, A. (eds) (1992). *Battlefields of Knowledge: The Interlocking of Theory and Practice in Social Research and Development.* Routledge, London.

Low, A. (1986). *Agricultural Development in Southern Africa: Farm Household Economics and the Food Crisis.* James Currey, London.

McGregor, J. (1991). 'Woodland resources: ecology, policy and ideology: an historical case study of woodland use in Shurugwi communal area, Zimbabwe'. PhD thesis, Loughborough University of Technology.

Mack, R. (1970). 'The great African cattle plague epidemic of the 1890s'. *Tropical Animal Health and Production* 2, 210–19.

Mascarenhas, J. *et al.* (eds) (1991). 'Participatory Rural Appraisal: proceedings of the February 1991 PRA Trainers' Workshop'. *RRA Notes* 13. IIED, London.

Maseko, Z., Scoones, I. and Wilson, K. (1987). 'Integrating research and extension: experiences from a participatory water development project in southern Zimbabwe'. *ILEIA Newsletter* 4(4), 18–19.

Mashingaidze, K. (1994). 'Maize research and development'. In: Rukuni, M. and

Eicher, C.(eds). *Zimbabwe's Agricultural Revolution*, pp. 208–18. University of Zimbabwe Publications, Harare.

Masters, W. and Nuppenau, E. (1993). 'Pan-territorial versus regional pricing for maize in Zimbabwe'. *World Development* 21, 1647–58.

Maurya, D., Bottrell, A. and Farrington, J. (1988). 'Improved livelihoods, genetic diversity and farmer participation: a strategy for rice breeding in rainfed areas of India'. *Experimental Agriculture* 24, 311–20.

Maxwell, S. and Bart, C. (1995). 'Beyond ranking: exploring relative preferences in P/RRA'. *PLA Notes* 22, 28–35. IIED, London.

Maxwell, S. and Frankenburger, T. (1992). *Food Security: Concepts, Indicators and Measurement: A Technical Review*. UNICEF/IFAD, New York and Rome.

Maxwell, S. and Smith, M. (1992). 'Household food security: a conceptual review'. In: Maxwell, S. and Frankenberger, T. (eds). *Household Food Security: Concepts, Indicators, Measurements*. IFAD and UNICEF, Rome and New York.

Mazvimavi, D. (1989). 'Analysis of annual rainfall in Zimbabwe for trends and periodicities'. *Geographical Journal of Zimbabwe* 20, 42–52.

Medawar, P. (1982). *Pluto's Republic*. Oxford University Press, Oxford.

Merrill-Sands, D., Biggs, S., Bingen, R., Ewell, P., McAllister, J. and Poats, S. (1991). 'Institutional considerations in strengthening on-farm client-oriented research in National Agricultural Research Systems: lessons from a nine-country study'. *Experimental Agriculture* 27, 343–73.

MLARR (1989). *The First Annual Report of Farm Management Data for Communal Area Farm Units, 1988–89 Season*. Farm Management Research Section, Economics and Markets Branch, Ministry of Lands, Agriculture and Rural Resettlement (MLARR), Harare.

MLARR (1990). *The Second Annual Report of Farm Management Data for Communal Area Farm Units, 1989–90 Season*. Farm Management Research Section, Economics and Markets Branch, Ministry of Lands, Agriculture and Rural Resettlement, Harare.

MLAWD (1994). *The Agricultural Sector of Zimbabwe: Statistical Bulletin, May 1994*. Economics Division, Ministry of Lands, Agriculture and Water Development (MLAWD), Harare.

Mombeshora, B. (1987). 'Practical application of farming systems research in Chivi communal area'. In: *Cropping in the Semi-Arid Areas of Zimbabwe*, pp. 397–416. Agritex, Harare and GTZ, Masvingo.

Moris, J. (1991). *Extension Alternatives in Tropical Africa*. ODI, London.

Morkel, A. (1925). 'A maize rotation experiment: combining green manuring and the application of fertilisers'. *Rhodesia Agriculture Journal* 22, 826, 830.

Mortimore, M. (1989). *Adapting to Drought*. Cambridge University Press, Cambridge.

Mosley, P. (1983). *The Settler Economies: Studies in the Economic History of Kenya and Southern Rhodesia, 1900–1963*. Cambridge University Press, Cambridge.

Moyo, S. (1991). *Institutional Support for Non-agricultural Rural Industries*. Working Paper 31. Zimbabwe Environmental Research Organisation (ZERO), Harare.

Mudenge, S. (1988). *A Political History of Munhumutapa, 1400–1902*. Zimbabwe Publishing House, Harare.

Mudhara, M. (1991). 'Economics and fertiliser use in maize in semi-arid environments: experiences of the Farming Systems Research Unit in Chivi communal area'. Unpublished paper, FSRU/IIED, Harare and London.

Mudimu, G., Chopak, C., Chigume, S., Govereh, J. and Bernsten, R. (1990).

'Household income, food production and marketing in low rainfall areas of Zimbabwe: status, constraints and opportunities'. In: Rukuni, M., Mudimu, G. and Jayne, T. (eds). *Food Security Policies in the SADCC Region*, pp. 169–90. University of Zimbabwe/Michigan State University Food Security Research in Southern Africa Project, Department of Agricultural Economics and Extension, University of Zimbabwe, Harare.

Mugwira, L. and Mukurumbira, L. (1984). 'Comparative effectiveness of manures from the communal areas and commercial feedlots as plant nutrient sources'. *Zimbabwe Agricultural Journal* 81, 241–50.

Mugwira, L. and Shumba, E. (1986). 'Rate of manure applied in some communal areas and the effect on plant growth and maize grain yields'. *Zimbabwe Agriculture Journal* 83, 99–104.

Muir-Leresche, K. (1985). 'Crop price wage policy in the light of Zimbabwe's development goals'. Unpublished PhD thesis, University of Zimbabwe, Harare.

Mukamuri, B. (1988). 'Rural environmental conservation in south-central Zimbabwe: an attempt to describe Karanga thought patterns, perceptions and environmental control'. Paper presented to the African Studies Association conference, September 1988, Cambridge.

Murray, C. (1987). 'Class, gender and the household: the development cycle in southern Africa'. *Development and Change* 18, 235–50.

Nhira, C. and Fortmann, L. (1993). 'Local woodland management: realities at the grass roots'. In: Bradley, P. and McNamara, K. (eds). *Living with Trees: Policies for Forestry Management in Zimbabwe*, pp. 139–56. World Bank Technical Paper 210. World Bank, Washington.

Nhuvira, P. (1992). 'Savings clubs: an alternative to agricultural loans in communal areas'. *Adult Education and Development* 39, 279–85.

Nobbs, E. (1915). 'Report on crop experiments at Government Farm, Gwebi, 1914–1915'. *Rhodesia Agricultural Journal* 12, 745–58.

Norman, D. (1980). *Farming Systems Approach: Relevance for the Small Farmer.* MSU Rural Development Paper 5. Department of Agricultural Economics, Michigan State University, East Lansing.

Norman, D., Siebert, J., Modiakgotla, E. and Worman, F. (1994). *Farming Systems Research Approach: A Primer for Eastern and Southern Africa.* Farming Systems Programme, UNDP, Gaborone.

Okali, C., Sumberg, J. and Farrington, J. (1994). *Farmer Participatory Research: Rhetoric and Reality.* Intermediate Technology Publications, London.

Otway, H. and Wynne, B. (1989). 'Risk communication and paradox'. *Risk Analysis* 9, 141–5.

Oxby, C. (1994). *Restocking: A Guide.* Vet Aid, Roslin, Scotland.

Palmer, R. (1977). *Land and Racial Domination in Rhodesia.* Heinemann, London.

Parry, M., Carter, T. and Konijn, N. (eds) (1988). *The Impact of Climatic Variations on Agriculture. Vol 2. Assessments in Semi-Arid Regions.* Kluwer Academic Publishers, London.

Phimister, I. (1978). 'Meat and monopolies: beef cattle in southern Rhodesia'. *Journal of African History* 19, 391–414.

Phimister, I. (1988). *An Economic and Social History of Zimbabwe: 1890–1948. Capital Accumulation and Class Struggle.* Longmans, London.

Popper, K. (1975). *Conjectures and Refutations: The Growth of Scientific Knowledge.* Routledge, Kegan and Paul, London.

Pottier, J. (ed.) (1993). *African Food Systems Under Stress: Issues, Perspectives and Methodologies*. SOAS, London.

Potts, D. and Mutambirwa, C. (1990). 'Rural–urban linkages in contemporary Harare: why migrants need their land'. *Journal of Southern African Studies* 16, 677–98.

Pretty, R. and Chambers, R. (1994). 'Towards a learning paradigm: new professionalism and institutions for agriculture'. In: Scoones, I. and Thompson, J. (eds) (1994). *Beyond Farmer First: Rural People's Knowledge, Agricultural Research and Extension Practice*, pp. 182–203. Intermediate Technology Publications, London.

Ranger, T. (1985). *Peasant Consciousness and Guerrilla War in Zimbabwe*. James Currey, London.

Rattray, A. (1950). 'Annual report of experiments, 1948–1949 season'. *Rhodesia Agricultural Journal* 47, 126–30.

Rattray, A. (1951). 'Maize: Hints for the new farmer'. *Rhodesia Agricultural Journal* 48, 123–34.

Reijntes, C., Haverkort, B. and Waters-Bayer, A. (1992). *Farming for the Future: An Introduction to Low External Input and Sustainable Agriculture*. Information Centre for Low External Input and Sustainable Agriculture (ILEIA). Macmillan, London.

Rhoades, R. and Bebbington, A. (1988). *Farmers Who Experiment: An Untapped Resource for Agricultural Development*. International Potato Centre, Lima, Peru.

Richards, A. (1939). *Land, Labour and Diet in Northern Rhodesia*. Oxford University Press, Oxford.

Richards, P. (1985). *Indigenous Agricultural Revolutions: Ecology and Food Production in West Africa*. Hutchinson, London.

Richards, P. (1986). *Coping with Hunger: Hazard and Experiment in an African Rice Farming System*. Allen and Unwin, London.

Richards, P. (1989). 'Agriculture as performance'. In: Chambers *et al.* (eds). *Farmer First: Farmer Innovation and Agricultural Research*, pp. 39–43. Intermediate Technology Publications, London.

Richards, P. (1993). 'Cultivation: knowledge or performance'. In: Hobart, M. *An Anthropological Critique of Development. The Growth of Ignorance*, pp. 61–78, Routledge, London.

Roberts, N. and Lambert, R. (1990). 'Degradation of dambo soils and peasant agriculture in Zimbabwe'. In: Boardman, J., Foster, I. and Dearing, J. (eds). *Soil Erosion on Agricultural Land*, pp. 537–58. John Wiley and Sons, London.

Rohrbach, D. (1988). 'The growth of smallholder maize production in Zimbabwe: causes and implications for food security'. PhD thesis, Department of Agricultural Economics, Michigan State University.

Rohrbach, D. (1989). *The Economics of Smallholder Maize Production in Zimbabwe: Implications for Food Security*. MSU International Development Paper 11. Michigan State University, East Lansing.

Röling, N. (1994). 'Facilitating sustainable agriculture: turning policy models upside down'. In: Scoones, I. and Thompson, J. (eds). *Beyond Farmer First: Rural People's Knowledge, Agricultural Research and Extension Practice*, pp. 245–7. Intermediate Technology Publications, London.

Roth, M. (1990). *Analysis of Agrarian Structure and Land Use Patterns*. Background paper prepared for the World Bank Agricultural Sector Memorandum. World Bank, Harare.

Roth, M. (1994). 'Critique of Zimbabwe's 1992 Land Act'. In: Rukuni, M. and

Eicher, C. (eds). *Zimbabwe's Agricultural Revolution*, pp. 317–34. University of Zimbabwe Publications, Harare.

Roumasset, J., Boussard, J. and Singh, I. (1979). *Risk, Uncertainty and Agricultural Development.* Agricultural Development Council, New York.

Royal Society (1992). *Risk: Analysis, Perception and Management.* Royal Society, London.

Rukuni, M. (1994). 'The evolution of agricultural policy: 1890–1990'. In: Rukuni, M. and Eicher, C. (eds). *Zimbabwe's Agricultural Revolution*, pp. 15–39. University of Zimbabwe Publications, Harare.

Rukuni, M. and Eicher, C. (eds) (1994). *Zimbabwe's Agricultural Revolution.* University of Zimbabwe Publications, Harare.

Russell, D. and Ison, R. (1993). 'The research–development relationship in rangelands: an opportunity for contextual science'. In: *Proceedings of the First International Rangeland Congress, Montpellier, France*, vol. 3, pp. 1047–54. Association Française de Pastoralisme, Montpellier.

SADC (1993). *Assessment of the Response to the 1991–92 Drought in the SADC Region.* Food Security Technical and Administrative Unit, SADC, Harare.

SADC (1994). *Drought Management Workshops in Southern Africa: Report of the Regional Drought Management Workshop*, Volume 1. Workshop Proceedings. Food Studies Group, Oxford and Food Security Technical and Administrative Unit, SADC, Harare.

Sahn, D. (ed.) (1989). *Seasonal Variability in Third World Agriculture: The Consequences for Food Security.* Johns Hopkins Press, Baltimore.

Sandford, S. (1979). 'Towards a definition of drought'. In: Hinchey, M. (ed.). *Proceedings of a Symposium on Drought in Botswana*, pp. 33–40. Botswana Society/Clark University Press.

Sayer, A. (1992). *Methodology in Social Science: A Realist Approach.* Routledge, London.

Schoffeleers, J. (1979). *Guardians of the Land.* Mambo Press, Gweru.

Scholes, R. and Walker, B. (1993). *An African Savanna: A Synthesis of the Nylesvley Study.* Cambridge University Press, Cambridge.

Schön, D. (1983). *The Reflective Practitioner: How Professionals Think in Action.* Avebury, Aldershot.

Scoones, I. (1989). *Economic and Ecological Carrying Capacity: Implications for Livestock Development in Zimbabwe's Communal Areas.* Pastoral Development Network Paper 27b. ODI, London.

Scoones, I. (1990). 'Livestock populations and the household economy: a case study from southern Zimbabwe'. PhD thesis, University of London.

Scoones, I. (1991). 'Wetlands in drylands: key resources for agricultural and pastoral production in Africa'. *Ambio* 20, 366–71.

Scoones, I. (1992a). 'Land degradation and livestock production in Zimbabwe's communal areas'. *Land Degradation and Rehabilitation* 3, 99–113.

Scoones, I. (1992b). 'The economic value of livestock in the communal areas of southern Zimbabwe'. *Agricultural Systems* 39, 339–59.

Scoones, I. (1992c). 'Coping with drought: responses of herders and livestock in contrasting savanna environments in southern Zimbabwe'. *Human Ecology* 20, 293–314.

Scoones, I. (1993). 'Why are there so many animals? Cattle population dynamics in the communal areas of Zimbabwe'. In: Behnke, R., Scoones, I. and Kerven, C. (eds). *Range Ecology at Disequilibrium: New Models of Natural Variability and Pastoral Adaptation in African Savannas.* ODI, London.

Scoones, I. (1995a). 'Investigating difference: applications of wealth ranking and household survey approaches among farming households in southern Zimbabwe'. *Development and Change* 26, 67–88.

Scoones, I. (1995b). 'Exploiting heterogeneity: habitat use by cattle in the communal areas of Zimbabwe'. *Journal of Arid Environments* 29, 221–37.

Scoones, I. (1995c). 'Politics, polemics and pastures: range management science and policy in southern Africa'. In: Leach, M. and Mearns, R. (eds). *The Lie of the Land: Challenging Received Wisdoms in African Environmental Change and Policy*. James Currey, London.

Scoones, I. and Cousins, B. (1988). 'A participatory model of agricultural research and extension: the case of vleis, trees and grazing schemes in the dry south of Zimbabwe'. *Zambezia* XVI, 45–65.

Scoones, I. and Cousins, B. (1994). 'The struggle for control over wetland resources in Zimbabwe'. *Society and Natural Resources* 7, 579–94.

Scoones, I. and Matose, M. (1993). 'Local woodland management: constraints and opportunities for sustainable resource use'. In: Bradley, P. and McNamara, K. (eds). *Living with Trees: Policies for Forestry Management in Zimbabwe*, pp. 157–98. World Bank Technical Paper 210. World Bank, Washington.

Scoones, I. and Thompson, J. (eds) (1994). *Beyond Farmer First: Rural People's Knowledge, Agricultural Research and Extension Practice*. Intermediate Technology Publications, London.

Scoones, I. and Wilson, K. (1989). 'Households, lineage groups and ecological dynamics: issues for livestock development in Zimbabwe's communal lands'. In: Cousins, B. (ed.). *People, Land and Livestock*, pp. 17–122. Centre for Applied Social Sciences, University of Zimbabwe, Harare.

Scott, J. (1985). *Weapons of the Weak: Everyday Forms of Peasant Resistance*. Yale University Press, New Haven, CT.

Scott, J. (1976). *The Moral Economy of the Peasant: Rebellion and Subsistence in Southeast Asia*. Yale University Press, New Haven.

Sen, A. (1981). *Poverty and Famines: An Essay on Entitlement and Deprivation*. Clarendon Press, Oxford.

Shaner, W., Phillip, P. and Schmel, W. (1982). *Farming Systems Research and Development: Guidelines for Developing Countries*. Westview Press, Colorado.

Simmonds, N. (1990). *The Social Context of Plant Breeding*. Plant Breeding Abstracts 60 (4).

Slovic, P., Fischoff, B. and Lichtenstein, S. (1980). 'Facts and fears. Uunderstanding perceived risk'. In: Schwing, R. and Albers, W. (eds). *Societal Risk Assessment: How Safe is Safe Enough?* Plenum Press, New York.

Southern Rhodesia (1939). *Report of the Commission to Enquire into the Preservation of the Natural Resources of the Colony* (McIllwaine Report). Government Printers, Salisbury.

Sperling, L., Loevinshohn, M. and Ntabomvuru, B. (1993). 'Rethinking the farmers' role in plant breeding: local bean experts and on-station selection in Rwanda'. *Experimental Agriculture* 29, 509.

Stack, J. (1994). 'The distributional consequences of the smallholder maize revolution'. In: Rukuni, M. and Eicher, C. (eds). *Zimbabwe's Agricultural Revolution*, pp. 258–73. University of Zimbabwe Publications, Harare.

Stack, J. and Chopak, C. (1990). 'Household income patterns in Zimbabwe's communal areas: empirical evidence from five survey areas'. In: *Integrating Food, Nutrition and Agricultural Policy in Zimbabwe*, pp. 118–25. MSU Food Security Project, Department of Agricultural Economics and Extension, University of Zimbabwe, Harare.

Stanning, J. (1985). *Contribution of Smallholder Agriculture to Marketed Output in Zimbabwe, 1970–85*. Working Paper 5/85. Department of Agricultural Economics and Extension, UZ, Harare.

Stanning, J. (1989). 'Grain retentions and consumption behaviour among rural Zimbabwe households'. In: Mudimu, G. and Bernsten, R. (eds). *Household and National Food Security in Southern Africa*, pp. 79–102. University of Zimbabwe and Michigan State University Food Security Research Project, Department of Agricultural Economics and Extension, University of Zimbabwe, Harare.

Starkey, P. (1987). *Animal Drawn Wheeled Tool Carriers: Perfected Yet Rejected. A Cautionary Tale of Development*. Vieweg und Sohn, Wiesbaden, Germany.

Stocking, M. (1978). 'Relationship of agricultural history and settlement to severe erosion in Rhodesia'. *Rhodesia Agricultural Journal* 73, 35–9.

Stocking, M. and Elwell, H. (1973). 'Soil erosion hazard in Rhodesia'. *Rhodesia Agricultural Journal* 70, 93–101.

Stocking, M.A. (1986). *The Costs of Soil Erosion in Zimbabwe in Terms of the Loss of Three Major Nutrients*. Working Paper 3. Soil Conservation Programme, Land and Water Development Division, FAO, Rome.

Stolzenbach, A. (1994). 'Learning by improvisation: farmers' experimentation in Mali'. In: Scoones, I. and Thompson, J. (eds). *Beyond Farmer First: Rural People's Knowledge, Agricultural Research and Extension Practice*, pp. 155–9. Intermediate Technology Publications, London.

Swift, J. (1989). 'Why are poor people vulnerable to famine?' *IDS Bulletin* 20(2), 8–15.

Takavarasha, T. (1993). 'Trade, price and market reform: current status, proposals and constraints'. *Food Policy* 18, 288–93.

Tattersfield, R. (1982). 'The role of research in increasing food crop potential in Zimbabwe'. *Zimbabwe Science News* 16 (1), 6–10.

Tattersfield, R. and Havazvidi, E. (1994). 'The development of the seed industry'. In: Rukuni, M. and Eicher, C. (eds). *Zimbabwe's Agricultural Revolution*, pp. 114–26. University of Zimbabwe Publications, Harare.

Tawonezvi, P. (1994). 'Agricultural research policy'. In: Rukuni, M. and Eicher, C. (eds). *Zimbabwe's Agricultural Revolution*, pp. 92–103. University of Zimbabwe Publications, Harare.

Thompson, C. (1993). *Drought Management Strategies in Southern Africa: From Relief through Rehabilitation to Vulnerability Reduction*. Food Security Unit, SADC and UNICEF, Nairobi.

Tobaiwa, C. (1993). 'Zimbabwe: the response to the 1992 drought in the context of long-term development objectives'. Paper prepared for the *SADC Regional Drought Management Workshop*, September 1993. SADC, Harare.

Toulmin, C. (1986). 'Pastoral livestock losses and post-drought rehabilitation in sub-Saharan Africa: policy options and issues'. *African Livestock Policy Analysis Network Paper* 8. ILCA, Addis Ababa.

Toulmin, C. (1994). Tracking through drought: options for destocking and restocking. In: Scoones, I. (ed.). *Living with Uncertainty: New Directions in Pastoral Development in Africa*, pp. 95–115. Intermediate Technology Publications, London.

Tyson, P. (1986). *Climate Change and Variability in Southern Africa.* Oxford University Press, Oxford.

Upton, M. (1987). *African Farm Management.* Cambridge University Press, Cambridge.

Walker, T. (1989). 'Yield and household income variability in India's semi-arid tropics'. In: Anderson, J.R. and Hazell, P. (eds). *Variability in Grain Yields: Implications for Agricultural Research and Policy*, pp. 309–19. Johns Hopkins University Press, Baltimore.

Walker, T. and Jodha, N. (1986). 'How small farm households adapt to risk'. In: Hazell, P., Pomareda, C. and Valdes, A. (eds). *Crop Insurance for Agricultural Development: Issues and Experience*, pp. 17–34. Johns Hopkins University Press, Baltimore.

Walker, T. and Ryan, J. (1990). *Village and Household Economies in India's Semi-arid Tropics.* Johns Hopkins University Press, Baltimore.

Walling, D. (1984). 'The sediment yield of African rivers'. In: *Challenges in African Hydrology and Water Resources*, pp. 265–83. Institute of Hydrology Publication 144. Wallingford.

Wallis, J. (ed.) (1954). *The South African Diaries of Thomas Leask.* Chatto and Windus, London.

Walters, C. (1986). *Adaptive Management of Renewable Resources.* McGraw Hill, New York.

Walters, J. (1915). 'Crop rotation in southern Rhodesia'. *Rhodesia Agricultural Journal* 12, 151–7.

Watson, J.P. (1977). 'The use of mounds of the termite *Macrotermes falciger* (Gerstacker) as a soil amendment'. *Journal of Soil Science* 28, 664-72.

Watt, M. (1913). 'The dangers and prevention of soil erosion'. *Rhodesia Agricultural Journal* 10, 5.

Watts, M. (1989). 'Coping with the market: uncertainty and food security among Hausa peasants'. In: De Garine, I. and Harrison, G. (eds). *Coping with Uncertainty in Food Supply*, pp. 260–89. Oxford University Press, Oxford.

Webb, P. and von Braun, J. (1994). *Famine and Food Security in Ethiopia: Lessons for Africa.* John Wiley, Chichester.

Webber, L. and Ison, R. (1995). 'Participatory rural appraisal design: conceptual and process issues'. *Agricultural Systems* 47, 107–31.

Weiner, D., Moyo, S., Munslow, B. and O'Keefe, P. (1985). 'Land use and agricultural productivity in Zimbabwe'. *Journal of Modern African Studies* 23, 252–85.

Weinrich, A.K.H. (1975). *African Farmers in Rhodesia: Old and New Peasant Communities in Karangaland.* Oxford University Press, Oxford.

Wellard, K. and Copestake, J. (eds) (1993). *Non-Governmental Organizations and the State in Africa.* Routledge, London.

Westoby, M., Walker, B. and Noy-Meir, I. (1989). 'Opportunistic management of rangelands not at equilibrium'. *Journal of Range Management* 42, 266–74.

Whingwiri, E., Natarajan, J., Makombe, G., Mataruka, D., Low, A., Cameron, T. and Kunjeke, P. (1987). 'The package for higher maize yields in the semi-arid zones: is it economical?' In: *Cropping in the Semi-arid areas of Zimbabwe*, pp. 384–96. Agritex, Harare and GTZ, Masvingo.

Whitlow, R. (1985). 'Dambos in Zimbabwe: a review'. *Zeitschrift fur Geomorphologie*, Supplementband 52, 115–46.

Whitlow, R. (1988). *Land Degradation in Zimbabwe: A Geographical Study.* Department of Natural Resources, Harare.

Whitlow, R. and Campbell, B. (1988). 'Factors influencing erosion in Zimbabwe: a statistical analysis'. *Journal of Environmental Management* 29, 17–29.

Wienmann, H. (1972). *Agricultural Research and Development in Southern Rhodesia, 1890–1923.* Occasional Paper 4. Department of Agriculture, University of Rhodesia, Harare.

Wienmann, H. (1975). 'Agricultural research and development in Southern Rhodesia, 1924–1950'. *Series in Science* 2. University of Rhodesia, Harare.

Wilken, G. (1987). *Good Farmers: Traditional Agricultural Resource Management in Mexico and Central America.* University of California Press, Berkeley.

Wilson, K. (1986). 'The human ecology of Zvishavance district'. Unpublished mimeo.

Wilson, K. (1987). *The Indigenous Genetic Resources of the Karanga Crop Production System.* Environment and Development Activities (ENDA)-Zimbabwe, Harare.

Wilson, K. (1988). 'Indigenous conservation in Zimbabwe: soil erosion, land-use planning and rural life'. Paper presented to the African Studies Association conference, September 1988, Cambridge.

Wilson, K. (1989). 'Trees in fields in southern Zimbabwe'. *Journal of Southern African Studies* 15, 1–15.

Wilson, K. (1990). 'Ecological dynamics and human welfare: a case study of population, health and nutrition in Zimbabwe'. PhD thesis, University of London.

World Bank (1991). *Zimbabwe Agricultural Sector Memorandum: Volume II, Main Report.* Southern Africa Department, Agricultural Operations Division, World Bank, Washington.

Worman, F., Heinrich, G. and Norman, D. (1991). 'Some organisational considerations in implementing FSR in a harsh environment: increasing farmer involvement in Botswana'. *Journal for Farming Systems Research and Extension* 2, 119–37.

Wynne, B. (1991). 'Knowledges in context'. *Science, Technology and Human Values* 16 111–21.

Wynne, B. (1992). 'Uncertainty and environmental learning: reconceiving science and policy in the preventive paradigm'. *Global Environmental Change* June, 111–27.

Zimbabwe Department of Meteorological Services (1981). *Climate Handbook of Zimbabwe.* Government Printer, Harare.

Zimbabwe Government (1987). *The National Conservation Strategy: Zimbabwe's Road to Survival.* Nature Resources Board, Harare.

Zimbabwe Government (1991). *Zimbabwe: A Framework for Economic Reform, 1991–1995.* Government Printer, Harare.

Zimbabwe Government (1992). *Livestock Policy.* Ministry of Lands, Agriculture and Rural Resettlement, Harare.

Index